Teaching Struggling Readers

How to Use Brain-based Research to Maximize Learning

Carol A. Lyons

HEINEMANN
Portsmouth, NH

Heinemann

361 Hanover Street
Portsmouth, NH 03801–3912
www.heinemann.com

Offices and agents throughout the world

The author and publisher wish to thank those who have generously given permission to reprint borrowed material:

Figures 1–2, 2–3, and 4–3 from *Human Physiology* by A. Vander et al. Copyright © 1990. Published by The McGraw-Hill Companies. Reprinted by permission of the publisher.

Figure 3–1 from *Rousing Minds to Life* by Roland Tharp and Ronald Gallimore. Copyright © 1988. Published by Cambridge University Press. Reprinted by permission of the publisher.

Excerpts from *Becoming Literate* (1991), *Reading Recovery* (1993), and *Change Over Time in Children's Literacy Development* (2001) by Marie Clay are reprinted by permission of Reed Publishing New Zealand and Marie Clay.

Excerpts from "Emotions, Cognition and Becoming a Reader and Writer: A Message to Teachers of Struggling Learners" by Carol Lyons in *Literacy Teaching and Learning: An International Journal of Early Reading and Writing* 4 (1). Reprinted by permission.

Excerpts from "The Role of Emotion in Memory and Comprehension" by Carol Lyons in *Extending Our Research: Teaching for Comprehension in Reading, Grades K–2* edited by Gay Su Pinnell. Reprinted by permission.

Library of Congress Cataloging-in-Publication Data
Lyons, Carol A.
    Teaching struggling readers : how to use brain-based research to maximize learning / Carol A. Lyons.
      p. cm.
    Includes bibliographical references and index.
    ISBN 0-325-00435-8
    1. Reading—Remedial teaching.   2. Educational psychology.
  3. Teacher-student relationships.   4. Affective education.   I. Title.

LB1050.5 .L97   2003
372.43—dc21   2002014596

Editor: Lois Bridges
Production: Elizabeth Valway
Cover design: Jenny Jensen Greenleaf
Composition: Publishers' Design and Production Services, Inc.
Photos on pages 77 and 135 by Margilee P. Hilson.
Photos on pages 100, 128, and 133 by Beverly Wells.
Photos on pages 142 and 179 by Ron Blome.
Manufacturing: Steve Bernier

Printed in the United States of America on acid-free paper
09   ML   10

To my son, Ken,
a caring pediatrician and exemplary teacher,
with admiration and affection.

Contents

Figures

Foreword

Carol Lyons has given us a book that is both accessible and fascinating. Two topics that are often overlooked or avoided by educators are the neurological basis of learning to read and write and the emotional underlay and overlay of the young child's learning. In Carol's wonderful examples we see how children's neurological impulses work with their strongest feelings to solve the challenges of learning. Her explanations of complex issues are clarified by brilliant accounts of young learners interacting with parents or teachers who seem to understand developing minds. I think readers will not only be challenged to think about brains and emotions but also will never again feel comfortable leaving them out of their thinking.

Important questions are explored in an easy-to-read text that is clear, flows well, and yet explains some tough concepts. How does the brain grow and function? You will remember the account of the button jar! As Patty tries to write her name, as Charles masters a simple set of words, and as Kevin tries valiantly to break "basketball" into three syllables, we begin to understand the developing minds of these students.

What groups of students concern us and how can we create social environments to help them achieve their full potential? In particular, how do developing minds become literate? The book discusses unmotivated students, low-progress students, students classified as learning disabled, students with attention deficit disorder, and language-delayed students.

What do teachers need to understand about these things to create effective practice? How can we make the most of what the neuropsychologists and medical researchers are finding out? And what does it take to change teachers' minds? Or their practices?

This delightful text should be read from cover to cover. Enjoy the things that are familiar to you and slow down to think about what is not familiar. Does it address some problems you recognize? Where do you agree and disagree? I suspect it would be easy for a reader to attribute the success of many of Carol Lyons' children to the "normality of the child," but the credit should go to the inspirational insights of the teachers and parents who are described as they worked with the children.

The author opens up the discussion for classroom teachers, psychologists, educational psychologists, school psychologists, neuroscientists, and brain researchers. Teachers in early intervention and those who work with learning disability and dyslexia will all recognize the relevance of this book for their work. Doctors and social workers should read it and consider recommending it to some of the families they work with.

There will always be some children who cannot make it without supplementary individual instruction. This will be most economically provided in the early stages of learning something. Rather than let them fall behind their peers we must find ways to accelerate children's learning, so that they catch up and join in with their successful peers. Better classroom education for the majority will never eliminate the need for individual teaching for some learners to acquire basic reading and writing skills.

Carol Lyons addresses a perpetual problem that will never go away in any education system, anywhere. There is a need to make a continuous supply of catch-up education available as a matter of course wherever children are in schools. We have done this with speech therapy for decades but have only recently begun to do this for literacy learning, and it is working well. Every child must be given the tools they need to succeed in later education, and sometimes that means giving individual instruction. And effective individual instruction of children with diverse needs can never stem from "a set of instructions for everyone to follow."

How can we best address the literacy learning problems of the lowest-achieving children? In particular, how can we deal with the raw anger, or intense fear, or stubborn resistance of the children who do not want to fail or comply? Teaching manuals do not tell the parent or teacher how to handle these emotions. Carol's examples are superbly chosen to show persistence and support from teachers who encountered such negative situations. How did Carol deal with the emotions of the thirteen older boys labeled LD and placed in a second-grade transition class, who responded to her opening request as their new teacher to take their seats ". . . soon there were thirteen boys walking in a circle on top of their desks, laughing and singing a rap song?" From that starting point she constructed thirteen favorable outcomes!

From reading this book it is easy to see why first-wave early intervention fits so well as an essential piece for producing two outcomes: (1) removing any literacy problems for most low achievers; and (2) helping identify students with a continuing need for learning that is adjusted to their several handicaps. This must continually be explained to a literate society. When early intervention does its job well, it is not clear to new leaders in education that there is any reason to support the successful endeavor. By its own efficiency it makes the problem invisible. As a result, the problem rapidly slips down on the agenda and risks falling into oblivion. This book will help raise the profile for what it is that we have to provide to get all children off to a good start in education.

Are there dangers in introducing teachers to a readable version of some insights from neurological science? Imagine, for example, the talk behind Reading Recovery's one-way screen. "Look, she's making him repeat it to strengthen the myelination of the pathways!" Carol Lyons' writing should not lead to that. She does a masterly job of introducing teachers to the valid concepts, categories, language, and arguments to do with the brain's control of what readers do.

The teaching described in the illustrative examples is reader friendly and it all looks easy. Adults may have to understand an elaborate argument, but that understanding could lead parents or teachers to a simple change of direction in practice. The illustrative examples show what changes occur. They are not performances to mimic, they cannot be captured in some PR slogan, and they cannot be listed as ten graded steps to success. Yet the messages in this book will encourage parents and teachers to work effectively alongside learners. I believe that deeply committed and questioning educators will ask, "Why haven't we discussed these topics before? This is so helpful."

Marie Clay

Acknowledgments

I began thinking about the ideas presented in this book while I was teaching third- and fourth-grade children from many different cultural backgrounds on an army base during the Vietnam War. These experiences, followed by another two years teaching poor, inner-city students on the East Coast, provided the impetus for writing about how best to teach children who struggle to learn. But it was my doctoral work at Ohio State University in the early 1980s that convinced me that until teachers had a better conceptual understanding of how children think and learn and the neuropsychology of learning, they would not come to fully understand *what* to do to facilitate learning, *why* it is so important, and *how* to develop rationales for their decision making to guide their practice.

I am grateful to two Ohio State University emeritus professors: Marlin Languis, professor of early childhood and science education and director of the Brain Behavior Laboratory; and Philip Clark, professor of psychology, who introduced me to the neuropsychology of learning and supported my research throughout my doctoral program. They helped me learn how to think about the mind and learning and listened, challenged, and encouraged my thinking. They also provided me with opportunities to start pursuing ideas juxtaposing brain mechanisms of learning, the relationship between cognition and emotion, and learning to read and write.

I am also grateful to emeritus professors Charlotte S. Huck, who helped me to understand the importance of emotion in learning and response to literature, and Martha L. King, whose interest and research in language development influenced how I thought about teaching and learning. Special thanks also goes to Marie M. Clay, whose exciting, visionary, groundbreaking research that began in 1960s and continues today has contributed significantly to both the theory and the practice of teaching children to read and write. Her thoughtful and challenging discussion about the ideas presented in this book informed my thinking and research.

I owe a great debt of gratitude to the following Reading Recovery and classroom teachers for sharing their reasoning, experiences, and reflections while working with struggling students: Gail Breslin, Blue Hill Consolidated School, Blue Hill, Maine; Kathy Hardman and Maryann McBride, Prince George's County Public Schools, Upper Marlboro, Maryland; Karolyn King, Southwestern City Schools, Grove City, Ohio; Cheri Slinger, Upper Arlington City Schools, Upper Arlington, Ohio; Carla Soffos, The University of Arkansas at Little Rock; Rose Mary Estice, Mary Fried, Emily Rodgers, The Ohio State University, Columbus, Ohio; and the late Sue Hundley, Lesley University, Cambridge, Massachusetts. These remarkable teachers offered insights, inspiring models of teaching practices, and suggestions for how to effectively work with the most difficult-to-teach students. I have learned so much from their work.

I would also like to thank the children in the lessons and stories described in this book. They have taught their teachers and me more than they will ever know. The children's and teachers' struggles and successes, as revealed through many real-life experiences, speak volumes.

Special thanks goes to Ken Lyons, M.D., for giving me so much enjoyment during the first five years of his life and for agreeing to let me write about it. Ken's careful editing of the neurology sections of this book and Marie Clay's motivating comments while reading early drafts of the manuscript were helpful and encouraging. I am also indebted to Rose Mary Estice, Mary Fried, Susan Fullerton, and Gay Su Pinnell for their comments, perceptive insights, interest, and enthusiastic responses to chapter drafts.

I wish to thank the following RR teacher-leaders for providing the photos for this book: Debra Duncan, Kathy Hardman, Maryann McBride, Beverly Wells, and Debby Wood, Prince George's County Public Schools, Upper Marlboro, Maryland; Betty Tompkins, Charles County Public Schools, LaPlata, Maryland; Paula Conner, Liberty Union-Thurston Schools, Baltimore, Ohio; and Phyllis Amicon, Wood County Educational Service Center, Bowling Green, Ohio.

I was fortunate to have the opportunity to work once more with the supportive, skilled, and creative editorial staff at Heinemann. I am grateful to my editor, Lois Bridges, who always provides wise counsel and responds immediately to every concern or question. Production editor Elizabeth Valway's artistic instincts, insights, and attention to detail facilitated the production process and made it an enjoyable experience. Karen Clausen, the editorial assistant, helped immeasurably, making sure that the manuscript was ready for production. Finally, I would like to thank editorial director Leigh Peake for her continued leadership and commitment to excellence.

As always, I want to express love and appreciation to my family and thank them for their continued support, especially Fran and Ken Lyons and my mother, Elizabeth Mueller. I would also like to thank my sisters, Barbara Caverly and Jan Humes; my brother-in-law, Dave Caverly; my niece Tracy Busse and her husband, Aaron; my niece Cori Caverly; and my nephews, Mike Caverly and Matt Humes, and my son Ken, who provided some of the examples and photographs in this book.

In addition to the researchers in neuroscience, learning, reading, writing, learning and reading disability, early childhood, and effective teaching from whom I have learned so much, I have also learned from extensive reading of the literature in teacher education. I would like to thank all of the scholars whose work is referenced here.

A final word of appreciation goes to the thousands of classroom, learning disability, special education, and Title 1 teachers; teacher-leaders; and literacy coordinators throughout the world who continue to work daily with students who struggle to learn to read and write. Your efforts are seldom known, recognized, or appreciated, but the children you reach and teach will be forever thankful, for you have prevented them from experiencing a lifetime of frustration and reading failure. On behalf of all the struggling children you have taught to read and write and their parents and families, thank you for making a difference in their lives.

Introduction

American education largely ignores the emotional origins of intellectual development, thinking, and reasoning. Some educators and politicians believe that more attention to the emotional side of learning would lead to touchy-feely pedagogy with focus on feeling good rather than learning the basics. This belief is pervasive because for years a dichotomy has existed between cognition or intellectual behavior and emotion or affective behavior (Greenspan 1997). The dichotomy is apparent in how schools are managed and teachers teach. For example, counselors are generally available to provide emotional support to individuals who are experiencing a personal crisis or traumatic event (e.g., the death of a classmate), but there is little or no emotional support for individuals experiencing learning difficulty.

Schools operate on the theory that cognitive and academic achievement are synonymous and distinct from emotion. While a school's mission statement may address self-esteem, respect for individual differences, and sensitivity to students from multilingual and diverse backgrounds, the fact remains that graded courses of study and curriculum plans are nearly always based on learning specified content and developing specific skills. During the last five years this attitude and approach to education has strengthened and informed educational policy and set the national education agenda.

The same situation exists in reading instruction. The emotional side of literacy learning is rarely mentioned in educational research and/or practice. Reading educators generally pay little more than lip service to the affective side of becoming literate. According to Athey (1985), diagrams of the reading process may identify affective factors, but beyond this acknowledgment, affective factors "receive little additional elaboration or explication" (527). This practice continues in spite of an extensive body of research that suggests that children with low reading skills experience loss of self-esteem, confidence, and initiative; suffer diminished self-worth; and have emotional traumas that may last for a lifetime (Parris, Wasik, and Turner 1991).

Some administrators, literacy educators, and policymakers assume that cognitive and academic development are equivalent. This assumption leads to the view that one approach to beginning reading instruction fits all. An example of this practice is the widespread use of phonics to teach young children how to read. School district personnel select the phonics curriculum, train teachers to deliver the regimented program in a prescribed and systematic way, monitor the delivery of the material, and administer standardized reading tests to measure the effect of the program on students' achievement.

Children who fail to meet required levels of reading achievement, as measured by the standardized tests, are suspected of having a learning problem . . . a deficit. Individual differences in learning to read are not generally considered unless they are large enough that the student is identified as having an attention deficit disorder and/or labeled learning disabled, emotionally disturbed, developmentally handicapped, or hyperactive (Coles 1998). Once tested and labeled, medication is often the first and only recourse.

Little consideration is given to helping teachers learn how children become proficient readers and writers. In most cases, teachers do not learn how to observe children's behavior while reading and writing nor do they observe how effective teachers adjust instruction and use a variety of effective techniques and approaches to meet students' idiosyncratic needs. Nor have they been introduced to recent developments in neuroscience that prove that emotions are integral to thinking, reasoning, and problem solving and cannot be divorced from learning (Damasio 1994) or learning to read and write (Coles 1998).

This lack of information is particularly unsettling because long-term follow-up studies of children who are having difficulty learning to read in first grade reveal that they struggle academically and socially throughout elementary and secondary school (Allington and Walmsley 1995; Juel 1988). Studies investigating student failure (see Wasik and Slavin 1993) show that literacy difficulties emerge during the first year of school and that individualized instruction, by a knowledgeable teacher, *early on* will prevent a lifetime of failure. The Reading Recovery[1] (RR) program, developed by Professor Marie M. Clay (1993b), is designed to prevent first-grade reading failure. And according to Cunningham and Allington (1994), "No other remedial program has ever come close to achieving the results demonstrated by Reading Recovery" (254).

I wrote this book for two reasons. First, educators, politicians, and academics in the educational and psychological community give little, if any, attention to the affective side of learning to read and write and I believe that is a grave mistake. There is an extensive body of neurological and psychological research (Greenspan 1997; LeDoux 1996) that demonstrates that emotions are essential to thinking and are an inseparable part of the learning process. This body of research is especially important for literacy educators to understand because unless students learn to read and write early on they cannot fully participate in classroom experiences during elementary school years and beyond.

The second reason I wrote this book is that learning to read is critical to students' academic success and has a tremendous impact on their emotional and social development throughout life. Therefore it is important that teachers learn how to design and implement effective literacy lessons that support students' cognitive and emotional needs and development. The teachers featured in this book illustrate this understanding in daily interactions with students. We can all learn from their expertise and example.

This book is based on what I have learned over a thirty-year period in five different settings. The first, raising a child, introduced me to the wonderment of how infants come to understand their environment and the powerful role parents play in the learning process. While taking graduate courses in child development and child psychology during my son, Ken's, infancy and preschool years, I was able to document changes in his cognitive and emotional development from age two months through five years. These weekly journal entries, reviewed many years later, revealed how learning occurs through the unity of thought, emotion, and action. Ongoing conversations with Ken throughout adolescent and adult years, especially while he was attending medical school and during pediatric residency, have provided insights into the affective dimensions of early learning and the critical role experience and conversation play in the process.

Second, teaching primary and intermediate grades for six years and special education students for two years helped me understand how emotions contribute to learning and teaching. Teaching in a suburban school district in Ohio; an Army/Airforce military base in Fort Lewis, Washington, during the Vietnam War; and, especially, working with ten-, eleven-, and twelve-year-old inner-city boys in a transitional first-grade class in New Britain, Connecticut, provided valuable lessons in how best to teach failing readers. I learned firsthand that during emotionally charged times, teachers must learn how to support the affective side of learning in order to help students become motivated, self-regulated, and independent learners.

Third, experiences accumulated over a period of twenty-seven years, seventeen of which have been spent at Ohio State University teaching and mentoring teacher-leaders, literacy coordinators, and university trainers in the RR and Literacy Collaborative[2] (LC) programs. These experiences have provided insights and a better understanding of how adults think and learn. I have documented and analyzed teacher and student interactions during RR and LC lessons to better understand the development of teachers' thinking, reasoning, and decision making. I have also spent the last few years examining videotapes and live demonstration lessons of effective RR teacher-leaders and teachers who have successfully taught the very lowest-achieving RR students to read and write. My work with the children, teachers, teacher-leaders, and literacy coordinators has helped me to better understand and identify the affective and cognitive dimensions of learning and learning to read and write.

Fourth, doctoral coursework in cognitive psychology and neuropsychology and research for an EEG dissertation investigating the thinking and reasoning of twenty-four prospective teachers while they completed various cognitive tasks revealed how feeling successful or frustrated during problem-solving activities impacts learning. The critical role emotion plays in thinking was also confirmed during experimental studies I participated in while working as a graduate research assistant at the Brain Behavior Lab at Ohio State University. Brain electrical activity mapping (BEAM) studies of autistic children, individuals who suffered head trauma, and special education and learning disabled youngsters as they completed various cognitive tasks provided a clear picture of how emotions may interfere with or support learning, thinking, and remembering.

Finally, for the last fifteen years, I have had the privilege of teaching twenty-one low-achieving first-grade RR students how to read and write. Nineteen of the twenty-one students were classified by teams of school and district professionals—including special education administrators, school psychologists, and reading specialists—as learning disabled, language delayed, or having an attention deficient disorder. My interactions with these struggling first-grade readers helped me to better understand the complexity of the reading and writing process and how best to address the idiosyncratic needs of all struggling students.

These five unique experiences have convinced me that certain kinds of nurturing and teaching propel children to intellectual development and that affective experience facilitates children's ability to engage successfully in the variety of problem-solving tasks needed to read and write. These varied experiences have also reinforced my conviction that cognition and emotion are inseparable and that teachers must be able to see thinking and emotions as integrative and interactive processes that begin at birth and last for a lifetime. Unfortunately, the body of research documenting how emotions and cognition cannot be separated has neither informed nor had an impact on literacy research, policy, or practice. This book is an attempt to remedy the situation. Throughout the book anecdotes from my life and from the lives of children and effective teachers help make this point.

I have relied heavily on my own examples and work because I understand it best. I have also tried to include current information on brain research specifically related to perception, attention, movement, motivation, memory, emotion, and language. This body of research is relevant to early literacy development and thus important to parents, literacy specialists and educators, academics, and psychologists.

The book is divided into three sections. In the first section, "Understanding the Developing Mind," I introduce the reader to recent discoveries in neuroscience. This exploration is informed by neurological and psychological research that demonstrates how the brain grows and develops and how cognition and emotion are closely linked through experience and are inseparable in the making of mind. This section necessarily includes a description of the structure of the brain and how the critical but subtle emotional transactions between infant and parent support and stimulate the development of the neural system. I take a closer look at the critical role attention, movement, language, and emotion play in learning and remembering. While the subject of the book is not the developing brain per se, a description of the physiology of the brain is relevant because it provides a foundation for thinking about processing in literacy tasks, and what can be done when a child's processing is inefficient. Research and new understandings about how the brain works and functions are investigated daily. This book does not begin to address the complexity of brain functioning. What is presented is tailored to help educators and parents better understand the impact of their actions on children's learning.

The second section, "Creating Literacy Environments to Help All Students Achieve Their Full Potential," provides a focused look at interactions between teachers and students that lead to accelerated reading and writing progress. These chapters describe specific teaching procedures and techniques expert teachers have used to help students build neural networks that process more efficiently and effectively. Vygotsky's (1978) zone of proximal development is used to discuss how children develop through participation in problem-solving activities with a more knowledgeable teacher, parent, and/or caregiver.

Children with low literacy achievement exhibit a variety of learning profiles that require idiosyncratic instructional solutions. Effective teachers engage these children in such a way as to support and nurture the affective and cognitive dimensions of their mind. I describe this dynamic interplay between cognition and emotion through specific examples from lessons with reluctant, unmotivated children—students classified as hard to teach, learning disabled (LD), language delayed, and having attention deficit hyperactivity disorder (AD(H)D).

The third section, "Understanding What Makes Teachers Expert," examines the thinking, reasoning, and practice of classroom and learning disability teachers, expert RR teachers, and teacher-leaders. Focused and informal interviews with these exceptional teachers reveal how they think, act, and feel about their work with children and adults. They discuss the formal experiences (e.g., seminars and course work) and informal interactions with children and colleagues that helped them develop the expertise necessary to meet the individual needs of struggling students.

The specific ideas explored in each chapter are designed to help parents and teachers make a positive difference in the emotional and cognitive development of their children and students. Each chapter ends with practical advice for creating effective contexts and opportunities to help all children reach their full potential.

I believe that our schools' failure to teach children who are fully capable of learning to read and write is not the children's fault, but rather, due to a reliance on methods of teaching that ignore the nature of the learning process—specifically, the cognitive and affective dimensions of learning. With our current understanding of the inseparable fusion between cognition (reasoning) and emotion in the development of the mind, all children, with the exception of those with severe neurological difficulties, should be able to become readers and writers. In order to accomplish this goal, however, teachers must learn how to provide the powerful and sustained opportunities that will enable students with varying needs and abilities to learn from the very act of reading and writing itself. This book clearly illustrates how this can be accomplished.

Endnotes

[1]Reading Recovery (RR) is a research-based early intervention program designed to assure that initially struggling students build effective reading and writing processes (Askew et al. 1998; Pinnell 1997). The lowest-achieving first graders are provided with one-to-one tutoring for thirty minutes each day in addition to their regular classroom literacy instruction. The program is defined as lasting a maximum of twenty weeks.

[2]The Literacy Collaborative (LC) is a long-term professional development program designed to provide a comprehensive, schoolwide approach to K–6 literacy instruction (Lyons and Pinnell 2001).

Understanding the Developing Mind

In the last ten years, technological advances in neuroscience have improved our understandings about how the brain grows, develops, and functions. Rather than examining brains of the deceased, researchers are now able to observe and analyze the processing of live human beings from infancy through adulthood. This research shows that theories developed in the past—for example, the notion that, after fifty years of age, individuals lose one thousand neurons every day—are no longer true. Today we have more precise and detailed information to better understand the development of human reasoning and how individuals think and act. We know, for example, that when infants and young children have many opportunities to become active, constructive learners, they learn by themselves and for themselves. This research is particularly important to parents and educators working with young children and students who find learning how to read and write difficult.

The four chapters in the first section of the book introduce the reader to recent discoveries about the growth and development of the mind. Chapter 1 provides foundational information about the neural development, structure, and organization of the brain. Chapter 2 describes through examples how the brain's attention and movement mechanisms interact to facilitate learning. Chapter 3 focuses on language acquisition and the roles speech and language play in thinking and learning. The last chapter in this section examines the foundation of learning—emotion and the critical roles emotion and motivation play in learning and memory. Information in the first section of the book helps the reader better understand and interpret chapters in Sections 2 and 3. Each chapter concludes with practical advice for parents and educators.

Chapter 1

How the Brain Develops and Functions

Twenty years ago, neuroscientists assumed that the structure of a newborn's brain is genetically determined. Today there is growing scientific evidence that early childhood experiences have a major and precise impact on how the neural networks that structure the brain are wired. Recent discoveries in neuroscience have revealed that human behavior is not solely biological or genetic. Culture, experience, the context for learning, and social interactions play major roles in who we are, how we feel, how we learn, and what we learn.

Research using magnetic resonance imagining (MRI), brain electrical activity mapping (BEAM), and positron emission topography (PET) have documented how individuals of all ages and with varying degrees of competence think and learn. Modern neuroscience is providing hard, quantifiable evidence to help physicians and scientists better understand and more precisely explain how the brain develops and works.

In this chapter, I discuss seven principles of learning that have emerged from recent discoveries in neuroscience (Figure 1–1) and draw educational implications for each. Experiences I have had with my son, Ken, from infancy through preschool, in my personal life, and in my teaching career are also used to relate each principle to learning in general and to learning how to read and write in particular.

Learning Depends on the Integration of Brain Structures

The human brain is a wet mass of nerve tissue that weighs a little over three pounds. It is an extension of the spinal cord. The brain has three parts: the

1. Learning depends on the integration of brain structures.
2. Neural development is continuous.
3. Perception forms the brain's structure.
4. Sensory experience builds our brains.
5. The brain is organized into functional systems.
6. The brain is a pattern synthesizer.
7. Neural plasticity of the brain gives every child the ability to learn and relearn.

Figure 1–1. *Seven Principles of Learning Drawn from Recent Discoveries in Neuroscience*

forebrain, which includes the cerebrum and diencephalon; the midbrain, which is at the top of the brainstem; and the hindbrain, formed by the cerebellum and the remaining parts of the brainstem.

The midbrain is far smaller than the hindbrain or forebrain, lies at the top of the brainstem, and is critical to learning. The midbrain governs reflex muscle activity such as adjusting the size and movements of the pupil in the eye. Deep inside the brainstem, from the medulla to the midbrain, runs the reticular formation, which controls consciousness. Even when we are asleep, the reticular formation is on guard, ready to alert the forebrain if it senses "danger." The role of the reticular formation in attention and learning will be discussed later in this chapter.

The hindbrain is made up largely of the cerebellum (little brain) and is connected to the underlying brainstem. The cerebellum is involved with skeletal muscle functions and is an important center for coordinating and learning movements, controlling posture, and balance. In order to complete these functions, the cerebellum examines sensory information from the muscles, joints, skin, eyes, and ears and, acting on this information, coordinates muscle movements ordered by the cerebrum.

The forebrain, which comprises most of the brain, consists of the central core—called the diencephalon—and the right and left cerebral hemispheres that together make up the cerebrum (Figure 1–2). The cerebrum represents 70 percent of the central nervous system.

The cerebral hemispheres of the cerebrum have an outer shell called the cerebral cortex and many nerve fibers (neurons) that bring information in and carry information out of the cerebrum and interconnect the neurons within the cerebrum. The right and left hemispheres are connected by a bundle of about 250 million nerve fibers (neurons) called the corpus callosum. The corpus callosum enables the brain to exchange information freely between the left and right hemispheres.

The cerebrum has a crossover pattern such that each side of the body communicates with the opposite hemisphere. The right hemisphere controls motor functions on the left side of the body. The left hemisphere controls motor functions on the right side of the body. When my mother had a stroke, the neurologist reported that the left side of the brain was damaged, which suggested that she would have some paralysis on the right side of her body. She could not lift her right arm or put weight on her right leg.

Although the left and right cerebral hemispheres appear to be symmetrical, each has anatomical, chemical, and functional specialization. In general, the left hemisphere sees the details first, processes information sequentially, and deals with logic and linear patterns. The right hemisphere sees the whole picture first, processes information more globally (the gestalt), and deals with intuition and images. The corpus callosum then acts as a superhighway allowing quick access to both the linear details in the left hemisphere and the overall image in the right hemisphere for integrated thought.

Both hemispheres contain all functions until specialization starts to occur. This specialization develops at a different rate and in a different way in each individual. If there are no physical or mental deficiencies, complete hemispheric specialization is in place between nine and twelve years of age (Gopnik, Meltzoff, and Kuhl 1999).

The diencephalon, the second component of the forebrain, contains the thalamus, a large cluster of nuclei (groups of neuron cells) that serves as a synaptic relay station and integrating center for most sensory input to the cortex. The hypothalamus, which lies below the thalamus, is crucial to regulating and stabilizing normal internal states, such as temperature, hunger, and thirst, and the principal site for regulating fear, sleep, and pleasure, behaviors essential to survival and comfort.

The cerebral cortex is an area of gray matter arranged into six rolling convoluted layers, which increases the area available for cortical neurons

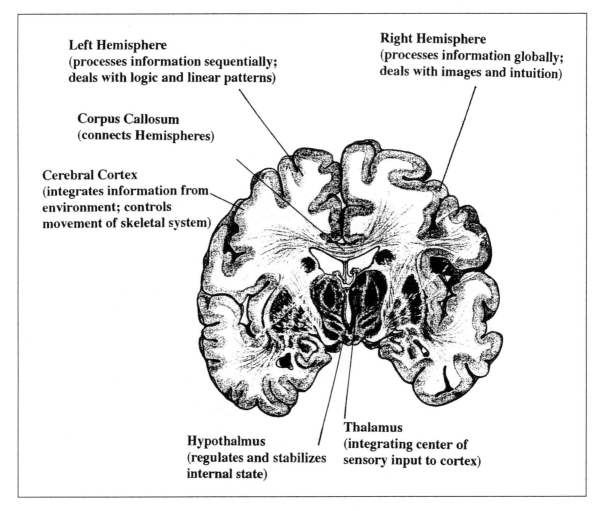

Left Hemisphere
(processes information sequentially; deals with logic and linear patterns)

Right Hemisphere
(processes information globally; deals with images and intuition)

Corpus Callosum
(connects Hemispheres)

Cerebral Cortex
(integrates information from environment; controls movement of skeletal system)

Hypothalmus
(regulates and stabilizes internal state)

Thalamus
(integrating center of sensory input to cortex)

Figure 1–2. *Side-by-Side Section of the Right and Left Cerebral Hemispheres*

without increasing the volume of the brain. It is the most complex integrating area of the central nervous system because it brings together the basic information received from the environment into meaningful perceptual images and refines and controls the movement of the skeletal system.

The outer layer of the forebrain (cortex) of each hemisphere is divided into four lobes: the frontal, parietal, occipital, and temporal (Figure 1–3).

The frontal lobes are responsible for planning, decision making, and thinking. They are also important to the working of memory and to learning new skills and behaviors. The temporal lobes, above and behind the ears, process sound and speech, which is more prevalent in the left hemisphere, and are involved in some aspects of long-term memory. The occipital lobes, located at the back of the forebrain, are used for processing vi-

sual information. Near the top of the cerebral cortex are the parietal lobes, which deal with touch, motor control, and orientation. Between the parietal and frontal lobes is the motor cortex, which controls body movement and works with the cerebellum to coordinate the learning of motor skills. Areas in the frontal, parietal, and temporal lobes also contain mechanisms involved in the motor aspects of language. A discussion of how these areas of the brain function is presented later on in this chapter.

Cerebral Dominance and Language

The use of language and its development clearly depends on brain structure. For approximately 90 percent of the population, the left hemisphere is superior at producing language and the conceptualization of what an individual wants to say and write. The assemblies of neurons in the left hemi-

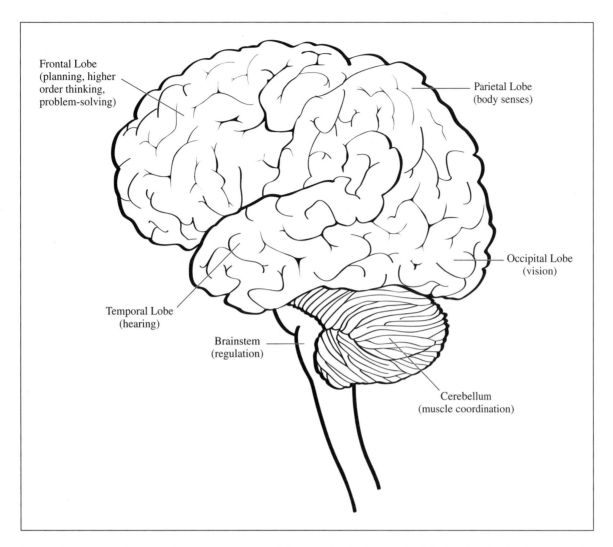

Figure 1–3. *Lateral View of the Outer Layer of the Forebrain (Cortex) of the Right Hemisphere with the Four Lobes, Brainstem, and Cerebellum Labeled*

Within the figure:

Frontal Lobe (planning, higher order thinking, problem-solving)

Parietal Lobe (body senses)

Occipital Lobe (vision)

Temporal Lobe (hearing)

Brainstem (regulation)

Cerebellum (muscle coordination)

sphere control the act of speaking or writing and recent verbal memory. The left hemisphere is also specialized for controlling the rapid changes and movement in motor neurons necessary for the production of speech sounds and for listening to someone talk. Understanding spoken and written language usually depends on the left hemisphere, although the difference between the hemispheres may not be as specialized for language comprehension as it is for language production.

My mother's stroke affected her left hemisphere. Damage to the left cerebral hemisphere, but not the right, interfered with her capacity for language. She could understand what we were saying but could not call up or produce the sounds or words to respond to our questions. As a result of daily speech and physical therapy after her

stroke and ongoing weekly therapy over a two-year period, Mom gained approximately 90 percent of her ability to walk, 80 percent of her capacity to speak, and 50 percent of her ability to write.

Anatomical and physiological asymmetries in the two hemispheres are present at birth but are fairly flexible in early years of life. For example, after damage to the left hemisphere of children under the age of two, adequate language develops in the intact right hemisphere. Even if the left hemisphere is traumatized in children after the onset of language development, functional language ability is reestablished in the right hemisphere. The transfer of language to the right hemisphere diminishes rapidly as the age at which the damage occurs increases, so that after the early teens, language development in the right hemisphere is interfered with permanently (Ratey 2001).

Just as the left hemisphere is dominant for events that occur in sequence over time—for example, language production—the right hemisphere is thought to be specialized for processing information that is treated as a unified whole, such as the perception of faces and other three-dimensional objects.

Memories are handled differently in the two hemispheres as well. Verbal memories are more apt to be associated with the left hemisphere and nonverbal memory—for example, visual patterns—with the right hemisphere. Emotional memories are stronger in the right hemisphere than in the left (LeDoux 1996).

Immediately after my mother's stroke, I asked my father to bring the family photo albums to the hospital. His mechanical engineer's mind could not understand the logic of my request, especially when I suggested that instead of reading a book, he sit next to Mom and discuss the photos in the album. Although Dad thought the idea was ridiculous, especially since my mother was in a coma, he reluctantly agreed to share the family album. After approximately eight hours, he began to see my mother respond to his one-sided conversation. She smiled and cried, her eyes wide open.

The neurologist speculated that the intact emotional right hemisphere of her brain was responding to the family photos, triggering pleasant memories from the past. Even though she could not express herself, Mom's nonverbal reactions suggested she understood what Dad was saying. By the time my sisters, brother, and I reached the hospital, Dad had set up a projector and screen in her room so that we could watch and discuss our family history chronicled in a slide show. He thought the more stimulation she received, the quicker she would recover and he was right.

Cerebral Specialization and Learning

Newest research on brain development reveals that the earlier and the more often both hemispheres are activated by use, the more dendrite connections form, extend across the corpus callosum, and myelinate. Myelin is a fatty white sheath that insulates each neuron and facilitates fast, smooth processing. The more myelin, the faster the processing between both hemispheres and the

rest of the brain. The sooner in life this occurs the more likely the individual will achieve perfection.

Tiger Woods' life from preschool to adulthood is a good example of how one can begin to attain perfection in an early age and develop into a competent, perfected golfer in later life. From the time he was a toddler, Tiger's father set about making his son into a professional golfer. Tiger learned how to swing a golf club and hit the ball when he was one and one-half years old. He started playing on a golf course when he was two and has never stopped playing. If Tiger hit a less-than-perfect shot, his father would show him how to adjust and correct his golf swing to make a better shot.

The mental task that is required to swing a club and stroke a golf ball at just the right time in the right spot does not occur in any single area or hemisphere of the brain. Instead, each hemisphere contributes assemblies of neurons localized in a specific part of the brain to complete the action. Because many assemblies of neurons are needed to produce a sequence of actions resulting in a specific movement, their function must be orchestrated in the performance of the task. In other words, even though mental acts seem intuitively to be a single act, they are not. Rather, each act is composed of many individual neural working systems in both hemispheres working in a coordinated, integrated fashion. And these two hemispheres of Tiger's brain began working in a coordinated way at one and one-half years of age.

As a toddler, Tiger Woods developed a complex, flexible, integrated, working processing system involving both hemispheres. The more he played, the more his neurons were organized into a sequence of movements that continued to myelinate through repeated use. The more myelination, the faster, more fluid, and more flexible the sequence of actions became. He learned how to adjust his swing no matter where the ball landed (e.g., in a sand trap, in tall grass) and effectively hit it, no matter how difficult the shot.

From a neurological perspective one might say that repetitive practice beginning at an early age and involving the coordination of a sequence of actions enabled Tiger to know how a perfect golf swing feels. Feeling involves tempo, pace, timing needed to swing the club, weight adjustment, and movement of the body as the golfer approaches and hits the ball. When the sensory information Tiger was processing in his right hemisphere did not feel right, he could make the necessary adjustment, modify his swing, and get back on track. The well-organized sequential movements involved in swinging the club, associated with the left hemisphere, are working in concert with the pleasing feeling of the whole, associated with the right hemisphere, to create harmonious action. The integration of both hemispheres at a very early age established a firm foundation upon which to improve and perfect his game, which was reinforced day in and day out throughout his life.

A similar analogy can be applied to preschool children who have opportunities to develop a firm foundation for learning to read and write. Researchers studying language development (Cazden 1988; Halliday 1975) and early literacy development (Clay 1975, 1979; Teale and Sulzby 1986) have found that early childhood experiences (e.g., hearing and sharing stories, dramatizing stories, painting and coloring, writing stories) and conversation play an important role in enabling children to read and write. The sooner children learn to coordinate the left-to-right movement of their eyes to follow the words on a page while listening to stories and attempt to write their name, which is also a controlled sequence of actions, the earlier they will learn to read and write.

Children who have experienced few literacy lessons are at a disadvantage when they enter school. While they can express themselves using language, they have not had opportunities to react to a story or express themselves in writing; therefore, they have not made connections between talk, reading, and writing. The children's brains are willing, ready, and able to develop these capabilities, but the people in their environment have neither created literacy opportunities nor initiated, supported, and responded to the children's early attempts to read and write, experiences that are necessary to help children benefit from more formal classroom instruction.

Neural Development Is Continuous

The second principle supported by recent research (see Ratey 2001) suggests that human beings have unlimited potential for learning that continues through old age. Until recently, scientists believed that once connections were made during childhood they were permanent. And after puberty, existing neurons could not become stronger, reorganize, or expand; they could only die. It was also believed that as individuals grew older, they have more difficulty learning and actually lose neurons. Recent developments in brain imaging have shown, however, that age-related neural loss is insignificant.

Controlled clinical studies provide concrete evidence that experience can reshape and reorganize our brain in the adult years. Thus, neural development is a continuous, unending process. Axons and their dendrites can be strengthened, modified, and regrown. If there is a deficit in the brain due to injury, stroke, or disease, for example, the brain is able to compensate for the lost function. My mother's recovery of approximately 90 percent of her motor and speech functions supports these data. The ability to regenerate or grow nerve cells could also help people who suffer damage from other parts of their central nervous systems, including spinal cords and nerves leading to body extremities. But how can the brain grow and develop new nerve cells? To understand the complexity of human brain growth and development, I will review some basic information about its structure.

There is no more emotionally secure experience for young children than to be held by a loving parent and read to on a daily basis.

What Is a Neuron and How Does It Work?

Human brain development begins at conception. At birth, infants have over 1 trillion brain cells. Approximately 100 billion are nerve cells, or neurons, and the rest are support cells called glia (Greek for *glue*), which hold the neurons together and filter out harmful substances. All individuals come into the world with approximately the same number of neurons and, thus, the same capacity to learn. Neurons are the functioning core of the brain and the entire central nervous system.

Each neuron has one axon and as many as 100,000 dendrites, strand-like fibers branching from the neuron (see Figure 1–4). Dendrites are the main way by which neurons get information (learn). Dendrites receive electrical impulses from other neurons and transmit them along a long fiber called an axon. Axons are treelike projections that send an electrical impulse to another neuron cell body through synapses. In the synaptic gap an electrical signal is briefly transformed into a chemical, called a neurotransmitter, and back again. The neurotransmitters either inhibit or excite the neighboring neuron. And they can either enhance or prevent further transmission of electrical impulses to dendrites of other neurons.

There are one hundred different kinds of neurotransmitters that operate naturally in our bodies. Two common neurotransmitters are considered important to learning; dopamine and serotonin. Dopamine coordinates movement and strengthens and prolongs the chemical firing between neurons. Without dopamine there is little or no muscular coordination. Parkinson's disease, for example, results from the death of neurons, which produce dopamine. Dopamine helps individuals sustain the attention needed to complete a task and, therefore, is oftentimes referred to as the learning neurotransmitter (Pert 1997). Ritalin, a widely prescribed drug for children with attention deficit disorder (ADD), increases the level of dopamine in the brain and helps children diagnosed with ADD to attend to a task.

Serotonin is a neurotransmitter associated with feeling good about ourselves and having a positive attitude and, thus, is called the mood neurotransmitter (Greenspan 1997). When individuals feel successful, happy, or proud that they have overcome a difficult task, serotonin levels increase. When they feel dejected that they can't learn or experience failure, serotonin levels decrease.

How Does the Brain Grow?

Neuroscientists believe that the brain grows in two ways. First, as neurons are stimulated, synapses are strengthened and the message-receiving dendrites develop new dendrite spines. If the neurons fail to develop synapses or the synaptic connections are weak, dendrites fail to grow. Thus, the brain grows through strengthening some connections and discarding weakened synaptic connections. It is estimated that each one of the 100 billion neurons may have anywhere from one to ten thousand synaptic connections to other neurons (Pert 1997).

The second way the brain grows is through myelination of axons. As electrical messages are processed over and over again, axons develop myelin. This insulating myelin sheath serves to insulate one axon from its immediate surroundings and speed up its message-transmitting capacity. The rapid conduction of the electrical impulses makes chemical transmission through synapses more efficient and allows electrical impulses to travel up to twelve times faster. The more myelin built up on the axons, the more automatic the processing. At first these neural pathways are faint, suggesting little myelin buildup, but with repetition myelin grows and the connections becomes stronger, easier. Repeated firings make successive firing easier and speedier and, eventually, automatic. When this occurs, a memory is formed. The more work the brain does, the more it becomes capable of doing.

There is little myelin present at birth, and it is estimated that it takes twenty to thirty years to finish the process. Myelin starts to grow from the lower structures in the brain, which are responsible for motor programs (e.g., crawling, walking, reaching, drinking), to the highest centers of the brain, the frontal lobes, which are responsible for abstract thought, problem solving, and decision making. Additional information about the role of myelin in learning is presented in Chapter 2.

The neurons and their thousands of dendrites intertwine in all directions to form an interconnected tangle with 100 trillion constantly changing connections and interactions. The trillions of connections guide our thinking, movement, and behavior. Experiences, environment, social interactions, what we perceive and attend to, as well

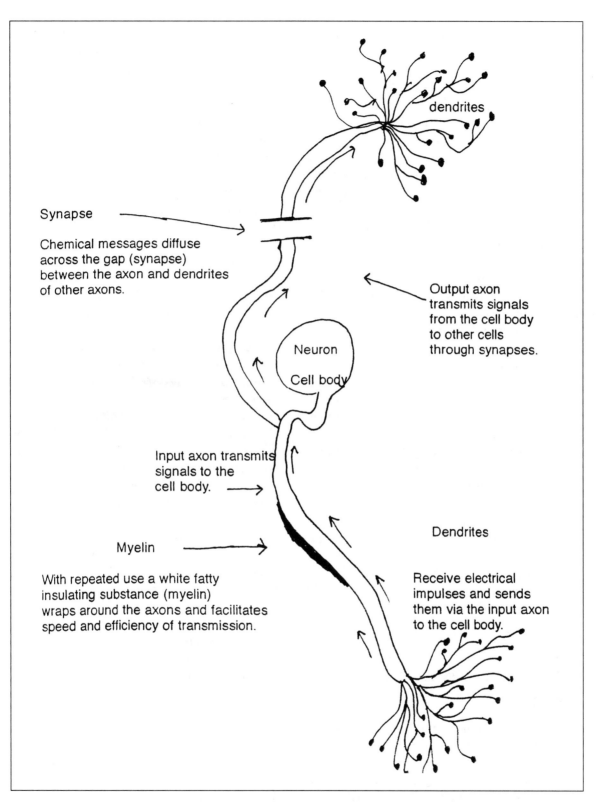

Synapse

Chemical messages diffuse across the gap (synapse) between the axon and dendrites of other axons.

dendrites

Output axon transmits signals from the cell body to other cells through synapses.

Neuron

Cell body

Input axon transmits signals to the cell body.

Dendrites

Myelin

With repeated use a white fatty insulating substance (myelin) wraps around the axons and facilitates speed and efficiency of transmission.

Receive electrical impulses and sends them via the input axon to the cell body.

Figure I–4. *The Transmission of Signals (Information) Through One Neuron with the Three Parts of a Neuron: Axon, Cell Body, and Dendrites Labeled. (The Synapse and Myelin are also Labeled.)*

as our emotional state determine how our brain gets wired.

Networks of Neurons Form Unique Maps

The brain does not process information and construct images by manipulating bits and pieces of data in a sequential manner like a computer, as was previously thought. Ratey (2001) explains that groups of neurons (not a single neuron) form maps that represent entire objects in different parts of the brain. Networks of neurons form in a unique way for each individual because no two individuals have the same experience or see the same thing the same way.

These maps interact simultaneously to help us form concepts and ideas. Then, working by analogy, the brain looks for similarities, differences, or relationships among them. For example, when an infant develops the concept *father*, groups of neurons (50 to 100 thousand) from various sensory regions of the brain interact simultaneously. An infant who has learned how to recognize his daddy when he walks into a room has used many groups of neurons comprising different sensory maps (smell, sight, sound, feel, and touch) to form a whole concept of his daddy. In order to distinguish his daddy from other men, the infant compares and contrasts his concept of Daddy, first with other people and then with concepts of other males he has seen. The many maps in the brain create a system of connections for whole categories of information. The result of these complex layers of maps is the infinite variety of each person's thoughts and behaviors.

Perception Forms the Brain's Structure

The third new insight about our brain is that through technology, neuroscientists are beginning to identify and describe how perceptions form the brain's very structure. We already know that networks of neurons (cognitive structures) develop our brains, working together to help us make sense of our world, and that learning is a product of an individual's experience. But in order to maximize children's opportunities to learn and to learn to read and write, educators must understand perceptual learning in general and visual perception in particular.

Perception Defined

Anybody who has taken a basic psychology course knows that the brain receives information from the environment through our sense organs (eyes, ears, nose, mouth, hands, etc.). Upon receiving stimuli, the brain decides how to interpret and transform what we see, hear, touch, smell, or taste and that becomes our conscious experience.

How our brains perceive, receive, and interpret information impacts how the assemblies of neurons organize and connect to build our brains. The brain makes judgments about what the eyes are looking at or the sounds the ears are receiving by creating an elaborate category system and then comparing the incoming stimuli with categories it has established from prior experiences. But how does it create this category system?

Developing a Category System

At a very young age, when children are just beginning to learn, they depend almost entirely on interactions with a more experienced other (adult or older child) to make sense of their experiences. Through these experiences with others, the brain begins to organize incoming stimuli into categories. Once an infant looks at an object and the brain receives the information, the brain puts it into a category. As the infant begins to make sense of his experiences, the brain continues to add to or refine the category system and create more categories. An environment that stimulates infants to do their own exploring and manipulating of objects provides many opportunities for the brain to construct this elaborate category system and, thus, the capacity to learn.

Infant studies (Greenspan 1997) have revealed that the development of a category system is dependent on how the child responds to environmental influences. Every response a child makes to sights, sounds, smells, taste, and touch facilitates the development of the category system. Involving children in multiple sensory experiences increases children's chances of developing more complex category systems. Young children need an environment that stimulates and engages them to explore and to manipulate their environment. Active exploration enables children to build motor and sensory pathways in the brain for future use.

Some children enter school with only limited category systems to help them make sense of their literate world. Limitations are not the result of brain deficits but rather of scarce opportunities to support the child's cognitive development. The following case illustrates this point.

On a letter identification test, when asked to name letter *B*, Michael said, "eight." He had been in kindergarten for one year and had been read to, yet he had no organized way of attending to the visual information in print. He had some knowledge of visual form—this was not random, for there is some similarity between a *B* and 8—but his knowledge was unorganized. During writing time, Michael drew a picture and, on occasion, dictated a sentence about the picture for the teacher to write. During independent writing, Michael wrote the first letter and the teacher wrote the rest of his name.

When asked to identify the letter *B*, the neural networks in Michael's brain classified *B* as the number 8; the letter *I* was 1, letter *S* was 3, letter *F* was 4. This was not random. Michael probably thinks they are all one set. Michael knew how to read numbers from 1 to 10; his brain had developed assemblies of neurons to categorize numbers, but none to categorize letters, although he was making connections.

Michael could see the letters; there was nothing wrong with his vision. But his brain had not developed the category system and capacity to transform the letters that he was looking at into a concept. It is impossible to recognize and name a letter if the brain has had no experience seeing and distinguishing the difference between letters and numbers.

According to Dr. John Ratey (2001), a clinical professor of psychiatry at Harvard Medical School, "we must *learn* to automatically and unconsciously fit our sensations, coming from all the senses, into categories that we have learned" (56). Michael had not been taught how to look at print. He never developed a way to start to categorize what to look at or where to look. He needed some explicit instruction in sorting letters and numbers. Michael's early literacy experiences had little impact on developing his reading and writing processing system.

Perception and Expectation

Perception requires a form of expectation and anticipation, of knowing what is about to confront us and getting ready for it. If you do not have an expectation of what you are looking at in your environment, your surroundings would be mass

confusion and each new experience would be overwhelming. We automatically and unconsciously fit our sensations into categories based on what we have learned. The following example illustrates this point.

When Kenny was thirteen months old, he had his first taste of a sweet bread-and-butter pickle and he liked it. For the next four months, he asked for pickles frequently and delighted in getting them out of the jar himself. We even talked about the crunching sound they made when he took a bite, which prompted him to take little bites to make more noise. Through repeated experiences, sensory neurons in Kenny's brain networked and shaped in a certain way to enable him to develop the concept *pickle* and an expectation of what a pickle looked like and how it tasted.

What we perceive is what the brain decides is in front of our eyes. When asked if he wanted a pickle, Kenny's brain used previously organized neural category systems to register what it looked like, how it felt as he took one out of the jar, how it tasted and sounded when he took a bite of the pickle. What his brain "saw" depended on decisions it had made and only indirectly on whatever stimulated his senses. His concept of *pickle* was reinforced every time he ate one until something happened that neither of us expected.

One day, after taking a bite of a pickle, Kenny made a terrible face and spit the pickle on the floor. He cried and tried to wipe the taste off his tongue. After several attempts to get the taste out of his mouth failed, he became very upset and started to choke and cough. It wasn't until I got him out of his chair and held him while dabbing a wet towel soaked in water on his tongue that he settled down.

I was surprised by his sudden reaction to the pickle until I looked at the jar and realized that I had mistakenly purchased a jar of dill pickle chips instead of sweet chips. The jars were the same size, shape, and color. The Vlasic labels were also similar except one label read "sweet pickle chips" and on the other label were written "dill pickle chips." I explained my mistake and told Kenny that I would read the label on the jar carefully before giving him a pickle. From that day on, he was hesitant and very cautious when biting into a pickle. For the next several months, he would make a face and say I had the wrong jar, even when I gave him a sweet pickle.

Recent research (Ratey 2001) provides some explanation for what was probably occurring in his mind. What we know, understand, and expect to see colors our perceptions. Neurons respond to input received from our senses and this input shapes the way we experience the next input. The more often the pattern is repeated, the more fixed the neural assembly becomes. Kenny's fixed assembly of neurons developed a concept for pickles based on tasting many sweet pickles for several months.

He expected to taste a sweet pickle, not a sour one. When he met an unfamiliar stimulus (a sour rather than a sweet taste), he perceived the input as new, which disturbed and confused him. This confusion caused him to react in a specific way . . . alarm, fear, fright. Once comforted, he was able to recover from the experience.

Ratey (2001) argues that confusion is positive when the outcome is positive because it enables the brain to adjust perception and reorganize neural networks, which explains why Kenny was able to recover. Tasting the dill pickle changed his concept of pickles. He was not the same child. His brain had assembled a new category system, sweet and sour. By his second birthday, Kenny enjoyed many different kinds of pickles. He had learned that pickles may look, smell, and feel the same, but taste differently.

Kenny's experiences with pickles led to the reorganization of neurons and resulted in the development of a new category system that changed the very structure of his brain. His perceptual system had also changed and improved its ability to respond to new challenges in his environment.

Visual Perception

When reading, your eyes look at the words on the page, but your brain tells you whether the marks you are looking at make the word *like* or *little*. Visual perception is the decision individuals make with the information they pick up with their eyes. The eyes look at the words on the page and the brain decides what they are (Smith 1994). The entire process is very complex and happens so quickly that it is difficult to measure or record. Marie Clay (2001) discusses the complexity of visual perception:

> Print information must pass through the visual sense for reading to occur and children have to learn what visual infor-

mation in print is usable, and how to use it. But the visual code of written language must also give access to the sounds of language and all other facets of the language code. (148)

In order to become literate, children must learn how to use visual information they perceive to anticipate the meaning of a word, sentence, or story. A good book introduction may set the child up to get the meaning of the story, but he must be able to look for visual information to confirm or reject what he anticipates. According to Clay (2001), "Becoming literate involves making the processes of visual perception operate under a new set of arbitrary constraints which apply to the written code of a language" (149).

Studies in neuroscience (Greenspan 1997) have shown the brain's structure is determined by how it perceives and interprets information. Assemblies of neurons are constantly making new connections through new experiences (i.e., literacy, play, culture) and strengthening existing networks through revisiting and repeating those experiences. Learning changes the very structure of the neural networks of the brain, which in turn change the structure of the brain.

Sensory Experience Builds Our Brains

The fourth principle of learning reveals the central and essential role experience plays in learning. Until recently, scientists had to dissect the brains of deceased individuals with various learning disorders and problems and compare them to deceased individuals who had minimal learning problems in order to speculate on the role of environment in learning. Today, through advanced technology (PET scans, MRIs, BEAM maps) neuroscientists are able to analyze children of different ages in various learning contexts learning new tasks.

What we have learned is that nerve networks growing out of our unique sensory experiences lay down intricate patterns and maps that govern how an individual's brain develops and functions. Through the senses, individuals construct understandings from which concepts and thinking develop. The richer our sensory environment and the more opportunity individuals have to explore

Six-month-old Mikey already knows how books work.

and become actively involved with it, the more intricate the patterns for learning, thought, and creativity become. The latest infant research reveals that the brain is profoundly flexible, sensitive, and plastic and deeply dependent on and influenced by events in the environment (Gopnik, Meltzoff, and Kuhl 1999). The following example illustrates this principle.

The Button Jar

When Kenny was five months old, he started to crawl. Once on the floor, he went immediately to the spare bedroom where I kept a two-gallon button jar on top of the sewing machine. I think he was drawn to the room because, on sunny days, the many colors, sizes, and shapes of the hundreds of buttons in the jar cast colorful shadows on the wall. As soon as he got into the room he pointed excitedly to the button jar. His baby-talk chatter told me he wanted the button jar. I would put the button jar on the floor so that he could take a closer look at the buttons, but looking was not enough. He wanted to touch the buttons. I would open the jar and dump a few buttons on the hardwood floor. He became very excited watching the buttons scatter across the floor.

To prevent him from putting the buttons into his mouth, I took his hand and showed him how to push the buttons one-by-one into a pile. Then with my help, the two of us would pick up each button and return it to the button jar. I watched him very closely so that he would not put the buttons into his mouth, which of course is what he

usually tried to do. After repeatedly telling him not to put the buttons into his mouth because he might swallow them and get sick, I had to tell him that the next time he tried to put a button into his mouth, I would put the button jar away.

The next day, Kenny learned a valuable lesson . . . Mommy means what she says. The button jar was put away. For the next three days, Kenny went into the button jar room and pointed to the jar, crying for me to put it on the floor. Mean Mommy said, "No, not until you tell me that you will not try to put the buttons in your mouth." The following day, when I asked if he was going to put the buttons in his mouth, he shook his head from left to right. The button jar game resumed immediately.

After about three weeks of pushing the buttons into piles, I showed him how to sort the buttons by color. While demonstrating the process, I would say, "Let's put all the white buttons in this pile." With my help, Ken learned how to make a pile of red, white, and black buttons. We would have a conversation about the color of each group. I did the talking and Ken made babbling sounds. He would look at me with that proud look mothers come to understand when a child feels good about what he has accomplished. We both had fun and I believe he knew that he was pleasing me.

When Ken was eight months old, he started to associate a color word with each pile of different-colored buttons. When I asked him to show me the red pile of buttons, he could point to the red pile. He could group the buttons according to a specific color, but could not yet produce the word to associate with each color. Once he could sort buttons by color, I showed him how to count the buttons in each pile. He started to learn the number concepts of one, two, and three and to say a word to represent each button he counted.

One day he pointed out that some of the buttons had holes and others had no holes on top. So we sorted buttons into holes and no holes. Ken, not I, had discovered another classification system. From that activity, we sorted buttons by the number of holes. Two holes, four holes, six holes, and so forth. He also noticed that some buttons were smooth, others were rough, some were square, others were round. Some buttons had people on them, others didn't. Some were shiny, others weren't. He had not acquired a word to label the concepts, but he noticed differences and similarities among buttons, thus completing the task visually. By the time he was one year old, Ken had developed a category system in which to classify and associate a specific button with specific words (e.g., color, shapes, number of holes).

Every day we played the button game. I would push all the white buttons together and ask him to tell me how I grouped the buttons. He would look at the pile of white buttons and say no holes, two holes, etc. Then our roles reversed. Ken would sort the buttons into specific groups and I would tell him how he had classified them. We took great delight in this activity, talking and laughing, trying to trick each other. Sometimes I would put a red button into the white pile and he would squeal and tell me no, and push it into the correct pile. Then I would watch him place a button in the wrong pile and he would watch me to see if I discovered his error. In his baby book I wrote that at twelve months of age, Ken's favorite pastime was playing with the button jar.

The Brain Is Organized into Functional Systems

The fifth principle of learning is that the performance of any one brain region is shared or influenced by structures in other areas. Until recently it was thought that most complex mental acts were handled almost exclusively by the frontal lobes in the cerebral cortex. Now it is understood that mental tasks are performed not by a single area of the brain but by the operation of many functional units, each of which is localized in a specific part of the brain. Because these basic organization units function even in simple mental tasks, for example picking up a pencil, widely distributed areas of the brain are involved and must be orchestrated in the performance of task.

This research is consistent with the theory of learning proposed by Alexander Luria (1973, 1976), a distinguished Soviet psychologist and neurologist. Luria's (1973) theory of the functional organization of the brain suggests that human mental processes involve complex functional systems that work together and make their own particular contribution to the organization of the whole. He proposed three functional units of the brain whose participation is necessary for any type of cognitive activity (Figure 1–5). Using Luria's description of the functional organization of the

brain, I can illustrate Ken's learning processes as he played the button jar game.

Unit I, located in the brainstem, is responsible for regulating tone or waking. The most important part of the first functional unit is the reticular activating system (RAS), a small structure located near the top of the brainstem. The RAS serves as a trapdoor or gatekeeper, allowing stimuli to enter the brain and be relayed through the limbic system to the appropriate cortical areas. This interaction helps us attend, think, keep our balance, and coordinate movement. Later, the child learns to send messages back down from the cortex to focus attention; for example, the child will attend to what the teacher is saying instead of looking out the window to watch the children on the playground. Without the reticular formation's alerting signals, the brain grows sleepy and disengages. The RAS plays a powerful role in directing consciousness and attention. How the RAS impacts attention is discussed in Chapter 2.

The RAS was responsible for focusing and sustaining Ken's attention while we played the button jar game. From the first moment the button jar was placed on the floor, he was focused, interested, and engaged in what I was doing and saying rather than on noises and actions taking place on the television outside the room. Sustained focused attention was maintained and continued even when the activities became more challenging. Unit I is responsible for focusing attention. Ken was always engaged when we played with the buttons. As he grew older, his participation in the activities increased and he could attend to a task for approximately eight minutes. He learned to

◆ attend to a variety of activities
◆ sustain attention for increasing amounts of time

The second functional unit (Unit II) is primarily responsible for the reception, analysis, integration, and storage of information. This unit occupies the posterior region of the cerebral hemispheres and incorporates the visual (occipital), auditory (temporal), and general sensory (parietal) regions. The temporal lobes, located near our ears, interpret basic characteristics of sound, pitch, and rhythm. The temporal lobes are areas believed responsible for hearing, listening, language, and memory storage. The occipital lobes receive sensory information from the eyes and

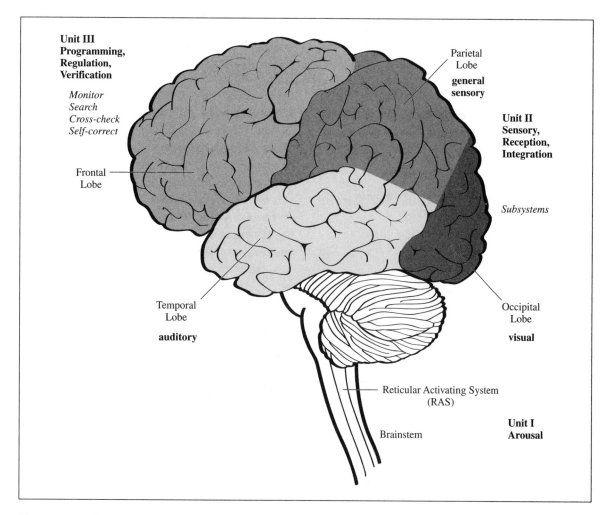

Figure 1–5. *The Surface of the Left Hemisphere of the Brain with Four Lobes and Their Functions Labeled According to the Luria Model*

interpret shape, color, and movement. The parietal lobes are the general sensory areas and are responsible for touch, pressure, cold, and heat and deal with the reception of sensory information, which involves movement. Each of these lobes processes the same information in different ways and different parts of the brain. There is much overlap in the functions of each of these lobes. These three parts of the brain appear to be involved with types of memory. The parietal, upper temporal, and occipital lobes seem to serve as short-term memory banks for auditory, visual, and kinesthetic (motion, perception) impulses. Actions described as subsystems, as discussed in Bruner's (1973) and Clay's (1991) work, are similar to behaviors associated with Unit II.

The sensing, receiving, and integrating unit is involved in specific interactions that involve cortical processing in the temporal, occipital, and parietal lobes of the brain. Through the button

jar game, Ken learned how to integrate and coordinate actions while involving these three lobes of the brain. For example, he learned to

◆ control arm, hand, and eye movements while placing buttons into discrete groups
◆ examine and make discriminations, thus fine-tuning his perceptual skills
◆ integrate and connect gesture, touch, sounds, and words with feelings

The third functional unit is located in the area around your forehead. It is involved in purposeful acts, which Luria termed *programming*, *regulation*, and *verification*. The frontal lobes play an essential role in regulating the state of the activity, organizing and changing it in accordance with complex intentions and plans formulated with the aid of speech. As the assembly of neurons in the frontal lobes mature, they team up with neurons in the RAS, which directs arousal and alertness, and with the limbic system, which regulates hormones and emotions, forming a loop that works to help us select and direct attention. An important function of this loop is regulating the child's ability to use "feedback" as an ongoing check on behavior. This feedback system helps us monitor and catch our errors and remember what we are supposed to do to resolve problems.

Varied experiences with the button jar provided opportunities for Ken to program, regulate, and verify his actions. For example he learned how to:

◆ categorize objects into discrete groups according to a plan of action
◆ develop a flexible classification system
◆ recognize similar and different patterns
◆ think creatively about how to classify and group buttons
◆ reorganize or reclassify individual buttons in a variety of ways
◆ find solutions or rationales for Mom's plan for organizing and developing categories
◆ regulate his behavior to develop his own plan for organizing information

As Luria's theory suggests, each unit of the brain is localized in a specific brain area, but because many brain units are involved, widely distributed brain areas take part in mental tasks. Thus the performance of any one brain region is shared or influenced by the structures and the functional organization of other regions of the brain. Additionally, the cortex and the subcortical regions of the brain, particularly the limbic and reticular systems, form a highly interconnected system in which many parts contribute to a particular mental task and both hemispheres are involved. In fact, the brain is so interconnected that it is difficult to know where any particular subsystem begins or ends.

The Brain Is a Pattern Synthesizer

The sixth principle, documented in recent clinical research, has shown that the brain is a natural pattern seeker and synthesizer and actively searches for patterns to categorize, organize, synthesize information, code it into memory, and then retrieve it. The brain's neural network categorizes stimuli into groups that form patterns and responds to patterns that have been established by past ex-

perience (Greenspan 1997). This research also reveals that our minds can instantly retrieve similarly coded information relevant in one situation and use this formerly coded information in a similar way for the new situation The following example illustrates how this can happen.

The Calendar Trick

Every year I buy a linen calendar towel, which depicts the days of the week for each month on one tea towel. I have a collection of towels that spans over forty years. When Ken was two, one of his favorite pastimes was going to the kitchen drawer and throwing the calendar towels out on the floor. Instead of sleeping during nap time, he would take several towels to his room and carefully line them up according to years on the floor. I never understood why he did this, but as long as he was quiet, I didn't care.

When he was two and one-half years old, Ken asked my husband and I to give him a date and he would tell us what day of the week the date fell on. We would say August 7 and he would tell us Thursday. After checking his response, we found out that he was right. We would ask him random dates in different months and years and he always would tell us the correct day of the week. What was particularly amazing was how fast he could do this calculation. But when asked how he did it, he said he didn't know. What we did learn, however, was that he recognized similarities and differences among dates for each month depicted on the towels and he recognized recurring patterns of numbers among the days of the week and months of the year.

The neighbors and relatives soon learned about Ken's calendar trick. He could tell people what day of the week their birthday would fall on two and three years later, or what day Christmas fell on four years ago. He could tell us the day of the week for specific dates in the past, present, and future years, even accounting for a leap year. We received an invitation to take Ken to appear on the Johnny Carson show, which we turned down; however, my husband thought about taking Ken to the local bar to make some money. I nixed this idea.

When he was three and one-half years old, Kenny finally told us how he did the calendar trick. He said that if you know what day of the week the first of the month falls on, you can figure out the rest of days for every month in the year, because the same day of the week has the same numbers all the time. If the first day of January falls on a Thursday, then the other Thursdays in January will be on 8, 15, 22, and 29. If the first day of March falls on Sunday, then the remaining Sundays in March will be 8, 15, 22, and 29.

Ken had discovered patterns among and across the dates of each day of the week and in each month of a specific year. He developed a more complex and intricate skill beyond what we had learned while playing with buttons. He generalized properties and skills learned in one context and applied them to a new context. Ken acquired the ability to go from concrete thinking and categorizing developed through various activities involving the button jar, to abstract thought developed independently, evident in the calendar trick. Ken was able to retrieve this stored information rapidly and reliably because his affective capacity organized information in an especially functional and meaningful manner. Because the information was dual coded according to its affective sensory and cognitive qualities, he had the structure and circuitry set up in his brain to enable him to retrieve it easily. He probably was also motivated to share the calendar trick with us because he had received such positive reinforcement in the button jar game. The pleasure he experienced was not simply one of mastery, but one of feeling good and seeing the pleasure of others.

Although Ken's discovery of number patterns and their relationships is sophisticated for a three-and-one-half-year old, there are many preschool children who know how to count to twenty, their phone numbers and home address, the letters of the alphabet, how to write their names and the names of family members, and how to read simple books.

Neural Plasticity of the Brain

The seventh principle, also documented in recent research (Gopnik, Meltzoff, and Kuhl 1999), reveals that the most phenomenal attributes of the brain are the abilities of the neural tissue to change through activation. Neural plasticity is an intrinsic beneficial characteristic of the brain that gives us the ability to learn and the ability to adapt in response to new stimulation—to relearn. Beginning shortly after conception and lasting throughout a lifetime, the neural system is dynam-

ically changing. As we develop, move, and learn, the cells of our nervous system connect in highly complex patterns forming many different neural pathways. The patterns are organized and reorganized throughout life, allowing us an ever-greater ability to take in additional information and learn.

Medical research using MRIs and PET scans of stroke patients has shown that if there is trauma or damage to one of the brain's hemispheres, the intact hemisphere will reorganize and rewire itself to compensate for the lost function. I experienced this phenomenon firsthand with my mother.

As reported earlier in this chapter, my mother's stroke affected her left hemisphere, which for most right-handed individuals is the seat of language production. She started working with a speech therapist as soon as possible, and, after eight months of therapy, she was talking again. Her intact right hemisphere took over. Mom, with the help of a speech therapist, rewired her brain. It has been sixteen years since her stroke and most people would not know she once had difficulty speaking.

This research has also shown that children living in impoverished surroundings (orphanages, third-world countries, countries involved in wars), develop different brain structures than children who have experienced enriched environments. Yet, once removed from the impoverished context and placed in a more stable enriched environment, they acquire more neurons. These enriched environments included ongoing positive social interactions, which induced dramatic anatomic changes in the individual's brains, particularly the cerebral cortex, hippocampus, and cerebellum.

Conclusion

The plasticity and exquisite organization of the brain and nervous system give us the potential for lifelong learning when two conditions are met. First, the individual experiences an enriched environment, which includes positive social interactions and meaningful conversations. Second, the individual has the will, which includes motivation and determination, to learn and relearn. When the first condition is met, the second condition should emerge. The seven principles of learning presented in this chapter should be of interest to parents of young children, early childhood educators, classroom teachers, and any educator looking to better reach all children and create opportunities that enable them to achieve their full potential.

Educational Implications

The juxtaposition of recent research on the brain with recent research in cognition and emotion suggests four implications about learning that can be translated into four applications for effective teaching.

Learning

- ◆ The brain's structure is determined by experiences. Primitive structures in the brain, such as those controlling respiration, heartbeat, circulation, and natural reflexes, are already wired at birth. But in the higher regions of the cortex, neural circuits are not developed. The 1,000 trillion synapses that will eventually connect infants' 1,000 trillion neurons are determined by their early experiences. The number of connections made in the brain depend on the amount of exposure infants have to language, sounds, and sights in their environment and the kind of emotional responses they have with parents and caregivers. This finding is encouraging because it implies that one's mental life is not wholly determined by genetics . . . environment and experience play prime roles in learning. Every child has the potential to learn.

- ◆ The growth and development of the brain, especially during the early years, depend heavily on the environmental input and the *kinds* of experience children have every day. New learning occurs as new sensory experiences modify and change. Moreover, because different regions of an infant's brain mature at different times, different neural circuits are more sensitive to experience at different ages (Levine 2002). It is critical that parents and teachers, especially those who work with young children, understand the various factors, discussed throughout this book, that influence how the brain develops and functions.

- ◆ Due to the plasticity of the brain, changes in the environment and experiences change the structure of the brain. That is why infants learn in the first place and can unlearn too.

Furthermore, the more infants repeat the same action, the more myelination of the neurons occurs, the more formation of certain neural connections in the brain, and the more fixed the neural circuits in the brain for that activity become. If the infant does not use the loosely myelinated brain circuits, the connections will not be adaptive; they will weaken and could eventually be lost.

The plasticity of the brain gives every child the ability to learn and relearn. This plasticity and exquisite organization of children's brains allow for unlearning and relearning when they experience an enriched, supportive, and challenging learning environment. Parents and teachers have enormous potential for providing opportunities to assist in the process.

- ◆ Children do not all learn in the same way. Rather, individuals have unique and specialized ways to develop concepts, think, and reason. Because children have different experiences to organize their brains, and each brain is uniquely structured as a result of these experiences, children must utilize many different ways or paths to learn. Therefore, it is preposterous to think that there is only one way to teach, especially something as complex as reading and writing.

Teaching

- ◆ Studies investigating children's learning (Greenspan 1997) show that variations in performance are due to the child's emotional state while learning and to how much immediate support the child receives. Therefore, parents and teachers who intervene early on when they observe the children's frustration while attempting to learn something are more likely to help them persevere and reach their full potential.

- ◆ Recent brain research shows that every child has unlimited potential for learning. This fact calls into question the notion that some children cannot learn. It also suggests that teachers who have a repertoire of ideas and techniques to draw upon will be able to trigger any one of the children's sensory maps. When one technique or approach to teach a child how to read or write is not working, they can rest assured that another will work.

Technological advances in neuroscience provide data showing that the acts of reading and writing depend on networks of neurons exchanging information and working together in an integrated way to extract meaning from sources of information (letters or sound, spelling patterns, cluster endings, syntax, and semantics) in written text. This research has revealed that learning to read and write is a very complex process. In order to help children construct a neural network to become proficient readers and writers, teachers must learn how to identify the complex and variable ways that children are attempting to process information and must provide differentiated instruction, using children's learning strengths to meet their idiosyncratic learning needs. As struggling children begin to actively and consistently initiate independent problem solving, they are able to reorganize their neural networks in more complex and efficient ways. Teachers must alter their instruction as children's competencies grow and develop.

◆ Every individual is always in the process of becoming . . . of developing neural networks. Limiting anyone, especially a beginning reader, with labels like "learning disabled," "language delayed," "developmentally delayed," or "emotionally handicapped" may prevent some children from having an opportunity to reach their full potential because the labels may interfere with teachers' attitudes and abilities to teach "labeled" children.

Throughout this book, examples of labeled children who learned to read and write are presented and discussed. Interviews and examinations of teacher and student interactions reveal that when teachers have high expectations and determination, they find a way to reach and teach all children, even those who are labeled. The remaining chapters in this section provide an in-depth look at the major factors that impact how the brain functions as children learn to think and act: attention and movement; language; and emotion and memory.

Chapter 2

Attention, Movement, and Learning

The notion that learning occurs when individuals are actively engaged in self-directed problem solving is not new. What is new is that recent discoveries in neuroscience have enabled researchers to gather more precise information about the development of the brain's attention and movement mechanisms and how they interact to facilitate learning. In this chapter I discuss the development of attention; the critical role movement plays in regulating, supporting, and directing attention; and the influence of attention and movement on learning in general and learning to read and write in particular.

Attention

Attention is a mental act of keeping one's mind closely on something—mental concentration—which is the foundation of learning. Individuals who are attentive have acquired the ability to focus their minds and sustain their foci until the task is completed; those who have difficulty attending experience difficulty learning. It is difficult to discuss attention without mentioning consciousness, which is awareness of one's surroundings, feelings, and thoughts. Although we do not have a clear description of consciousness, research in neuroscience has provided insights into the basic properties, functions, and roles of attention (Ratey 2001).

We know, for example, that attention is much more than simply taking note of sensory information coming in from our environment. Our brain's attention system:

◆ constantly surveys the environment to determine what is and is not important;

◆ decides how much and what kind of sensory information is needed to complete a task;

◆ allocates varied amounts of mental energy depending on task demands;

◆ sustains focus when the task is not interesting;

◆ determines if and when the task will be completed;

◆ persists in tasks long enough to finish them despite distractions;

◆ disengages from a current task when something more important requires immediate attention, response, or action.

All these aspects of attention are critical to learning.

In a recent study, Gopnik, Meltzoff, and Kuhl (1999) found that (1) preschool children vary in the length of time and developmental path they take toward regulating attention and (2) the lengths of time children sustain their attention is externally controlled by the physical properties of the object. For example, when toddlers can see, touch, move, manipulate, hear, and feel an object, they will attend for several minutes. And, when a parent or teacher engages in a conversation with the child (even if the parent does all the talking), the toddler's attention span increases by several minutes. The research has also shown that preschool children who have opportunities to make up a story, fantasize, and pretend while playing with an object or toy (e.g., boxes, dolls, or cars) are generally more attentive and stay absorbed in the activity for longer periods of time. Furthermore, their attention nearly doubles if they are engaged in conversation with others while playing. But when given a teacher-directed activity that is too difficult or uninteresting, preschool children disengage and become unmotivated and inattentive.

The Development of the Brain's Attention Mechanisms

Infants are born with assemblies of neurons to facilitate attention. Until recently, we had a limited understanding of the neurological and biological basis and development of these neural networks and structures that control attention. Today, with help from advanced technology and research, we have a clearer picture of how the brain's attention mechanisms work together to monitor and process information.

Neuroscientists have identified four distinct components within the attention system: arousal, motor orientation, novelty detection and reward, and executive organization (Ratey 2001). These four components of attention interact to detect and select what is important, focus the mind, and sustain the focus until the task is completed (Figure 2–1).

Component	Definition	Location of Brain Structures
1. Arousal	Ability to suddenly increase alertness	Reticular activating system (RAS) located in brainstem; connects brainstem, sense organs, limbic system, and frontal lobes
2. Motor orientation	Facilitates and maintains arousal	Cerebellum
3. Novelty detection and reward	Focuses and sustains attention	Limbic system includes portions of frontal lobes, temporal lobes, thalamus, hypothalamus, and pathways that connect them
4. Executive organization	Directs actions and integrates entire attention system	Prefrontal cortex and cingulate gyrus

Figure 2–1. *Components of the Attention System and Location in the Brain*

Arousal

Arousal is the ability to suddenly increase alertness. It is the first site and lowest level of our attention system. The brainstem is responsible for one's general state of arousal. The brainstem controls the necessary functions of the body that support life, such as breathing, circulation, heartbeat, and reflexes. The brainstem is the stalk of the brain. Through it pass all the nerve fibers that relay signals between the spinal cord and the cerebellum.

Running through the core and situated at the top of the brainstem is the reticular activating system (RAS), which is composed of a large number of neurons that receive and integrate information for all regions of the central nervous system (Figure 2–2). The RAS connects the brainstem, sense organs, limbic system, and frontal lobes, which interact to form the arousal circuit. The RAS is the part of the brainstem that is absolutely essential for life. When a baby is born, these primitive neural structures in the brain are already wired.

At birth, infants engage in brief, unfocused receptions of sensory stimuli from the environment. This passive process is helpful because it allows infants to process as much sensory information as possible while actively searching for anything that might require immediate attention. For several months, newborns do not perceive everything that takes place before their eyes or hear all the sounds in their complex environment. They limit the sensory information and increase alertness to specific aspects of the environment that pique their interest. The intensity with which infants process sensory information depends on

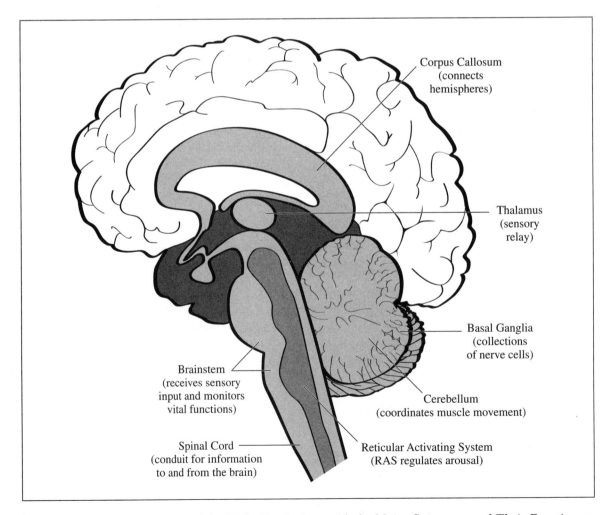

Figure 2–2. *The Midline View of the Right Hemisphere with the Major Structures and Their Functions Labeled*

their level of interest and alertness as determined by the RAS.

The RAS serves as a trapdoor, deciding what incoming information from the senses will be sent to the rest of the arousal circuit for processing in the frontal lobes and what will be kept out of consciousness. This selective attention mechanism saves information an individual thinks is important and discards the rest. Individuals have voluntary control over the RAS.

The RAS first focuses on the physical environment and directs our conscious attention to the comfort and maintenance of our bodies and to our well-being. For example, if you see a dog barking and running toward you, your attention is riveted on the approaching dog. The RAS immediately sends the information to the frontal lobes for processing. Is this dog friendly or mean? Will the dog bite me?

When trying to learn something new, your attention might focus on the environment. Is the room too dark or bright, hot or cold, noisy or quiet? Is this desk too low or high? Am I hungry? For some children these factors impact their ability to attend. Children who are easily distracted or respond indiscriminately to irrelevant noises or sights have difficulty focusing their attention and sustaining their focus.

Next, the RAS directs conscious attention to sensory information the individual thinks is important. Because our brain cannot process all the information we are receiving, it selects specific aspects of the environment that contain potentially useful information and ignores the rest. Recent research (Gopnik, Meltzoff, and Kuhl 1999) reveals that infants only a few days old will focus their attention on human voices and faces. Each time an infant gazes intently at a mother's face or listens to a lullaby she sings, neurons are activated and knitted together to start a memory of the mother's face and tone of her voice.

Arousal is critical to becoming literate. Emergent readers and writers must know what to pay attention to and how to focus their attention. They must be able to determine and select what is relevant to the task and discard irrelevant information. For example, they must learn how to attend to the distinct features of a letter so that they can distinguish between an *m* and an *n*. But before they can begin to process any information at the higher cortical regions of the brain, they must be aroused and actively engaged in the process.

Motor Orientation

At the next level of attention, motor orientation facilitates and maintains arousal. Located in the cerebellum, the motor centers enable us to physically reorient our bodies so that we can immediately direct our senses and attention. Motor orientation occurs as our sense organs turn to focus on the task at hand, which generally involves new, unexpected, or startling information and/or ideas. Motor orientation allows us to involve our senses in a concrete, coordinated manner and to process the new information in as short a time as possible. Like the arousal system, motor orientation is basically involuntary and will first be directed to the comfort and maintenance of our bodies. When we notice that the approaching dog is a large German shepherd who is not barking but growling and baring his teeth, we immediately orient our bodies to protect ourselves from danger.

Ratey (2001) described a three-step process by which individuals develop motor orientation: disengage, move, and engage. As the German shepherd approaches, you stop what you are doing (disengage), get a stick (move), and put the stick in front of you to protect yourself from an attack (engage).

Motor orientation is also apparent in the first few weeks after birth. Newborns will follow a moving object with their eyes or turn their heads in the direction of a sound. Eye movement studies (Gopnik, Meltzoff, and Kuhl 1999) reveal that when given a complicated picture, infants will look at the edges of the picture first, suggesting that they are imposing order to their world. Paying attention to the edges of a picture is a good way of dividing a static picture into separate objects. Attention requires motor orientation in order to initially engage the infants' neurons required to initiate, complete, and sustain attention. Motor orientation directly influences infants' ability to learn because it organizes the environment and directs attention in a sequenced way to specific aspects of the task. For example, after the buttons were spilled on the floor, Kenny directed his attention (arousal) and oriented his body to push each button with specific colors into separate piles (see discussion in Chapter 1).

Motor orientation is critical to learning anything. Paying attention to a growling dog or too many words on a line of print requires focused sustained attention. Moving your eyes, gesturing with your hands, positioning your body, listening (the movement of your ear drum), and moving your lips, mouth, tongue, and so on when speaking contribute to a unified, controlled, focused motor orientation and action while reading and writing. The three-step process involved in motor orientation (disengage, move, engage) is illustrated by a six-year-old reading *Cat on the Mat* by Brian Wildsmith.

MARY: "The cat on the mat."
TEXT: The cat sat on the mat.
MARY: [stops reading (Disengage); extends her finger and places it on the first word of the text (Move); rereads the sentence pointing to each word in left-to-right sequential order (Engage)]

Using her finger to guide the processing, Mary redirected her eyes and voice to match what she said, saw, and heard to the specific words on the page. Once an individual is aroused, has selected what to attend to, and has oriented her sensory organs and body to the task at hand, the third process, novelty detection and reward, is operationalized.

Novelty Detection and Reward

The limbic system is responsible for the third component of attention, novelty detection and reward. The limbic system is an interconnected group of brain structures, including portions of the frontal lobe cortex, temporal lobe, thalamus, and hypothalamus as well as circuitous fiber pathways that connect them (Figure 2–3). The limbic system is associated with learning and behavior.

The limbic system provides emotional overtones and motivation for learning . . . two critical functions for focusing and sustaining individuals' attention. It is an integral part of the attention circuitry that activates and directs messages to the frontal lobes. The limbic system can either facilitate or shut down the processing system if it fails to find some kind of challenge (novelty detection) and personal and emotional connection for whatever the brain is being asked to do (the reward). Moreover, if an individual displays strong emotion (either negative or positive), less emotionally charged information may never make it through the limbic system to be processed by the frontal lobes.

According to Ratey (2001), detecting novelty and seeking reward are the two primary sources that determine where we focus our attention. The novelty system takes note of new stimuli or information. The reward system produces sensations of pleasure, assigning an emotional value to a stimulus, which also helps the child remember. If the German shepherd runs away and you are left standing alone (novelty detection), you will breathe a sigh of relief and feel pleased that you have successfully defended yourself (the reward).

Infant research (Gopnik, Meltzoff, and Kuhl 1999) has shown that mothers who put their faces very close to the child and address their baby by name, use shorter lively utterances, and speak in an unusually melodious fashion are more likely to capture the children's attention. If mothers direct their children to look at a colorful object (novelty detection), the infant will smile and coo with delight (reward). These types of activities will hasten the child's process of connecting words to objects. Additionally, infants who have such experiences on a routine basis will continue to want to play in a similar way throughout their lives. They have learned early on the wonders and joys of discovering new things about their environment.

Studies of parent and child interactions during play time (Berk 2001) reveal that overloading preschool children with too much information and stimulation leads to disorganization and causes them to withdraw from the parent and the task. These findings suggest the detrimental impact of excessive adult tutoring on young children. Parents should not make play into "lessons" to teach children color words, numbers, animal names, and so forth.

The novelty detection and reward system is critical to literacy learning as well. Providing children opportunities to read challenging books that will support their developing problem-solving strategies is very satisfying. The following transcript reveals one six-year-old child's excitement when she had found too many words in the line of text and corrected her error without help from the teacher.

MARY: Mrs. Roberts, I found what was wrong. [novelty detection] and I fixed everything by myself. [reward]
TEACHER: You sure did and I knew you could do it! You should be very proud of yourself. I am.

Children who have positive experiences while reading and writing are more likely to try different ways to solve the problem. They also enjoy

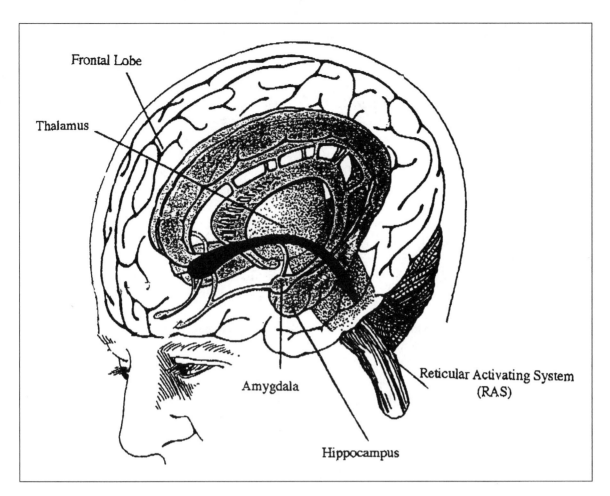

Figure 2–3. *The Limbic System with Major Structures Labeled*

engaging in the process of novelty detection and experiencing the reward when they self-correct.

Research has also shown that challenge fosters children's selective attention, motor orientation, and ability to detect what is novel and new. If a child is introduced to something new—for example, the slightly more complex processing involved in increasing the text difficulty—and has learned the necessary strategies to succeed, she will be motivated to try the novel task and gain personal and emotional satisfaction for her attempts. Children who are successful may become upset if the teacher or parent intervenes and tells them what to do because they are confident that they will eventually succeed without help.

Children who have negative experiences while trying to problem-solve during reading because the task is too difficult or they have not learned a repertoire of ways to resolve their conflict may quit trying. There is no reward in repeated failure. Children who continually experi-

ence failure are more likely to wait for the teacher to tell them what to do. Memories of the positive and negative emotional reactions will direct and dictate how individuals respond. If children generally have a positive response while learning, they will persevere; if the response is negative they will oftentimes avoid the task.

Researchers investigating preschool children's attention system (Ruff and Lawson 1990) report that threats (real or perceived) cause the limbic system to withdraw from the situation or task and not send information to the higher cortical regions of the brain, resulting in little motivation to attend and continue to problem-solve. Furthermore, the limbic system does not respond to reason. Telling a child to pay attention or get motivated is about as effective as telling a finicky cat to eat certain cat food. The limbic system is integral not only to attention but to many other brain functions, notably the emotional and social brain. A discussion of the limbic system and the role it plays in emotion, motivation, and learning is presented in Chapter 4.

Executive Organization

The fourth component of our attention system, the executive organization, directs our actions and integrates our entire attention system (Figure 2–4). It is comprised of the prefrontal cortex and cingulate gyrus, which are anatomically interconnected and command action and reaction, integrating our attention with short- and long-term memory. The executive organization components complete our attention network, which is a cognitive system involved in selective attention, mental resource allocation, problem solving, decision making, and voluntary movement control (Ratey 2001).

The cingulate gyrus region mediates communication between the prefrontal cortex and limbic system and is active when we need controlled, distributed attention such as attending to the words on the page we are reading while building up meaning from pages of text previously read. It can also regulate its own dopamine levels, which stimulate the reactivity of neural networks to enhance learning. The cingulate gyrus determines which bits of sensory information we are to attend to and sends that information to the prefrontal cortex.

The primary emotional signal the anterior cingulate gyrus receives comes from the amygdala, at the core of the limbic system. The amygdala influences attention by assigning emotional significance to incoming information. Because the cingulate gyrus is part of the limbic system, its participation in the control of attention suggests strong ties between emotion, motivation, and attention. Although the control of attention is related to the child's increasing awareness of what he can do unassisted and helps him complete a task through demonstration and conversation, the shift from external to internal control of attention is related to changes in motivation.

The prefrontal cortex in the frontal lobes controls the executive function, determining which information should be dealt with, for how long, and with how much energy. It decides if the incoming information should be mulled over or forgotten. The executive function plays a major role in the ability to sustain attention by blocking out irrelevant information or stimuli. It allows you to ignore or tune out noise in a classroom or conversations

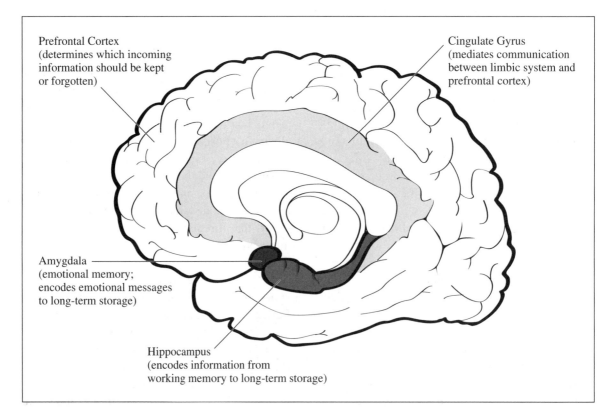

Figure 2–4. *The Limbic System: Executive Organization with Major Structures Labeled*

of others while reading a book and to sustain attention even when the material is not terribly interesting.

Pulling It All Together: The Brain's Attention System

Four components within the attention system—arousal, motor orientation, novelty detection and reward, and executive organization—contribute to the brain's overall ability to monitor incoming information from the environment. These components work together in the following way.

The reticular activating system (RAS), located at the top of the brainstem, allows stimuli coming from the environment to enter the brain and be relayed through sensory organs—the occipital lobes (vision), temporal lobes (hearing, language, and smell), and parietal lobes (general sensory, touch)—of the right and left hemispheres of the brain to the limbic system and to the frontal lobes. As the frontal lobes mature, they team up with the RAS, the brain's gatekeeper, which directs arousal and alertness, and with the limbic system (memory, emotion, and cognition) forming a loop that works as a gating system to select and direct attention. An important function of this loop is to regulate the ability to use verbal feedback (language directives) and nonverbal feedback (ideas and actions) that provide an ongoing check on one's own behavior. The feedback loops help children focus attention, remember previously learned information, and persevere until they resolve the problem.

As children learn to control where to focus attention, they must also learn to develop a plan; act on it in an organized, efficient manner; and maintain attention until the task is completed. Infants have a very short attention span and are easily distracted. As they enter early childhood, however, their attention span becomes more sustained and stable.

Recall Kenny's interest in playing the button jar game. At the age of seven months, he could remain actively involved and attentive while manipulating the buttons for about five minutes. He enjoyed seeing and hearing the buttons scatter on the floor, feeling the texture of a button, and tasting them (until I stopped him). Kenny could also point to the pile of white buttons when asked, even though he could not say the word *white*. As the game became more difficult—for example, he had to identify distinct features of a button, categorize it, and put it into specific group (e.g., colors, shapes, sizes)—his attention span increased. By the time he was twelve months old, Kenny could remain attentive for approximately fifteen minutes at one sitting.

Kenny developed the flexibility (1) to control and manage attention requiring activation of the brain's attention mechanisms and (2) to prevent inappropriate or competing responses. Because attention and motor orientation are linked, limits on attention are related to how many times the child repeats the activity. Activities that have been repeatedly performed become extremely efficient, less demanding, and automatic.

Once tasks become automatic, they are completed without conscious thought. The more often this occurs, the more quickly and efficiently the memory of that

Infants who are read to regularly learn how to focus their attention, manipulate books physically, and make "reading-like" sounds.

action can be retrieved with little conscious thought, which may explain why some children, when confused while reading a more complex sentence, automatically and without prompting take their finger and point to the words to get back on track. Pointing controls and focuses their eyes on the words in the text. Once they comprehend what they read, children will remove their finger and regain speed and fluency. As the new skill becomes routine, attention is freed for learning new concepts, which will lead to more complex reasoning. In this way, learning to read and write influences the development of attention as much as attention affects learning.

Selective attention and the organization of a response to act are critical to learning how to read and write. Ratey's (2001) explanation of how these four components of the attention system work together quickly to develop our attention mechanisms are useful in thinking about how emerging readers learn to attend to print. The following example illustrates the process.

Patty, a first-grade student, is reading *Willy the Helper* by Catherine Peters. In the story the family dog, Willy, tries to help the mother, father, and two children with their chores, but he always ends up making a mess. On page 2, Willy is sitting on the bed waiting to help the little girl, who is looking at a bed covered with clothes.

PATTY: "On Monday Willy helped me . . ." [stops (arousal)]

TEXT: On Monday Willy helped me fold the clothes.

PATTY: [long hesitation, looks closely at the unknown word *fold* while running her finger under the four letters, moves her mouth, and whispers the sounds she hears as she reads the word (motor orientation, novelty detection)]

PATTY: "fix," It can't be "fix," there is no *x*. [(executive organization) realizes that *fold* does not end in an *x*.]

PATTY: [long hesitation; looks closely at the unknown word, *fold*, while running her finger under the four letters; moves her mouth; and whispers the sounds she hears as she reads the word (motor orientation, novelty detection)]

PATTY: "find!" It can't be "find," there is no *n* in the middle. [(executive organization) realizes that *fold* does not have an *n* in the middle of the word and heard the *n* when she said *find*.]

PATTY: "Fold," I got it. "Fold" looks right. "On Monday Willy helped me fold the clothes."

In less than one minute, Patty chose between three meaningful and syntactically appropriate alternatives and found the one best-fit solution.

Ratey (2001) points out that "understanding attention and consciousness is fundamental to understanding ourselves . . . how we perceive information, how we attend and become conscious of it, and how we know. Attention and consciousness are the foundations on which we create an understanding of the world. Together they form the ground upon which we build a sense of who we are . . . the basic functions that give rise to "the mind" (111).

The more we understand the complex and elaborate interplay of the brain and body to regulate attention and consciousness, the clearer it becomes that movement is essential to learning. The next section discusses how and why movement is crucial to learning.

Movement and Learning

Today, neuroscientists have convincing evidence that cognitive processes involved in learning and remembering are carried out by the different regions of the brain responsible for movement. Ratey (2001) argues, "There is mounting evidence that shows that movement is crucial to every other brain function, including memory, emotion, language, and learning . . . and that higher brain functions have evolved from movement and still depend on it" (148). But what role does movement play in thinking and learning and how does this develop?

The Development of Movement

Anyone who has observed an infant for only a few minutes knows that primitive reflexes (e.g., sucking and thrusting arms and legs) dominate a newborn's movement. By two months of age fine motor skills begin to develop. Infants can open and close their hands around someone's finger and may hold an object for a few minutes. By the time they are four months old, infants can hold a rattle and put it in their mouths. Babies develop massive amounts of nerve networks to coordinate a repertoire of movements to go from lying to sitting, crawling, standing, and walking during the first ten to twelve months of life.

At the same time assemblies of neural networks to produce language are developing in the infants' brain. During the first six months of life, infants' small throaty sounds turn into cooing, crying, grunting, squealing, gurgling, and eventually words. All these acts involve motor networks of the brain.

Recent research (Gopnik, Meltzoff, and Kuhl 1999) has revealed that during the first year of life, reflexes fade and are replaced with intentional actions. Intention involves the planning, deliberating, and decision making that precede the child's action. In order for infants to translate thoughts into movements, neural networks located in the frontal lobes must be recruited. As Ratey (2001) points out, even emotions are intertwined with the brain's motor networks; the root of the word *emotion* is motion, which means *to move*.

Brain Structures That Control Movement

The brain operates as a whole in producing movement. The primary motor area in each hemisphere (see Figure 2–5) is devoted to movement.

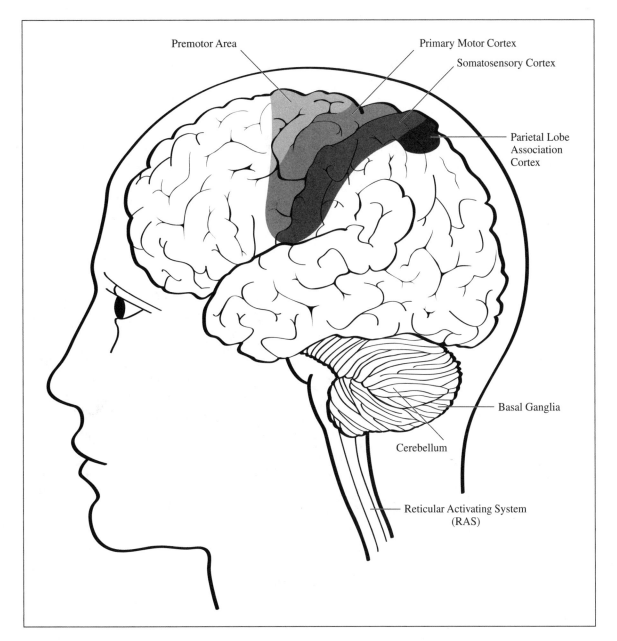

Figure 2–5. *The Primary Motor Areas of the Cerebral Cortex*

The motor cortex controls movements that involve learning, such as moving your eyes in a left-to-right order to read; movements made in response to an expected signal (e.g., too many words on the line of print, so I must reread). The primary motor cortex is more involved in controlling skilled, accurate movements than in producing automatic ones and seems to be unable to generate voluntary movement without input from the subcortical motor centers located in the brainstem, the basal ganglia, and cerebellum (see Figure 2–2).

Two other important structures regulate the performance of specific, directed voluntary movements: the basal ganglia and cerebellum. The basal ganglia are a collection of nerve cells at the base areas of the cortex that appear early in brain development. The cerebellum regulates the performance of specific, directed voluntary movements. The cerebellum sits on top of the brainstem, as can be seen in Figure 2–2, and coordinates the muscle activity in posture and movement of the hand, arm, leg, eyes, and so forth. It is critical for the performance of rapid, consecutive, simultaneous movements such as the sophisticated movements of a musician or a proficient reader and writer.

The cerebellum does not initiate movements, but rather modulates movements initiated by the motor cortex. Until recently, neuroscientists thought the cerebellum to be solely associated with control of muscle movement. Today, with advanced technology, it is clear that the basal ganglia and the cerebellum are also important in coordinating thought and action (Ratey 2001). These areas are connected to the frontal lobes, which are responsible for planning, problem solving, and timing of behavior.

The limbic system, which is a center for emotion and motivation, also plays an important role in movement. The limbic system determines which control system will be used for a given set of muscles, depending on the reasons for movements. For example, you would use one set of movements to escape if you thought a dog was going to attack. You would use a different set of movements if you were reading a book, encountered difficulty, and had to use several sources of information to self-correct.

How Movement Impacts Learning

Initially an infant has a difficult time learning how to organizing a sequence of actions to pick up an object, but eventually, after repeated and successful attempts, she can perform this task automatically and with little effort. Processes that are fundamental and mastered, such as picking up a toy, are eventually stored in and executed by the basal ganglia and the cerebellum in the lower brain. But this automaticity could not have occurred without the infant's intentionally activating assemblies of neurons in the motor areas of the cerebral cortex during the acquisition stage of development.

A similar principle can be applied to learning how to read and write. Initially the child may have difficulty learning how to read in left-to-right serial order across a line of print. The teacher will show her how to consciously direct this movement by taking her hand and finger to point to each word, one after another, in a left-to-right fashion, an action sequence carried out in the motor cortex. Eventually the child will use her eyes alone, still a motor movement, to read a book because

Eight-month-old Cori has started to develop the attention and movement mechanisms necessary to read her book.

the left-to-right directional scanning movement has become automatic and relegated to the basal ganglia and cerebellum to be carried out. When encountering harder texts, however, she may need to resort to overt movement and use her finger to guide the processes, a decision made in the frontal lobes in her brain.

Writing is also a sensory-motor skill that involves a coordination of a range of muscles in your fingers, hand, arm, neck, and shoulder. Writing directs the eye and the brain where to attend, focuses the mind on various features of print, and helps to develop visual analysis skills. The eye, ear, and hand are involved in a coordinated movement as a young child writes. Movement is thus tied to cognition because the higher cortical motor regions and frontal lobes of the two hemispheres are responsible for learning, routinizing, and processing motor and mental functions in parallel.

Parallel processing of motor and cognitive functions also helps us when we are experiencing learning difficulties. For example, when a child is having difficulty remembering how to make a letter, saying the words to direct her action will generally assist recall. The child is activating numerous motor centers, either deliberately or automatically, to form the letter. As tasks become more complex, the interconnection of movement and cognitive processes becomes stronger. When working well, the motor system allows individuals to shift back and forth between deliberate and automatic movements and deliberate and automatic cognition.

How Movement Facilitates Early Learning

Infant research has shown the important role movement plays in early learning. Bruner (1973) studied infants developing the skilled actions required to successfully grasp an apple sitting on a table. He describes a six-stage process in the development of the sequenced movement that enables infants to perform this skilled action.

Stage 1   The infant attends to the task and performs some anticipatory actions. In this stage the child's selective attention system (RAS) focuses her mind on the apple. The infant's eyes are focused on the apple and her entire body moves in anticipation of getting the apple. Her brain receives sensory perceptions from the environment. These sensory signals occur before the action takes place and are called feed-forward signals.

Stage 2   A loosely ordered series of actions occur, only roughly approximate, variable, and requiring much effort. The child extends her hand and fingers to grasp the apple but she cannot orient her body—specifically, hand, eyes, and fingers—in an action sequence to reach the apple. The movement is clumsy and the apple falls on the floor. Every time the infant attempts to get the apple, her brain is receiving feedback that will help to redirect and reorganize the sequence of actions.

Stage 3   The clumsy stage changes to success with a short series of acts in proper sequence (serial order). For example, she may on occasion control the extension of her arm, hand, and fingers to touch the apple but cannot put her fingers around the apple to grasp it. Through repeated actions, false moves, and self-corrections the infant becomes more skilled and there is a noticeable change in the sequence of acts, suggesting that she has acquired a new structure. This new structure is the neural development of motor and sensory pathways in the brain.

Stage 4   Reinforcement or success modifies the action pattern so that it becomes less variable. The more often the infant tries to get the apple from the table, the more likely she is to develop an effective sequenced series of movement patterns. The motor and sensory pathways in the brain are developing myelin. The more successful the infant becomes, the less feedback is needed.

Stage 5   With practice the infant does not need to attend to all sections of the sequence. Subroutines (Unit II of Luria's model of the brain; see Figure 1–5) are formed, which the child executes with little attention. The infant has learned how to coordinate sensory movement patterns to grasp the apple. As subroutines in the brain are formed and linked, the infant's movements become more automatic and require less attention and effort. The subroutines became part of a new series of actions in a higher-order structure (Unit III in Luria's model—the frontal lobes). This stage is a transition between receiving feedback (the infant was not successful in grasping the apple) and knowledge of results, which occurs when the infant has successfully grasped the apple.

Stage 6   With more practice, the skilled performance becomes less variable, anticipation becomes more accurate, and speed and fluency increase because an economy of attention and effort has been achieved. The infant can easily reach the apple and anything else she wants to grasp. The more myelin that is built up on the neurons, the more automatic the processing. With repetition myelin grows, the connections become stronger and easier, and a memory is formed. When the infant has learned how to organize and coordinate a sequence of actions to successfully complete the task at hand, she is freed to anticipate how to organize and control a sequence of actions on another occasion with similar results.

Bruner's careful description of infants developing a skilled sequence of actions illustrates the critical role attention and movement play in learning. It also shows that in order to learn and function well, the RAS, brainstem, cerebellum, motor cortex, frontal lobes, limbic system, and other areas of the brain must interact, coordinate, and provide feedback to the other organs.

Clay (1991, 2001) adapted Bruner's explanation of the development of skilled actions, referred to as a theory of serial order, to understand sequential acts required in learning how to read and write. The young reader must learn to control left-to-right directional scanning behaviors of sentences in a story, words in sentences, and letters in words. He must learn to look at and perceive the circles, curves, tails, and squiggles that make up an individual letter, and discriminate one letter from another. The young writer must learn how to attach lines, circles, dots, and tails in just the right way to make a specific letter.

Teachers can speed up children's development of these reading and writing skills by directing the child's attention through movement; for example, by

◆ taking the child's hand and pointing his finger to guide the directional behavior across a line of print;
◆ guiding the child's movements to write her name;
◆ clapping the child's hands to help her hear syllables in a word;
◆ guiding the child's hand while providing a verbal description of movement she is using to form a letter.

These movement actions ensure that the child is actively involved and attending to the task, which will facilitate the ability to remember the action. And as discussed earlier, many regions in the brain are working together to accomplish the task.

The coordination of body, hand, and eye movements are required if young children are to develop skilled actions to grasp something, bring a fork to the mouth, or ride a bicycle. Similarly, beginning readers and writers must acquire left-to-right directional scanning behaviors to attend to print and develop visual analysis skills to attend to the distinctive features of fifty-four upper- and lowercase letters of English and discriminate them one from another.

Clay (1991) points out that "when the child can point [to] one [word] after the other and can find the words in his speech, he still has the problem of coordinating the two activities, that is, making the motor pattern of his hand coincide with the word-finding activities of his ears and eyes" (164). Children who are having difficulty learning to read and write may not have learned how to attend to or coordinate their speaking, pointing, and looking behaviors.

Clay (2001) reports that in order to be successful, young readers and writers must focus and control their attention in three different ways:

1. Direct attention outward to print. In order to do this they must learn about directional rules and how the print is laid out in a book, where to start on a page to begin to read and write, how to move from left to right across the page, and how to return to the left side of the page to continue to read and write.

2. Switch attention from oral language (speech) to printed language (words) in the text. This process involves the coordination of their eyes, voice, and ears as they match what they say with the words that they see printed on the page.

3. Direct attention inward and think about many sources of information simultaneously to gain meaning from the text. These processes involve attending to different knowledge sources (e.g., visual, phonological, meaning, and structural information) as well as the print layout and so forth, making sure everything fits together and they understand what they read.

The complex processing necessary to become a proficient reader and writer will not occur without the integration of brain structures involved in attention and movement.

Movement and Learning to Read and Write: Research Studies

The critical and essential role movement plays in learning to read and write is documented in three unique studies. McQueen (1975) taught twenty-one student teachers to record in minute detail the body, head, hand, and eye movements of children between the ages of five and one-half and six and one-half years who were reading individually to their teacher. He reported differences among children in the degree to which they used their hands to guide their eyes while reading. McQueen found that wandering eye and hand movements provided information about the beginning reading status of the child, and he concluded that better readers may have developed controlled and persistent eye movements for visual scanning and attending to print.

Robinson (1973) conducted an investigation of beginning readers and writers in four schools to find evidence of a relationship between descriptors of literacy behaviors, including writing vocabulary and phonemic awareness in writing, and progress in reading. Fifty children ages five and one-half to six years and forty-five children ages six to six and one-half years were studied over a six-month period to capture changes in reading and writing progress over time. Robinson found that the main predictor of early reading

progress across all groups, including the proficient group, was the number of words a child could generate and write in ten minutes.

In order to quickly generate and then write many words in a ten-minute time frame, children must be able to hear the sounds, quickly call up the visual pattern of known words such as *are*, *you*, and *my*, and write each letter of the word in sequence simultaneously. There is a high degree of motor activity required to complete this action. Children must use the mouth, larynx, tongue, and so on to say the word orally and use the hand to form individual letters in one coordinated fluid movement.

Lyons (1995) studied the reading and writing behaviors of seventy-two first-grade children who were identified by Reading Recovery (RR) teachers as having the most difficulty learning to read and write. Analyses of lesson records and teacher interviews conducted over a five-year period revealed that all seventy-two students experienced the most difficulty learning

◆ how to make and label letters;
◆ how to attend to, focus on, and point to one word after the other when reading a line of text;
◆ how to hear and record sounds in words.

Interestingly each learning difficulty identified requires that the children attend and coordinate the movement of their bodies, hands, eyes, ears, and mouths. Once the RR teachers demonstrated how to control, coordinate, and regulate the necessary sequence of movements to complete each task, the children made better progress. The teachers reported that when compared to other RR students they had previous taught, the seventy-two children took from three to five weeks longer to develop these skills (Lyons 1995). This research supports Clay's (1993b) theory that struggling readers and writers must learn how to attend to the details and features of print with respect to rules of direction, formation of letters, and the sound sequence in words through active participation and movement.

The RR teachers' experiences working with these seventy-two children also support Bruner's (1973) description of a child's development of a skilled action and the emphasis on the role of movement in the process and Clay's (1991) reference to this theory of serial order to better understand how children learn to read. As shown in

Bruner's studies with infants, the coordination of a skilled behavior requires anticipation, focused attention, repeated attempts, sequential movement patterns, feedback, and reinforcement. With practice the processing becomes more accurate, fluent, and efficient. In my view the three studies reported in this section demonstrate how movement becomes a vital link to learning and thought processes.

Pulling It All Together: Movement Facilitates Learning

When babies are born they have virtually no motor control and only rudimentary reflexes. By six months most infants can sit up, raise their head, and turn to look at their parents. These actions involve three parts of the brain: the motor cortex, which initiates the action; the basal ganglia, which store the programs for habitual movements; and the cerebellum, which activates the motor nerves to make the movement. These three regions of the brain are involved in this movement pattern every time children crawl, put food in their mouths, and grab for a toy to hold in their hands.

As infants continue to try to grasp an apple (see Bruner's theory discussed earlier in this chapter), they receive feedback in the form of emotional satisfaction and praise from a parent. The neurons in the brain involved in the action myelinate and serve to permanently support the action sequence. Feedback serves to strengthen the encoded program of action (getting the apple and putting it in the mouth).

Without movement babies would not be able to explore their world and attempt to understand it. And it is from this world that all new learning comes. Physical activity (movement) involves all sensory motor components and requires that the entire brain work together in an integrated and coordinated way. Through play young children develop large and fine motor skills, connect sight, sound, touch, and body awareness, and understand the relationships among them. It is especially important to focus on helping the child make physical and mental connections through lots of self-organizing play activities while the brain is still developing rapidly, before ages four and five (Gopnik, Meltzoff, and Kuhl 1999).

Conclusion

Attention and movement are an integral part of all mental processing. They orchestrate the brain mechanisms and neural networks that create thought and facilitate learning regardless of the individual's age. In order to become self-directed and independent learners, children must attend and be actively engaged in a task. Movement is an indispensable part of focusing attention while an individual is interacting with her environment.

Movement facilitates learning by focusing children's attention and activating, integrating, and anchoring sensory information and experience in their neural networks, which is essential to learning. Movement is necessary to build thought and keep it from drifting out of individuals' consciousness so that they can develop and expand their understandings. For example, movement is essential to complete everyday routines that require focused attention, such as reading, talking, and writing. Individuals might think about something to say, but it is not until they choose the words to speak or move their hands to write that thoughts are anchored. Writers might not immediately read what they wrote, but movement required during the act of writing is oftentimes necessary to gain and gel thought.

I doubt that the low-progress students featured in this book would have learned to read and write without the help of expert teachers to focus and sustain their attention through movement. Examples of expert teachers' interactions with struggling students reveal the critical role movement plays in focusing and sustaining children's attention throughout the learning process.

Educational Implications

Attention is fundamental to all human thinking and learning. It determines what information children observe and what tasks they choose to do. Attention also determines when and if the task is completed and how well it is done. Parents and teachers play a major role in developing children's capacity to attend and to sustain their attention. It is critical that parents and teachers seize many opportunities to create learning environments to focus children's attention so that they learn during the years of greatest neurological malleability, which is from birth to eight years.

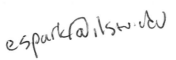
The following advice, offered to parents and teachers, supports the development of children's attention.

◆ Provide many opportunities to facilitate the development of the children's attention so that they are joyful, independent, self-directed learners from infancy and beyond. Keep tasks enjoyable and simple enough that children can feel successful and avoid making a "lesson" out of the activity. The parent who reads to a child to teach the letters of the alphabet and then quizzes her on the letter names when finished reading the story is robbing both of them of opportunities to enjoy and learn about each other.

◆ To help children control their attention, engage in conversation that is genuine and tied to a specific activity or task. Focus children's attention by relating the ideas to their experiences and personal world whenever possible. Drawing upon the children's experiences, interests, and ideas focuses and sustains their attention. Help children access prior knowledge that is not currently active but could be relevant to the current activity.

For example, as you read a story ask children what they think the characters will do and say. Ask children what they would do in a similar situation. Conversations about story characters and the problems they may be facing keep young children from becoming distracted, sustain attention, and show interest in children's opinions, which will motivate them to continue to be involved in the activity. Although attention becomes more sustained as children get older, experiences in early childhood equip children for more concentrated attention, which will be essential for success once they enter school.

◆ Develop activities and tasks that are challenging and well within children's capabilities. Challenging activities help to sustain children's attention *if* children feel they have a reasonable chance for success. To help them succeed, parents and teachers should show children how to quickly identify and focus on the most important information when attempting and completing a task. Selecting what children should attend to and not giving them too much information to process at once will prevent children from becoming discour-

aged and encourage perseverance. Shifting children's attention to relevant new information and helping them ignore nonrelevant, unimportant information builds a firm foundation for learning to read and write.

Recent research in neuroscience has demonstrated that movement is critical to every other brain function, including language, memory, emotion, thinking, and learning. A cognitive decision to move may involve billions of neurons, many of which include motor neurons to activate the muscle groups that enable children to move. Because children live in a wide variety of environments, their sensory-motor development beyond their innate survival needs (e.g., sucking and breathing) must be taught. Movement in the environment integrates and anchors new experiences and information and connects the neural networks in children's brains so that they can learn more complex movements. Parents and teachers can facilitate learning while actively engaging children in actions that require movement. The following suggestions are offered to support their efforts.

◆ Children need to use many sensory modalities to explore every aspect in their environment. Encourage children to move around, touch, smell, and, when appropriate, taste objects. The more senses involved in investigating an object, the more likely they are to develop ways to remember the object or recall their experiences. Reflection helps children incorporate prior knowledge into new information, which is essential to learning.

◆ The role of movement in connecting and developing neural structures is well documented (see Ratey 2001). Facilitate coordinated processing of motor, eye, and hand movements by using specific language and words to guide the children's behavior. For example, to teach children to write the first letter of their name, move their arm while directing their actions verbally.

MOTHER: Let's write the first letter in your name, Donna. [taking the child's hand] Start at the top and go down. [Mother and child make a vertical line down.] Move the pencil up. [Mother and child trace over the vertical line.] Now move the pencil around and touch the top of the line to the bottom of the line. [Mother and child make a curved line to complete the *D*.] That's the first letter in your name, Donna. What is the name of the first letter in your name? What letter did we just make?

DONNA: *D*.

The verbal direction helps Donna to attend to the sequence of actions required to make the letter *D*. It also directs Donna's attention while engaged in the process and cements the movement necessary to begin to develop a processing system that will eventually help her learn ways for remembering the letter name and recalling how to form the letter. Providing verbal directions while guiding children's movement is the form of encouragement and support that is critical to developing their ability to become successful readers and writers.

Parents, teachers, and other adults have tremendous influence on children's learning. They convey their culture to children and help them form attitudes, beliefs, and feelings of self-worth that will last a lifetime. Depending on the experiences they offer, these important adults can either support or stifle children's learning and learning potential.

Chapter 3

Language and Learning

Language, critical to nurturing and human survival, enables individuals to carry out five fundamental, compelling human urges: to show and receive love, to connect with others, to be emotionally secure, to understand the world and the people in it, and to reveal needs and desires. Most individuals think that language is the ability to express oneself with words, but it is much more. Language is any means of expressing or communicating to another through gestures, signs, and sounds. For example, when a two-month-old infant moves both arms up in the air, he is expressing a desire to be lifted. The child's movement is a form of language, an instinctive reflection and expression of the infant's need to communicate and make himself understood.

If asked when children learn language, most parents report the time when babies say their first words, which generally occurs between the ages of twelve and fourteen months. Neuroscientists have recently discovered, however, that this time period is not accurate. Infants know things about language, such as the sound system, long before they say their first words. Before birth, they hear the melody of their mothers' voices and by six months of age the native language a baby hears creates a permanent record in his brain that lasts a lifetime (Gopnik, Meltzoff, and Kuhl 1999). But how does this happen? And why is language critical to cognitive, social, and emotional development?

This chapter discusses recent scientific research about language acquisition, the social origins of language, the critical role language plays in learning and teaching, and the relationship between thought and language. Examples from my work with parents, children, and teachers help illustrate how to effectively interact and talk with children to support their developing language and ability to read and write.

The Biological Basis of Language

The basics of language are hardwired into the human brain before birth. The motor networks in the left and right hemispheres of the brain begin to form as the unborn infant moves with the mother's vibrations, rhythm of her heart, sound and tone of her voice. The movement resulting from the intricate combination of all these elements is the infant's means of expression. Movement through the motor cortex is very much a part of language production and thought.

As newborns hear the sounds of their native language, their brains construct auditory maps out of the smallest units of sounds in a language (phonemes). Different clusters of neurons in the auditory cortex respond to each phoneme and each cluster responds only when a nerve from the ear carries that particular sound.

Infants not only can hear the sounds in their environment; they can divide them into unique abstract categories. This process enables them to make all the distinctions that are used in all the world's languages (Gopnik, Meltzoff, and Kuhl 1999). Sounds that are clearly distinct ("da" and "ee") create clusters of neurons that are far apart in the auditory cortex of the brain. Sounds that are nearly the same ("da" and "ra") form clusters of neurons that are at close proximity.

The sounds infants hear and encode in the auditory cortex determine the very structure of their brains. Because infants have different experiences, their brains are organized differently, which explains why speakers of different languages hear and pronounce sounds differently. By the time he is twelve months old, the child's auditory map is formed and he will have difficulty hearing phonemes he has not heard before because there is no cluster of neurons to respond to that sound (Kuhl 1998).

Infants as young as five months can carry on a conversation without speaking one word. For example, when Kenny babbled while pointing to the button jar, I knew that he wanted me to put the jar on the floor. When he said, "daaaaa" while touching the cover of the jar, he wanted me to take it off and dump the buttons on the floor. Kenny was not only a full participant in our conversation, but he also initiated and controlled it.

As the infant plays with sounds (babbling), he develops neural networks. With repeated use, the neurons myelinate to form nerve fibers in the muscles of the voice box (larynx). The infant is then able to synchronize the tonal vibrations he is hearing with the sounds he makes by learning to contract or relax the muscles of the larynx. The ability to discriminate rhythm and tone along with the newfound ability to form words allows the child a greater sensitivity to dialect or accent. This heightened awareness makes learning a second language easier for a child than an adult.

In order to learn to speak so that they can be understood, infants must be able to hear the full tone, including the higher and lower tones that occur in normal speech. When these capabilities are impaired, language acquisition suffers. Some pediatricians believe that children who have many ear infections in the first years of life may miss these complex tones and are more at risk for specific hearing and speech difficulties (Gopnik, Meltzoff, and Kuhl 1999). Children who do not have opportunities to interact with others or are silenced have more difficulties learning how to communicate through language.

The neural connections between the motor cortex and the formal reasoning area of the frontal lobes are responsible for initiating and planning the complex movements crucial to language. These regions of the brain allow for constant interaction of muscle movements that enable infants to code words. For example, when an infant says, "Mama," the motor cortex stimulates muscular movements of the larynx, tongue, mouth, jaw, facial muscles, and eyes that form and give expression or emotion to the words. Without movement infants would not be able to express themselves. When babies are approximately twelve months old, patterns of their muscle movements help them code specific sounds into certain words.

The Social Origins of Language

Language is the primary avenue of communication with others and the means through which we represent our experiences. Young children learn and practice language by participating in purposeful activities organized by parents and other members of their cultural communities. In order to understand how children learn language, it is necessary to understand the nature of the social activities and interactions that adults devise for them.

During infancy babies learn to smile and babble while playing with toys as they interact with people, although these two activities are generally not happening simultaneously. But after nine months of age, a new stage of development is reached—social referencing. Social referencing marks the child's ability to coordinate their interaction with a person and with objects and respond to another's reaction to an object. For example, at three months old, Kenny would smile and babble while I gave him a bath and not pay much attention to the rubber toys floating in his bath water. When he was four months old, Kenny would babble and coo, talking to the toys in his bath water as he kicked them around. By five months, he could coordinate the two actions; interact with me and with the ducks floating in the bath water. Sometimes he would hide a duck from my view by pushing it to the bottom of the bathtub and engage in conversation.

MOM: I wonder where the rubber duck is hiding?
KEN: Coo, coo, da, da, da [laughs and smiles, holding the duck under the water and watching me look for it]
MOM: I can't seem to find that yellow duck anywhere. Come out yellow duck, please come out of the water.
KEN: [laughing, lets the duck go and it pops out of the water]
MOM: I am so glad to see you, yellow duck. Please don't hide from me anymore.

Kenny's babbling, laughing, and actions suggested that he understood our conversation and knew something about playing hide-the-duck, the rules of the game, and how to take turns. He also thought it was a very funny game so we played it often.

Our conversations during bath time were really an interaction of our minds, of our mental states whereby we let each other know what we were thinking. They probably had some effect on developing his ability to communicate with others. Peek-a-boo is probably the most common language game that adults play with infants. It teaches children how to wait their turn as they imitate adult's sounds and actions. Communication is fundamental to social interaction.

Gesture and Language

Studies of children from five to twelve months of age reveal that long before they start to talk, babies become skilled at using eye contact, facial expressions, and nonverbal gestures to communicate (Gopnik, Meltzoff, and Kuhl 1999). Infants at the one-sound (babbling) stage of language development spontaneously produce gestures along with their speech. I was watching my nephew put fruit on his eight-month-old daughter's plate. Suddenly Jordan threw her plate on the floor and, looking directly at my nephew, said, "da" in a loud, commanding voice. Her message was clear. "I am done and do not want any more food."

Jordan demonstrated that gesturing and speech are closely bound. She delivered a coherent message to the listener despite the fact that it consisted of two different modalities of expression. This coherence is possible because, before the communication unfolds, gesture and speech are part of a single idea. An expression proceeds the message, with most information channeled into speech and some information channeled into gesture. A mother might see her child running down the street and shout, "Stop" at the same time that she is putting up her hand to prevent the child from running into the street.

Gesture also plays a critical role in communication. Ratey (2001) reports a study conducted at the University of Chicago that involved eight unrelated deaf children—four from the United States and four others living in Taiwan. None of the children were the same age and none had been trained in standard sign language. They were individually administered problem-solving tasks in their home country. Each child was able to communicate through gesture to form complex sentences to solve the problem. The researchers found that the eight children made use of over ten thousand individual gestures and that their gesture system, rather than being associated with either English or Chinese, was similar.

Developing Concepts

Between the ages of fourteen months and four years, children develop a functional sense of objects and learn how to categorize and label them. Interactions grounded in purposeful, everyday activities facilitate the child's conceptual understandings. For example, when Kenny was about fifteen months old, he knew that the kitchen clock had something to do with bedtime. I would look at the clock and say, "It is seven o'clock, time to go to bed." After several weeks he would point to the clock and say in a questioning voice, "clock bed?" He could not tell time, but as he watched me looking at the clock he began to realize the clock had something to do with the day's ending and the time to go to bed. He was developing the concept of time by incorporating the word *clock* into a system of things related to time.

If the adult goes beyond the name to the object's function, the child can broaden his understanding (Gopnik, Meltzoff, and Kuhl 1999). Mom is getting daughter Kathy ready to go for a walk in the snow. She approaches the child saying, "Kathy here are your boots, help me put them on your feet." This one-sided conversation will help Kathy, associate the thing in the Mom's hand with the word *boot*. But if the parent added the following phrase, "and the boots will keep your feet dry and warm," while putting them on, Kathy would begin to understand the function of boots and build a broader context in which to create meaning. Since speech and language help us to define our world and our thinking, more open-ended conversations tied to an action may strongly facilitate language acquisition and creative thought processing.

Sharing a book with friends is a powerful way to learn how to think and communicate ideas.

Developing Vocabulary

The process by which children integrate their experience into a growing understanding of the world is how they learn to use language to convey specific meanings. Conversations with others build vocabulary before the age of two. Recent research shows that the size of a toddler's vocabulary strongly correlates with how much parents talk to the child (Gopnik, Meltzoff, and Kuhl 1999). The critical factor in developing vocabulary is how many times the child hears different words and the complexity of sentence structures. Parents who use complex sentences rather than baby talk to converse with their toddlers are more likely to have children with larger vocabularies.

Additionally, only face-to-face conversations, not television, facilitate children's language and vocabulary development. Children cannot have a two-way conversation with people on a television set. They learn how to use language in relation to talking with others about ongoing events. For example, toddlers are more likely to learn the concept "more" if it is tied to the mother asking if they want more milk. Or the concept "done," as Jordan demonstrated, will be more easily learned when associated with eating.

Thought and Language

No discussion about language would be complete without examining the theory of Lev Vygotsky (1978), a Russian psychologist who theorized that language is the major bridge between human beings' social and mental worlds and the most significant milestone in children's cognitive development. Vygotsky viewed language as an indispensable and distinctly human capacity that serves to integrate knowledge and facilitate thought. He regarded language as the primary avenue to communication with others and the means through which children learn to communicate thoughts, represent their ideas in words, and share their experiences.

Language is also a ready-made product of sociohistorical development. Alexander Luria (1976), a neurologist and colleague of Vygotsky, explained that from birth on, children live in a world of things that individuals in a society have created. These things are products of a particular culture and history. Beginning at birth, infants learn to communicate with others and develop relationships with things and concepts through the help of adults. Without this social interaction, children would not learn how to talk.

Studies of language learning (Bruner 1983) reveal that as infants construct meaning, they use each new experience to think how to reorder and expand their knowledge. Then they demonstrate that understanding through language. This concept became very clear to me during a family trip.

My husband and I took Kenny to his first parade when he was about ten months old. He loved it so much that we attended most of the parades in our county. The most memorable parade we watched was on the Fourth of July in 1974. We had already been to a parade in the morning and at the last minute decided to see a parade in a neighboring town. When we got there, hundreds of people were lined up along the parade route. I wanted to go home and tried to convince Kenny and my husband that the crowd was too large and we would not be able to get close enough to see the parade.

Ken, who was two years old, asked, "What is a crowd?" I explained that a crowd means too many people standing close to each other in one area. I pointed out how the people waiting for the parade were squeezed together. And when they squeezed together the arm and a shoulder of one lady touched the arm and shoulder of the man next to her. He seemed satisfied with my explanation, but it was not good enough to convince either of them to go home. We joined the crowd and stayed for the entire parade.

The next morning, Kenny and I went to the Farrow's Meat Market. We arrived just before 9:00 A.M. My car was the only one in the parking lot. It was a brilliant sunny day and as I was getting him out of the car, Kenny said, "Look at the crowd." I looked around the deserted parking lot and thought my explanation of a crowd went right over his head. So I asked, "What crowd?" "There," he said, pointing to the man walking down the street toward us. I said, "That's not a crowd, there is only one man. A crowd means a lot of people squeezed together, standing so close together that their arms and shoulders are touching each other just like we saw at the parade yesterday."

He said, "The man has a crowd on his face." Now I was really confused. I looked at the man again. I thought about what Kenny had said and then began to see the man's face differently. The

sun was shining directly in the man's eyes so he had to squint to see. His eyes were partly closed because the sun's light was too strong. When he squinted his eyes, nose, eyebrows, and forehead puckered. His nose appeared to touch his lips and forehead. He was squinting so much that the lower and upper lids of his eyes seemed to be touching. His face was contorted; it looked squeezed together.

Kenny had taken my description of the crowd at the parade to talk about the man he saw at the meat market. In trying to understand Kenny's understanding, I realized why he said the man has a crowd on his face. It made sense in this context. He had to learn when and how to use the word *crowd*, so that others would understand what he was trying to say. I acknowledged his use of the word *crowd* to talk about the man's face and then explained that crowd is used to talk about a lot of people—a crowd of people. I think he understood what I was saying because he would comment on the crowd of people at the grocery store or church.

Luria (1969) provides some insight into Ken's developing reasoning and understanding about how to use specific words to convey meaning.

> Language . . . is the source of thought. When the child masters language he gains the potentiality to organize anew his perception, his memory; he masters more complex forms of reflection of objects (and ideas) in the external world; he gains the capacity to draw conclusions from his observations, to make decisions, the potentiality of thinking. (85)

Toddlers are introduced to new concepts and new words every day. With feedback tied to a specific action, they begin to learn how to use language to analyze, generalize, and represent experience. Thus, language is an early self-extending system.

Conversation also helps children learn how to attend to various aspects of the task, guide their behavior during the act, and manage their actions—all important prerequisites to learning. The following conversation between a mother and her three-year-old daughter illustrates the process.

MOTHER: I need to measure out a cup of milk. Mary, will you help me?
MARY: OK [climbs on stool]

MOTHER: Help me look for the mark that means one cup. [shows Mary where to look on the measuring cup]. I will pour the milk and you tell me when to stop. [pours the milk slowly while Mary watches]

MARY: Stop! [Mom stops]

MOTHER: Did I get it right?

MARY: [looking closely at the mark her mother showed her] Yeah, you got it right.

The conversation between mother and child reveals how language served as a mediating mechanism that helped develop Mary's capacity to think. But how can adults build interdependent relationships with children that foster the development of meaningful skills that lead to independent, self-directing thinking and problem solving? Vygotsky proposed the concept of the zone of proximal development (ZPD) to accomplish this feat. Understanding how the ZPD works will help parents and teachers interact in such a way as to lead children forward and develop their capacity to think and learn.

Language and Assisted Performance in Developing the Mind

Two of Vygotsky's most compelling and profound ideas are the role of assisted performance (teaching) in the development of mind (learning) and the central role language plays in the process. Vygotsky (1978) believed that through language, higher mental functions (e.g., problem solving and decision making) are transferred and eventually acquired by learners, a process that occurs in the zone of proximal development (ZPD). He defined the ZPD as the distance between the child's actual development (the tasks the child can do independently) and the child's potential development (the tasks the child can do with adult help or in collaboration with more capable peers) (Figure 3–1). Vygotsky (1978) proposed that:

Every function in the child's cultural development appears twice; first, on the

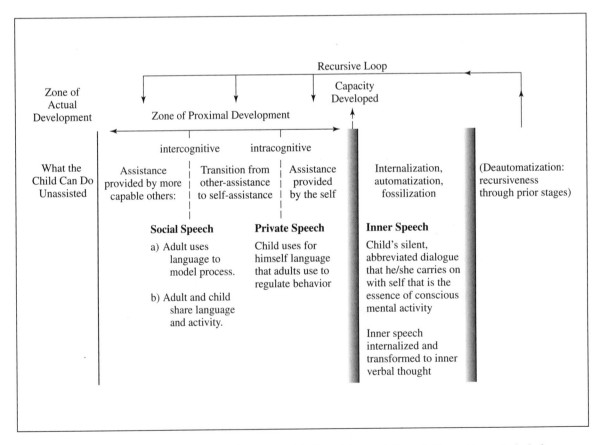

Figure 3–1 *The Zone of Proximal Development with Cognitive and Speech Transitions Labeled*

social level, and later, on the individual level; first, between people (inter-psychological), and then inside the child (intra-psychological). This applies equally to voluntary attention, to local memory, and to the formation of concepts. All the higher functions (problem solving, independent thinking) originate as actual relations between human individuals. (57)

Vygotsky (1978) argued that instruction (teaching) leads to the development of the child's mind and contributes to emotional growth and well-being. The purpose of instruction is to provide children with experiences in their "zone"—activities that are challenging but that can be successfully completed with sensitive adult guidance. The ZPD therefore depends on the teacher's potential to create opportunities to further children's development rather than on the children's potential.

Parents, as children's first teachers, have many opportunities to maximize children's learning potential every day. For example, Mary's mother engaged her daughter in an activity that required her to indicate when she had poured a cup of milk. This task created a "zone" for Mary and, by keeping the task "proximal" (slightly above independent functioning), Mary was able to successfully complete the task and tell her mother when the milk reached the specific mark on the cup. Does Mary understand what a cup of milk means? Probably not; but she had an experience that may help to develop the concept.

In order to maximize children's learning opportunities, parents and teachers must know how to create "zones" of proximal development and seize opportunities when they arise in natural contexts and conversation. But where do you begin? In the following section, I will describe each of the five phases of the ZPD shown in Figure 3–1 and illustrate how teachers and children move through the process.

The Zone of <u>Actual</u> Development

The zone of actual development refers to what the child already knows and can do unassisted and independently. Through close observation,

teachers can determine basic concepts and skills the child has already acquired. *An Observation Survey of Early Literacy Achievement*[1] (Clay 1993a) is designed to uncover what the child knows and can do with no assistance and reveal aspects of the child's problem solving that have already matured, that is, the end products of the child's cognitive development.

An Observation Survey of Early Literacy Achievement was individually administered to every child in David's first-grade classroom during the first two weeks of school. After reviewing the results of David's assessment, the teacher in the following transcript had some evidence about what David knows and can do. She also has an idea about David's strengths and limitations however, she wanted to determine if her assumptions were accurate.

TEACHER: David, write your name here.
DAVID: OK. [Immediately starts at the top-left corner of the page. Putting his pencil at the top of the page he makes a straight vertical line as if to make the first part of the *D*.]
TEACHER: What did you write, David?
DAVID: My name, but it is not done.
TEACHER: What do you have to do to finish your name?
DAVID: Something else but I don't know what.
TEACHER: I can help you. Let me show you what to do next.

The teacher determined David's actual development by watching him attempt to write his name. She observed that he knew to start writing on the top left-hand side of the page and how to make the first part of that *D*, the stick. She does not know if he is able to write an upper- or lower-case *D* or if he knows the difference between them. Nor does she know if he understands that to write his name, he must use a capital *D*.

When he said that he does not know how to write the rest of his name, David revealed the starting point of his zone of proximal development. The teacher will seize the opportunity to show him how to complete the task. For Vygotsky, the difference between unassisted performance (David writing the stick of the *D*) and assisted performance (completing the rest of the *D* with teacher support) identified the fundamental nexus of development and learning within the ZPD.

The Zone of <u>Proximal</u> Development

Vygotsky (1978) defines the zone of proximal development, as the "distance between the actual development level as determined by independent problem solving and the level of potential development as determined through problem solving under adult guidance or in collaboration with more capable peers" (86). The ZPD defines those functions that have not yet been learned (not matured) but are in the process of being learned (maturation), functions that will almost be automatic (mature) tomorrow or next week. The ZPD has three overlapping phases: Assistance provided by more capable others; transition from other-assistance to self-assistance; and assistance provided by the self.

Assistance Provided by More Capable Others

The first phase of the ZPD defines what the child can do with help and support of others. Before young children are independent, they must rely on adults or more capable peers for outside regulation to complete a task. The amount and type of outside help depends on the child's age and experiences.

Cori loves to read a story to her little brother Mikey.

Studies by Wertsch (1985) revealed that in the earliest phases of the ZPD, children have a very limited understanding and knowledge of the task or the goal to be achieved. The parent or teacher must organize an activity and facilitate learning by regulating the difficulty level of the task. They model mature performance and provide demonstration of the action so that the child can try to do what the parent or teacher is doing.

For example, when Kenny and I had our first interactions with the button jar, I spilled the buttons on the floor and, taking his hand, showed him how to push each button into a pile according to a specific color. I was deliberate in my actions, but did not intentionally create a "lesson"; however, in our joint interactions a tacit lesson was learned. I did not explicitly and intentionally focus on instruction or set out to teach him color words that would have been too difficult a task. I followed his lead.

In the following example, David's teacher consciously and intentionally creates an activity that engages him in such a way that he is able to use what he knows to complete the task . . . writing the capital letter *D*.

TEACHER: David, let me show you how to make the first letter in your name. [Taking David's hand, she demonstrates the movements in the air.] down, up, and around. That is how you make the first letter in your name, David. This is the capital letter *D*.

DAVID: I want to try it. What do I say?

TEACHER: You already know how to make the first part of your name, David. Take the pencil and while you are making the stick down, say the word "down."

DAVID: OK, I can do that. [proceeds to say the word "down" while making the first part (stick) of his name]

TEACHER: Now say "up" as you are moving your pencil up to the top of the line that you have already made.

DAVID: Like I am tracing over the first part I already wrote?

TEACHER: Yes, exactly . . . that is right!

DAVID: [says "up" while moving his pencil to the top of the first line]

TEACHER: [Taking David's hand, she demonstrates how to finish making the letter.] Now say "around" and move your pencil from the top part of the line around like this to meet the bottom part of your line.

DAVID: Let me do it by myself. [attempts to write his name but does not remember what to do after he makes the first part]

TEACHER: Let's say the words that will help you remember how to make the letter. [Taking David's hand, she and David form the letter.] Say the words with me. [She and David say, "Down, up, and around" while coordinating their movements with precise words to guide the process.]

DAVID: My turn. [makes the first part of his name and stops, looking at the teacher]

TEACHER: What can you do to remember how to make the rest of the *D*?

DAVID: Say the words . . . "Down, up, and around." [repeats "down, up, and around" and coordinates the words with the movement of his pencil]

TEACHER: Are you right? Is that a capital *D*?

DAVID: Yes it is, I just made the first letter of my name!

TEACHER: Wonderful. How can you help yourself to remember how to make capital *D*?

DAVID: Just say "down, up, and around" and presto—the capital *D*.

This transcript shows how the teacher structured David's participation so that he handled manageable but comfortably challenging portions of the activity. She used explicit language to organize and direct his movement while demonstrating how to form a capital letter *D*. When he had difficulty completing the task, she reminded him that there is something he could do to help himself.

The teacher created a scaffold, which was effective adult support, as David worked on tasks. She provided a scaffold to direct and move David's hand that enabled him to move his pencil down, up, and around to form *D*. The scaffolding included movement coordinated with verbal directives to guide his behavior.

Recent research conducted by Berk (2001) revealed that during the preschool years, scaffolding becomes increasingly verbal and directive. As children get older, teacher language becomes less directive but is used to convey meanings and thus becomes a powerful tool through which minds meet and the child begins to use language to think.

Notice the changes in the teacher's scaffold in facilitating David's process to make the letter *D*, from her verbalizations accompanying his movement, through speech attempting to direct him through the task, and finally to a more passive role as he became more capable of independent action. Through routine and, often, tacit guided participation and accompanying language to guide the process, David gained more control of letter formation.

Vygotsky (1978) emphasized conversations, which he referred to as social speech, learned in social interactions, as the most powerful tool for thinking and communicating ideas. Two types of social speech were evident in the preceding interaction between David and his teacher. Initially the teacher used specific language (speech) to model and guide the process of making the letter. As David became more involved in the activity, he appropriated the teacher's words (speech) to regulate his behavior. Once David could control his actions, the teacher used social speech to adjust their conversations and structured tasks to provide increasingly more challenging activities. For example, she asked him what he could do to help himself remember how to form the *D*. Thus, both the teacher and child, through structured tasks and guided performance, used social speech in different ways.

Conversations (social speech) between David and his teacher changed over time. Initially the teacher directed the activity, and as David demonstrated more understanding of the process, she released her control and transferred the responsibility of directing the activity to David. Vygotsky (1978) described this type of interaction as *inter*-cognitive—two minds (brains) working together to create a shared understanding and successfully complete the task at hand.

Gradually David came to understand how the parts of the activity fit together. It is through conversation during the task that this understanding developed. Once David had the overall idea about forming a *D*, the teacher could provide assistance in the form of feedback (specific questions and comments) to further his learning. As David gained competence, his role increased and the teacher's support and control diminished. David had moved to the next phase of the ZPD.

Transition from Other-Assistance to Self-Assistance

Transitions from phase one (assistance provided by more capable others) to phase two (transition from other- to self-assistance) is represented by a line with spaces to show the fluid and flexible adjusting of parent-and-child and teacher-and-student interactions, roles, and responsibilities that must occur within the ZPD. This transition requires teachers and parents to assess a child's level of performance and then create and arrange activities that are challenging but well within the child's ability with help. Before the teacher can determine the context in which to create these opportunities, she must assess the child's level of independent performance. On a subsequent day, David's teacher wanted to know if he could remember how to make the first letter of his name quickly, fluently, and independently.

TEACHER: David, come to the board and make the first letter of your name.

DAVID: Do you mean a *D*?

TEACHER: Yes, do you remember how to get started?

DAVID: I think so. I have to remember the words. [begins to make the stick] Down, up, and around. [slowly writes the capital *D*]

TEACHER: Are you right? Does that [points to the *D*] look like the first letter of your name?

DAVID: Yes, that is a capital *D*. I can write it now without your help. [picks up his pencil and writes another *D*, this time whispering] Down, up, and around [while coordinating the action and words]

TEACHER: Can you write the first letter of you name five more times on the board?

DAVID: OK!

1. Down, up, and around [coordinates the action with words in a loud voice]
2. Down, up, and around [mutters the words while making the *D*]
3. [Incomprehensible muffled speech while making the *D*]
4. Around. [no other speech]
5. [whispers] *D*

The teacher found out that David knew his name began with a capital letter *D* and that he could make the letter using abbreviated verbal directions when necessary.

The transcript also illustrates a shift from social speech, which remains directed at conversing with others (e.g., the first six lines of the transcript) to private speech, which is communi-cation with self for the purpose of self-guidance and self-direction. David's speech patterns shifted each time he made the capital *D*. He did not need language to recall how to make the letter and used fewer words to guide the process each time he wrote *D*. The fourth time he wrote the letter, David said "around" while moving his pencil in the appropriate way. Prior to writing the letter for the last time, a single abbreviated whispered utterance, "*D*," was spoken. This single utterance, made without hesitation, was all that David needed to remember how to form the letter. As private speech developed, it became abbreviated and lost its structural similarly with social speech.

According to Vygotsky (1978), children's private speech shows a progressive tendency toward abbreviated expression between three and seven years of age. The spontaneous use of private speech to meet challenges provides concrete evidence of children's use of language as a tool of thought. Vygotsky hypothesized that interaction between thought and language occurs through private speech.

Self-regulatory private speech is not a mechanical process involving direct transfer of exact copies of adult verbal prescriptions and reinforcements. It is the child's spontaneous speech to regulate his actions.

The development of David's "thinking out loud" or private speech reveals how language is used not as a means to communicate with others but as a way of planning and ordering experience for the self. Private speech involves thinking and problem solving out loud, which is used for self-reflective purposes within the child's brain (*intra*cognitive); *one* mind (brain) working alone to successfully complete the task at hand.

Assistance Provided by the Self

Transitions from phase two (other-assistance to self-assistance) to phase three (assistance provided by the self) completes the zone of proximal development. The line with spaces represents teachers' challenging and supporting children in a process of posing and solving problems that the teacher and, eventually, the child have created, as activities and tasks become more challenging and complex. As this process occurs, the child's thinking and problem solving are his alone; they occur within the child's mind (*intra*cognitive). During this process, the child uses private speech to regulate behavior. Once this occurs, the child has developed the capacity to initiate and successfully complete a task, as is evident in David's increasing ability to remember how to write the letter *D*.

Private speech is language for the self used as a strategic cognitive tool that continues throughout life. Adult's private speech generally occurs when faced with new tasks such as going back to college to learn computer science or a foreign language. Adults often talk to themselves to guide their thinking and restructure their previous behavior when they become confused or disoriented—for example, when they have lost their keys or made a wrong turn and must find a way to get back on track.

Internalization, Automatization, Fossilization

Internalization, automatization, and fossilization occur when the child has emerged from the ZPD and the concept and/or skill is internalized in his brain. From a neurological perspective, one could say a network of neurons in an individual's brain that were assembled and organized to perform a specific task has myelinated. Vygotsky (1978) described it as the "fruits" of the development, but he also discussed it as "fossilized," which suggests the fixity of the process. During this period of development there is a transition from private speech to inner speech.

Vygotsky categorized inner speech as the child's silent, abbreviated dialogue that he carries on with the self; that is, the internalization of the originally communicative function and the essence of conscious mental activity. Vygotsky (1978) argued that "language arises initially as a means of communication between the child and people in his environment. Only subsequently, upon conversion to internal speech, does it come to organize the child's thought, that is, become an internal mental function" (89). When this occurs, assistance from the adult is no longer needed. The following example shows David's development into this phase, evident when his private speech became inner speech as he read *If I Were You* by Brian Wildsmith.

Text	*David reads . . .*
If I were an elephant,	"If I were an elephant,"
I would lift a tractor	"I would lift a truck" [checks the end of the word] No *k*.
	"I would lift a *trailer*" [runs his finger under the word] No *l*.
	"I would lift a tractor." Yea, right,
	"If I were an elephant,"
high into the air.	"I would lift a tractor high into the air."

David made two meaningful and syntactically acceptable attempts (*truck* and *trailer*) to figure out the problem word *tractor*. You could hear his stream of consciousness as he talked to give himself direction. "No *k*, no *l*, yea right!" The stream of consciousness is essential to thought. Fortunately, David's self-talk (private speech) revealed his thinking. Based on my prior observations, I believe his thinking might have progressed in the following manner.

David said *truck* and then noticed that there was no *k* at the end of the problem word so *truck* was not right. David's second attempt to figure out the word was not successful. He listened to the sounds he heard in *trailer,* paused and looked at the middle of the problem word (as if to think) and noticed there was no *l* in the word *tractor*. He immediately redirected his behavior and said aloud, "tractor." Private speech had been transformed into soundless inner speech (verbal thought).

Vygotsky (1978) points out that the syntax of inner speech is highly abbreviated because the topic of conversation (in this case how to resolve the problem) is already known to the speaker and does not need to be stated. Eventually David's inner speech will be internalized and transformed to inner verbal thought. His behaviors suggest a smooth integration of several task components, each of which was taught and retaught three to four weeks prior to this lesson. He had developed a flexible strategic system for problem solving that enabled him to predict and confirm words that would make sense, look right, and sound right in a particular sentence. David had developed the ability to regulate his own behavior.

Both Vygotsky (1978) and Luria (1979) claim that children's use of language for self-regulation is intimately linked in its origins to the language used by adults to regulate children's behaviors. Thus private speech is both the precursor of consciousness and self-regulatory thought (evident in David's successful reading of *tractor*) and a critical link to the cultural transformation of cognitive skills from one individual (e.g., parent, teacher) to another.

David's teacher created meaningful activities for both of them to participate in and used specific language (social speech) that became David's tools of thought as they participated in the shared activity. From those conversations, David appropriated cognitive strategies and then constructed private speech utterances uniquely suited to overcome the problems he encountered. This process enabled him to successfully read the text. The shared activity and talk were incorporated into David's private speech and, consequently, into his thinking. Figure 3–2 illustrates the relationship between speech and cognition.

Neurological studies (Greenspan 1997) have demonstrated that experiences organized and directed through specific speech and language patterns develop the growth of brain structures and minds in such a way that you can see connections among neurons and dendrites, which, through repetition and myelinization, become stronger, speedier, and more flexible.

Level of Control	Speech
Adult Control Adult plans, organizes, guides, monitors, and regulates child's behavior.	*Adult Speech* Adult uses language to model and guide the process.
Shared Control Adult and child share activity and responsibility for planning, organizing, guiding, monitoring, and regulating child's behavior.	*Social Speech* Language and activity are shared by adult and child through conversation.
(**inter**cognitive—shared control between adult's and child's brains)	
Self-Control Child has the ability to perform action in the absence of the adult.	*Private Speech* Origins in the adult's verbal commands and directives. Child uses for himself abbreviated language that adult used to guide behavior.
(**intra**cognitive – within the child's brain)	
Self-Regulation Child's self-formulated plan, not yet internalized, to guide action.	*Inner Speech* Child's silent, abbreviated dialogue that he or she carries on with self that is the essence of conscious mental activity.
Child guides, plans, monitors his or her behavior from within (in the brain) and flexibility according to changing circumstances.	Inner speech internalized and transformed to inner verbal thought.

Figure 3–2. *The Relationship Between Level of Control and Speech, with Transitions from Adult Control to Shared Control to Self-Regulation*

De-Automatization of Performance

Lifelong learning involves the same overlapping sequenced ZPD phases—from assistance provided by a more capable other, to transition from other-assistance to self-assistance and, finally, independent assistance provided by self. In order to develop knowledge and skill, these phases of learning must recur over and over again. And for every learner, regardless of age, there is a mix of other-assistance to regulate processing, self-assistance or self-regulation, and automatic processing that requires little or no attention (Tharp and Gallimore 1988).

Every learner experiences points in time when the task they are working on becomes more difficult, hindering or preventing automatic processing. This deautomatization of performance leads the individual to phase five of the teaching and learning process—recursion through prior phases of the ZPD.

Individuals who experience difficulty have three options in the recursive loop. The first and oftentimes most expedient option is helping yourself. Self-talk (private speech) is a useful feedback system to help one recall prior learning and regain self-control.

David talked to himself to remember how to form a capital *D* and figure out the word *tractor*. When children (and adults) cannot remember how to write a word, spelling it orally helps recall. Adults talk to themselves when they try to remember where they left the car keys. When confronted with a difficult situation, older children and adults will sometimes remember what their mother or father told them to do when they were in a similar predicament.

If self-help and self-talk do not remedy the situation, the individual will need more expert help from a parent, caregiver, teacher, or peer. The degree and amount of help depends upon many variables, including the task demands, where the individual's processing is breaking down, the level of performance, the goal of instruction, and the teacher's assessment of the learners' strengths and needs.

The adult or expert other must be able to assess the situation and find out the minimum level of help that the child needs in order to proceed and adjust the help accordingly. The continual adjustment of the level and amount of help is responsive to the child's level of performance and shifts accordingly as the child becomes more capable. This adjustment is provided in the ZPD and the learning process begins again.

Conclusion

Children apply their ability to use language not only to communicate with others but to plan and organize their thoughts in order to direct future actions. Moreover, it helps children (and all human beings) to hold their thoughts in short-term memory so that they can refine and improve their thinking, as is evident in the examples in this chapter.

Language helps individuals communicate and understand not only the literal meanings of words but their emotional meanings as well. Research suggests that in order to understand and interpret the emotional aspects of language or speak with feeling, individuals must understand the literal meaning of words (Ratey 2001).

Vygotsky regarded teaching and learning as fundamental processes and forces in cognitive and social-cultural development. I would add

Reading to toddlers helps them to hear the sounds of language and develop rich vocabularies.

that teaching and learning are also critical to children's emotional development. Although language and thought are not the same thing, they are certainly tightly interwoven and inseparable. Individuals think in words. Communication—both verbal, through language and emotion, and nonverbal, through body movement and gesture—is important to children's ability to adapt to their environment cognitively, emotionally, and socially, at home and in school.

Educational Implications— Language and Learning

Every child is capable of learning given the right opportunities, context, and assistance. Through language children learn to make sense of and interact with their environment, which is critical to learning. Parents, as their children's first teachers, caregivers, and family members who interact with children on a daily basis play a critical role in helping young children acquire language. Research has demonstrated that purposeful, contextualized conversations with young children impact their emotional, cognitive, and physical development. This research suggests four key implications for parents and caregivers who interact with infants and toddlers on a daily basis.

◆ When talking with children, interact in a warm and personal way. Have pleasant conversations with them. Children become frightened when they routinely hear loud, bossy, mean voices. Listening carefully to children and showing an interest in their discoveries and how they talk about them will put them at ease.

◆ In order to support children's language development, play with young children and make the play enjoyable, not vocabulary lessons. Babies and toddlers understand loving physical contact better than long strings of unrelated words. To increase a child's vocabulary, refrain from using baby talk.

◆ Young children's attention span is generally limited to a few minutes; however, conversations related to play or a meaningful activity, such as going for a walk or eating a cookie, will sustain their attention, and concepts are more likely to be developed (see discussion in this chapter). When introducing a new concept or language, be sure to make it explicit and relate it to an action.

◆ In order to feel competent and successful, children must learn how to express what they understand and make themselves understood. Parents and caregivers can facilitate the processes by listening to children and showing interest in their many discoveries and how they talk about them. When children are old enough to convey meaning, let them know if they have not made themselves understood. And when adults do not understand children, they should continue the conversation until they do understand what the children mean.

In order to provide the appropriate amount of assistance to shift children's ability to express their thoughts and reasoning, teachers must be sensitive and careful observers of the children's current level of understanding expressed through verbal and nonverbal actions. The following six implications, drawn from language and sociocultural research, provide effective ways to work with children, especially those who are struggling to learn.

◆ Observe and listen carefully to what children are saying while engaged in a particular task. This assessment cannot be done without concrete information. Opportunities to get this knowledge must be organized by the adult and involve the child in an activity. For example, teachers who want to know what strategies children are using while reading will select a text they believe is not too difficult and ask children to read it. Taking a running record of a child's reading of the text and his processing will help the teacher determine which strategies the child is using or neglecting. Such assessments will help teachers know what children can do unassisted while performing a particular task. Making careful and sensitive assessments often (daily) to determine what the child can do without help is a requirement of good teaching.

◆ Effective teaching leads and enhances development. It is future oriented. Effective parenting and teaching occurs when assistance is offered at points in the zone of proximal development (ZPD) where children's performance requires assistance. Offering assistance at too low a level will interfere with children's learning because they have already developed the knowledge and skills. When teachers engage children in activities they can already do, they focus on the past and children learn nothing new. Offering assistance at too high a level will disrupt children's performance because they will not understand what to do.

◆ The best thing teachers or parents can do to help children who are experiencing difficulty learning something is to ask them to discuss or demonstrate what they understand, then watch and listen to the answer. Teachers who do this may be able to see whether the children are on the right track and what they need to learn next. If children are confused, the teacher will be able to pinpoint the confusion and clarify their thinking. Without that information, powerful and effective teaching will not take place.

◆ Create opportunities for children to learn how to learn as they progress from other-assistance to self-assistance within the ZPD. Identify specific behaviors to look for that may indicate shifts in children's learning and conceptual development. Create opportunities (through the arrangement of materials and conversations) to accommodate specific student needs and shift instruction when student behaviors suggest a task is too easy or too hard.

◆ Listen carefully to children's language for transitions from social speech between the teacher and child to private speech, when the child uses the language of the teacher to control his reading and writing behaviors; to inner speech, the child's abbreviated dialogue that he carries on with himself; to inner verbal thought. Do not put words in children's mouths to control their actions. Self-regulatory speech is not a mechanical process involving direct transfer of adult verbal prescriptions and reinforcements *except* very early in development. Children's spontaneous speech regulates their actions (see discussion in this chapter).

◆ Children's evolution of social development and learning processes begins at birth as they interact with parents and caregivers and continues through schooling as they interact with teachers. Communications with others is the heart of this learning process. Children who have been particularly successful language learners and users are surrounded by adults who

  ◆ create many opportunities for children to use language to think, problem-solve, and reflect on their learning;

  ◆ recognize and praise children often for little successes;

  ◆ provide specific praise when children accomplished something they initially found difficult learning;

  ◆ show, through their actions and words, high expectations for children's ability;

  ◆ understand that children and students will live up to the expectations of their parents and teachers.

Research (Levine 2002) consistently demonstrates that language development in early childhood is strongly related to later reading and writing competence and to academic achievement in general. Therefore, conversations with parents, caregivers, and other adults is vital to language proficiency and, in turn, to becoming a proficient reader and writer.

Endnote

[1] *An Observation Survey of Early Literacy Achievement* consists of six assessments: letter identification, word test, concepts about print, writing vocabulary, hearing and recording sounds in words, and text reading.

Chapter 4

Emotion, Memory, and Learning

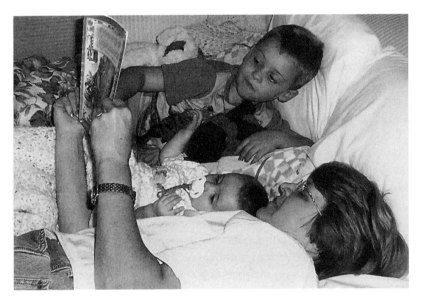

During the last ten years, research in neuroscience has confirmed that emotions are essential to thinking and remembering and are an inseparable part of the learning process (Greenspan 1997; LeDoux 1996; Levine 2002). The meaning children bring to and take from their experiences has power, not only because they are constructing knowledge by assimilating new information into previously learned information, but also because of the emotional responses the experience triggers.

As any parent or teacher knows, there are individual differences in children's emotional response to a situation. For example, one child may be outgoing and will immediately run to people when they first enter a room and appear to be eager to talk and learn. Her older sister, on the other hand, may be shy and slow to warm up to people and not appear eager to converse and learn. There are also differences in children's emotional response to working on a problem and to responding to challenge and defeat. Some children, when facing difficulty the first time, may quit immediately, while others will enjoy the challenge of trying to figure out the problem and be tenacious in their attempts.

No matter how children react to a situation, however, parents' and teachers' responses to them have a positive or negative impact on their future emotional, social, and cognitive development. In fact, children's ideas and feelings about themselves reflect, in large measure, parents', teachers', and significant others' attitudes toward them (Greenspan 1997).

In light of the intimate connection between cognition, emotion, and social development, each aspect of children's functioning is expected to affect the other. Since emotions are such an important and inseparable part of the learning process, it is important that educators and parents understand the critical role emotions play in learning and how they can create positive learning opportunities to help children become independent, secure lifelong learners.

In this chapter I (1) define and discuss emotion and its inseparable fusion with cognition; (2) describe the neurological roots of emotion; (3) discuss the role of emotion in memory; and (4) examine the impact of emotion on motivation, learning, and remembering. Educators generally agree that the goal of reading and writing instruction is to develop children's capacity to independently read increasingly more complex texts with ease and understanding. Emotions have a significant role in students' ability to achieve this goal. The examples in this chapter reveal how the meaning children bring to and take from their literacy experiences is related to their ability to invest positive emotions throughout the learning process. Understanding the impact of emotion on learning is necessary if parents and teachers are to help all children to reach their full potential.

What Is Emotion?

The term *emotion* is derived from the Latin word *movere*—"to move." Emotion is defined in *Webster' New World Dictionary* (Neufeldt 1988) as "a state of consciousness having to do with arousal of feelings and distinguished from other cognitive states such as volition and awareness of any physical sensation." It is a movement outward and the way individuals communicate to others their most important internal states. There are two aspects of emotions: (1) inner emotions such as feelings of joy, fear, love, anger, and anxiety, which are entirely within an individual; and (2) the outward expressions and displays of emotion such as laughing, crying, sweating, blushing, or tone of voice, which provide an outward sign that an inward emotion has occurred.

From infancy through adult life, human beings read faces and body language to determine what is going on inside an individual's mind. Is there a smile or a frown? Does the person look at you or away from you during a conversation? When you make a speech, does the audience smile and nod their heads in agreement or shake their heads and frown? Is the child you are teaching slumping in her chair or sitting straight?

Interpreting Emotional Behavior

Bodily expressions, especially of the face, are the first means of communication between a baby and her mother. Movements that express—a kiss or slap, a smile or a shake of the head, arms extended to lift a child, ignoring a child's extended arms, moving toward a child or away from a child—are outward signs of a parent's emotions, providing meaning without words. Greenspan (1997) believes that, for the rest of our lives, the seemingly trivial gestures of emotion first understood in late infancy serve both to anchor our human relationships and to support our thought processes and learning.

Observing body language provides reliable clues from which to interpret individuals' inner emotions—their state of mind. Children can tell when their mother or teacher is upset. One child knew his reading teacher did not like him because she threw the books down on the table every time they started a lesson. After observing a videotape of the teacher interacting with this child, I agreed with him. The teacher's inner emotions (anger about having to work with this child) were displayed when she slammed the books on the table and said in a loud and angry voice, "Pick one."

We have all had personal experiences in which another person's movements reveal her inner emotions. For example, if you are talking to someone and she starts to look away, stare blankly, gaze off into space, or search the room with her eyes, you get the feeling that what you have to say is unimportant, and you feel undervalued. Studies of preschool children reveal that the inner emotions of teachers or parents may have a detrimental impact on learning. When parents or caregivers do not pay attention to children—by gazing off or staring without reacting to what the children are doing or saying, as if they were not in the room—preschool children's speech becomes disorganized, and their attempts to learn gradually decrease (Greenspan 1997).

Most of us have also had an experience when our internal state or frame of mind (emotion) has impaired or prevented our ability to think. Several years ago, while driving my usual route to an elementary school in the South Side of Chicago, I approached a car accident and was forced to take a detour. I soon found myself on unfamiliar roads and, after several miles, I realized that my car was the only one on the road. The street signs were not familiar and I knew that I was lost in a neighborhood that to me looked dangerous.

My heart started beating, my palms were sweating, my face felt flushed. I gripped the steering wheel harder and made sure the car doors were locked. I tried to calm myself down, even started talking to myself in an attempt to determine which direction I was going in and what I needed to do to get back on track. But the more I thought, the more anxious and confused I became. I decided to keep driving until I found the main road and could go to a gas station and ask someone for directions.

After about ten minutes of driving around, I saw a gas station. I ran in to ask the attendant for directions but when he asked where I was going, I could not think of the name of the school or street the school was on. All I could tell the attendant was that it was on the South Side of Chicago and about fifteen minutes from the gas station. After he rattled off several schools in the area, he finally said, "Chapman," the school that I was looking for. The attendant started giving me directions orally, and I asked him to please draw a map and write down the names of the streets. I did not trust my memory to find my way back to the school. I got into the car and read the directions out loud giving myself verbal directives—when to turn, what stores to look for, how far to drive on each street. When I saw the Jewel store sign, I breathed a big sigh of relief because I knew where I was and didn't need the directions anymore.

Antonio Damasio (1994) provides a plausible explanation of what happened when I was forced to take a detour to the school. The neural substrates for cognitive responses (initially trying to find another route to get to school) associate and interact with neural substrates for emotions (inner feelings of fear and anxiety) and these acquired connections merge from a unique experience (the detour) for an individual. When there is an upset to the routine, which occurred when I was forced to take the detour, the emotional response, often unconscious, automatic, and involuntary, is activated in various parts of the brain. This activation is actually a full-body activation of the endocrine system, which includes the heart, blood pressure, pulse, and other regulations of the body that affect cognition and emotion.

The psychological changes in my body revealed that it is not the brain but the totality of the person that is the unified whole of thinking.

Furthermore, as Damasio points out, because the emotional system can act independently of the cognitive system, emotional reactions and emotional memories can be formed without conscious, cognitive participation at all. Emotions are played out physically in our bodies through internal motor activity, such as a rapid heartbeat, sweaty palms, and flushed face—all of which I experienced. I could not get a plan to guide and monitor my behavior when things changed. The routine that I was comfortable with was upset. I experienced and exhibited a physical response to an emotional override. My behavior was an outward expression of an inward emotion that affected my ability to think (cognitive processing).

The Emotional and Cognitive Foundations of Learning

In Chapter 1, I discussed my son Ken's cognitive development as we played with the buttons in the button jar. Now we will examine his emotional development during the same activity. Recent neurological research (see Damasio 1994; Gopnik, Meltzoff, and Kuhl 1999) provides concrete evidence that cognition (reason) and emotion (feeling) interact to support the learning process, which includes the acquired abilities of problem solving, decision making, planning, and self-regulation. Furthermore, these interactions begin early on in life and continue through adulthood.

Greenspan (1997) discusses three major principles that support the links between infants' emotional and cognitive development (Figure 4–1). First, the foundations of learning are the infant's own natural intentions. This principle suggests that it is the *child*, not the parent or caretaker, who determines and controls what to attend to and subsequently what is learned. The child's reticular activating system (RAS) is responsible for arousal and consciousness and is critical to focusing our attention system. Attempting to develop Ken's ability to learn color words or number concepts by manipulating buttons would probably not have worked if it were my idea. Greenspan's research shows that when an infant is confused, senses disapproval, or feels anxiety or stress, there is a psychological and physiological reaction in the brain that inhibits processing. The child's RAS

1. The foundations of learning are the infant's own natural intentions.
2. Emotions organize intellectual capacities and create the sense of self and well-being.
3. Parts of the brain that deal with emotional regulation play a crucial role in cognition (thinking).

Figure 4–1. *The Fusion Between Emotional and Cognitive Development: Principles of Learning*

shuts down and he will look away. But if the parent follows the child's interest, many learning opportunities will arise because the infant has voluntarily attended and engaged.

The second principle suggests that each sensation a child registers also gives rise to an affect or emotion. Greenspan (1997) called this process "dual coding" of experience, which is the key to understanding how emotions organize intellectual capacities and create the sense of self and well-being. Greenspan argues that emotions and intellect are *not* two separate parts of a person. Emotions are the organizer or the "super-sense," helping to organize all the sensory information coming our way. Experience is stored and organized in the brain with a dual code. The dual code consists of the sensory experience and the emotional or affective reaction to the experience, both of which will be coded together in the brain. Greenspan (1997) believes, "This double coding allows the child to cross-reference each memory or experience in a mental catalog of phenomena and feeling and to reconstruct it when needed" (21).

The dual coding phenomenon may help to explain the relationship between Ken's cognitive and emotional development. I believe that his capacity to reason (i.e., sort buttons in discrete categories) was followed by mechanisms of emotions, which occurred as he began experiencing feelings of affirmation and support from me. Once this occurred, systematic connections between categories of objects and situations, on the one hand, and emotions, on the other, were formed in his mind. He labeled and coded the buttons as bright, smooth, red, and so on, but also labeled and coded them by emotional qualities connected with feelings he exhibited while playing with the buttons.

This double coding allowed him to cross-reference the category system with a positive memory.

The third principle supports the notion that the parts of the brain and nervous system dealing with emotional regulation play a crucial role in planning, discriminating and choosing between alternatives, monitoring and self-correcting, and regulating one's behavior. Neurological research (Damasio 1994) shows that neural development in the prefrontal cortex regulates emotions. Furthermore, damage to the prefrontal cortex seriously impairs a child's ability to evaluate the consequences of his acts, which is important to judgment and regulation of behavior. When the regulatory system is working well, infants between the ages of three and eight months can register the appropriate sense perceptions presented with sights and sounds, attend and discriminate among them, and comprehend sensations that they see, touch, and hear (Greenspan 1997).

Ken squealed with delight while touching and pushing the buttons on the floor, but he also came to understand that if he tried to put a button in his mouth, the button jar would disappear and the game would end. He responded to the button jar game in terms of its emotional as well as physical effect on him. He learned how to emotionally regulate his behavior by not doing what he wanted to do, which was eat the buttons.

In one study, Greenspan (1997) found that measurements of emotional regulatory function taken at eight months of age correlated with children's mental capabilities as indicated on standardized IQ tests of four-year-olds. Greenspan believes that "intellectual learning shares common origins with emotional learning. Both stem from early affective interactions. Both are influenced by individual differences. The sort of learning a child acquires in kindergarten and the early grades is not the true foundation of her education. In fact, early schoolwork cannot proceed without previous mastery of various mental tasks" (219).

The Neurological Roots of Emotion and Cognition

The child's brain forms microscopic connections responsible for feeling, thinking, learning, and remembering. As depicted in Figure 4–2, the lobes

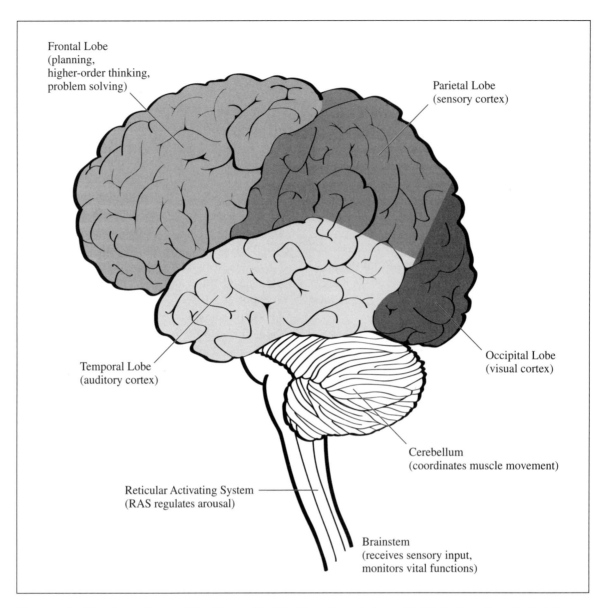

Frontal Lobe
(planning,
higher-order thinking,
problem solving)

Parietal Lobe
(sensory cortex)

Temporal Lobe
(auditory cortex)

Occipital Lobe
(visual cortex)

Cerebellum
(coordinates muscle movement)

Reticular Activating System
(RAS regulates arousal)

Brainstem
(receives sensory input,
monitors vital functions)

Figure 4–2. *The Outer Layer of the Cortex Divided into Four Lobes with Their Functions Labeled*

of the cortex (temporal, occipital, parietal, and frontal) work together to integrate thought.

A mother cannot see the electrical activity that occurs as neurons in her child's retina make a connection to neurons in the visual cortex (occipital lobe) of the child's brain. But when this happens, the mother's face becomes a memory in her child's mind that will last for a lifetime.

Nor can the mother see the release of a chemical substance, a neurotransmitter, as neurons in the baby's ear, carrying an electrical encoded sound of "ma," connect to neurons in the auditory cortex (temporal lobe) of the child's brain. Yet the sound "ma" has created a cluster of cells in the infant's brain that will respond to no other

sound for the rest of her life. Neuroscientists are realizing that

◆ experiences after birth, rather than something innate, determine the organization and structure of the human brain;
◆ early childhood experiences exert a dramatic impact, physically determining how the intricate neural circuits of the brain are organized.

These early experiences influence the cognitive and emotional structures of the brain itself (Gopnik, Meltzoff, and Kuhl 1999).

We know, for example, that in order for these connections to be made—for the child to distinguish her mother's face from any other female she encounters and also distinguish her mother's voice from any heard—the reticular activating system (RAS) must be engaged.

The RAS is critical to every individual's attention system because it regulates all incoming sensory information. Our attention mechanisms are primed to focus automatically on sensory patterns that contain high contrasts and/or emotional intensity. High contrast, for example, might mean hearing many voices talking at once but being able to hear *only* the teacher's or parent's voice clearly.

A sensory pattern containing emotional intensity may occur while listening to someone read or tell a story. Suddenly the memory of a related personal experience may pop into your mind. You'll shift your attention to your own mental story and merely monitor your friend's story while processing your own, blocking out the story that is being told.

Neural Structures and Memory

The inner layers of the cortex (forebrain) contain neural structures essential to learning and memory. The RAS sends messages coming from the five senses to the thalamus, which sorts the information and sends it to the three pairs of lobes:

◆ to the temporal lobes to process auditory information;

◆ to the occipital lobes to process visual information;

◆ to the parietal lobes for sensing information, where it is processed in short-term memory (Figure 4–2).

The information is then sent to the frontal lobes, which decide what should be stored in long-term memory.

This information is sorted in two ways and sent to two different structures, the amygdala and the hippocampus, which are critical to memory. These two structures are found deep inside the medial part of the temporal lobes. The amygdala lies adjacent to the hippocampus and underneath it (Figure 4–3).

The Amygdala

The thalamus relays sensory information to the amygdala, a site of basic emotion memory, and to the cortex, where cognition occurs. From the cortex, the stimuli go on to the hippocampus, a site

involved in memory and linked to the amygdala. The amygdala catalogues, files, and stores emotional information and determines if it is emotionally important for long-term storage. The amygdala's response to a situation can drastically affect how well it is remembered.

LeDoux (1996) believes that the amygdala is a critical site of learning because of its central location between input and output stations. Each route that leads to the amygdala—from the sensory thalamus, the sensory cortex, and the hippocampus—delivers unique information to the organ.

The emotional responses begin in the amygdala before we completely recognize what it is we are reacting to or what we are feeling. Because our neural emotional system can act independently of the neocortex (frontal lobes), some emotional reactions and emotional memories can be formed without any conscious, cognitive participation at all (LeDoux 1996). This means that an emotional response can precede a cognitive perception and response.

Before a sensory perception has reached the frontal lobes, where it enters conscious awareness and undergoes fine categorization, the amygdala has already branded it with a raw emotional continuum from mildly interesting to not interesting at all. It activates the body and the rest of the brain in response to how significant it deems the information to be. The amygdala provides a preconscious bias of intensity to every stimulus you come into contact with, even before you actually pay attention to it. It can, and does, operate outside consciousness.

The amygdala's emotional tagging occurs in consultation with our memories of similar situations. It allows us to instantly judge and then react to the situation we are in. If we have a bias, an expectation that the same thing will happen that happened the last time, it will impact how we react. For example, I once heard a broadcaster discussing an upcoming football game between the University of Michigan and Ohio State University.

> The University of Michigan quarterback who defeated Ohio State University (OSU) last year is starting today's game. His passing game demolished the OSU Buckeye offensive line last time. He is stronger and more accurate this year, and the OSU offensive line is

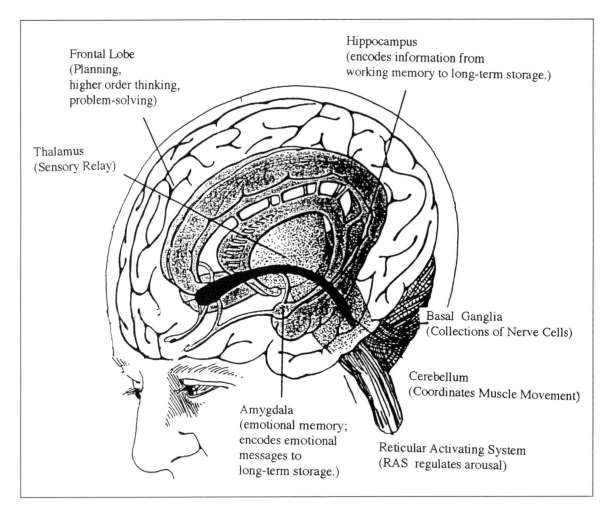

Frontal Lobe
(Planning,
higher order thinking,
problem-solving)

Thalamus
(Sensory Relay)

Hippocampus
(encodes information from
working memory to long-term storage.)

Basal Ganglia
(Collections of Nerve Cells)

Cerebellum
(Coordinates Muscle Movement)

Amygdala
(emotional memory;
encodes emotional
messages to
long-term storage.)

Reticular Activating System
(RAS regulates arousal)

Figure 4–3. *Memory Systems with Major Structures and Functions Labeled*

weaker than it was two years ago. The writing is on the wall.

The sportscaster had already decided who would win the game before it took place. A teacher may decide that Johnny will have difficulty learning to read because she taught his brother last year and he experienced reading difficulty.

Children who struggle to learn oftentimes expect failure. Recall the child who told her Reading Recovery (RR) teacher that it was a waste of her time to try to teach her to read. This child prejudged the situation because she had recalled previous situations and learned to expect failure. This bias prevented her from trying. Strong emotions based on prior experiences cause some children to prejudge the learning situation.

The Hippocampus

The hippocampus catalogues, files, and stores factual information. It communicates this information back to the surrounding regions of the brain. The maintenance of the stored information for a few years requires that the components of this system store the memory trace, which is maintained by repeated interactions between the temporal lobe system and the frontal lobes. Gradually over time, the hippocampus relinquishes its control over the memory to the neocortex, and the memory appears to remain for a lifetime.

This model of memory has helped physicians and neuroscientists better understand what occurs over time in Alzheimer's disease. The disease begins its attack on the brain in the temporal lobes, particularly in the hippocampus, thus explaining why forgetfulness is the first warning sign. But the disease eventually creeps into the cortex, suggesting why, as the disease progresses, all aspects of memory (old and new) are compromised. Understanding how the disease compromises the mind and brain in tandem is helping researchers figure out approaches to preventing, arresting, or reversing the cognitive meltdown that occurs.

Thus, as noted above and in Chapter 1, information is coded two ways, which Greenspan, (1997) refers to as dual coding. It is coded both emotionally and cognitively in two different regions of the brain, each specifically designed and responsible for learning and memory.

◆ The hippocampus is responsible for planning, problem solving, and reasoning related to factual information.
◆ The amygdala is responsible for telling us how we feel about that information, which is then stored in our emotional memory.
◆ The hippocampus files, catalogues, and stores factual information.
◆ The amygdala files, catalogues, and stores emotional information.

Emotional and cognitive memories are stored and retrieved in parallel, and their activities are joined seamlessly in our conscience experience.

LeDoux's research (1996) suggests that neural pathways are set so that a learning situation may evoke an emotional response that may be helpful. Or a rapid negative emotional response can precede cortical cognition and impair learning, memory, and thinking. Understanding how the hippocampus and amygdala function in learning and memory provides a plausible explanation for an unforgettable high school incident I experienced.

How Emotions Affect Learning and Memory

In my junior year of high school I took trigonometry. The teacher would routinely ask every student to come to the blackboard to work out trigonometry problems, which she orally gave to the class. There were only sixteen students in the class so there was plenty of room for all of us to have a place at the board. I dreaded going to the board because during the first few weeks of "board work" I usually did not get the problem right.

Sister Agatha would ask members of the class to examine the problems on the board and look for errors. The students oftentimes found errors in my work. They would then discuss my mistakes. I always hoped that I would get the problem correct and, if I was wrong, that the teacher would not single out my work for everyone to examine. When she did, I was embarrassed because my errors seemed obvious to my classmates. After several weeks of embarrassment, I asked my dad for help.

Dad watched me working on several different types of equations and asked me to talk about what I was doing. He then pointed out an error in my reasoning that was causing me to consistently make similar mistakes. Sister Agatha may have explained my pattern of errors the same way that Dad had explained them, but I was too upset to listen well enough to understand and remember what she said. Through my Dad's interest and help, a negative experience became positive and I continued to grow in my understanding of trigonometry.

The negative experience that occurred during the first few weeks of class triggered a stress response as soon as the teacher said, "Let's go to the board." I felt myself get flushed, my stomach started to churn, my heart beat faster, and I started to sweat. The physiological changes that took place in my body occurred because previous experiences in going to the board to solve trigonometry problems were not positive. These physiological changes were the product of the dual coding of emotions and cognition.

I couldn't think because I was worried that I would get the problem wrong again and Sister Agatha would ask the rest of the class to examine my work. I couldn't hide the steps I took to resolve the problems because they were written on the board for everyone to see. As soon as Sister Agatha said, "Everyone to the board," I panicked.

My RAS sent the information immediately to the amygdala (seat of the emotional brain), bypassing the thalamus, which would have sent it to the frontal lobes to examine the situation. When this occurred, chemical signals, neurotransmitters, were released and my body started to prepare for flight. My heart raced faster to get my blood flowing again. This stress response was triggered by a few words from the teacher that I associated with embarrassment and failure. The stress response can save your life or it can cause you great embarrassment, which it did in my case. The emotional memory took precedence and, as LeDoux (1996) points out, the brain always gives priority to emotions.

Thus, learning is not solely a cognitive process. Recent research in neuroscience provides concrete evidence that learning is much more. Learning involves emotional, cognitive, and social functions that are not a hierarchy, that are not acquired in sequence. Nor is one function more important than the others but rather, all functions are a *synergy,* a combined and correlated force of united action. This synergy among emotional, social, and cognitive functions cannot be prevented because it is occurring within, as neurons in our brain communicate with each other. Emotion is the building block of all learning, from birth throughout life. Emotions build memories.

Memory Systems of the Brain

Memory is an internal process that pulls together learning, understanding, and consciousness. In the past, scientists believed that one neuron in the brain equaled one memory and that each region of the brain performed its particular operation. Today we know this is not true. In fact, there is no single center for memory, no region of the brain responsible for locating and retrieving memories. Memories are made and stored in different networks of neurons throughout our brain. Scientists also report that there are two major types of memory—short-term and/or working memory and long-term memory.

Short-Term and Working Memory
Short-term memory initially lasts for only fifteen to thirty seconds. Some researchers say that individuals have limited space for short-term memory and that the older they are the more space they acquire. Individuals can generally hold up to seven items in working memory. Working memory can be used for several hours and gives individuals the ability to form more lasting long-term memories.

We have all used our working memory to cram for a test. We study hard the night before, and this information is stored in working memory long enough to take the test, but it is forgot-

The expression on ten-month-old Cori's face shows she finds reading books a very pleasurable experience.

ten after taking the test. In fact we would have a difficult time recalling the information the following week.

Working memory is temporary storage and critical to recall. If information is not meaningful or not allowed to form patterns in the brain, it will be lost. Information in temporary storage is sent to the frontal lobes, which decide whether it should be stored in long-term memory. Working memory also registers our current mental activity while retrieving information from long-term memory and holds it until it is ready to be processed in long-term memory. Children classified as having attention deficit disorder are believed to have problems with working memory.

Long-Term Memory
Long-term memory receives information from working memory and stores it for an indefinite period. There are four different kinds of long-term memory—procedural (automatic), semantic, episodic, and emotional—which are used to access and store information for a long period of time (Figure 4–4).

Type	Function
1. Procedural (skills)	Starts as explicit and changes to implicit (automatic)
2. Episodic	Puts facts and events in time
3. Semantic	Retains facts and holds information learned in words
4. Emotional	Retains positive and negative occurrences

Figure 4–4. *Long-Term Memory Systems*

Procedural Memory Procedural or skill learning is the first memory function to develop in the brain's early stage of growth. A baby learns how to extend his arm to reach an object. Recall Bruner's (1973) theory of developing a skilled action reported in Chapter 2. Procedural memories start as explicit memories and change to implicit or automatic memories (Ratey 2001). Explicit memories are directly accessible to our conscious awareness. For example, when a teacher takes a child's finger and shows her how to match and point to individual words one after another across a line of text, the action is explicit.

Implicit memory is responsible for the establishment of a skill or set of skills. These skills become automatic once they are learned. For example, through repeated reading, the child will be able to move her eyes across a line of text without either teacher support or using her pointing finger to match what she says to what she sees. She will be able to complete a task without thinking about how she did it in the past. The procedural memory, at first explicit, has become implicit and automatic.

Episodic Memory Episodic memory is the capacity to set facts and events in time and to refer to them freely. It is the ability to look into the past and remember the birth of your child or your wedding. Some children will remember when a teacher showed disgust when they couldn't remember how to make a letter or the letter sound after it was taught. The teachers' responses to a child's inability to recall information may impact her memory more than the teacher will ever know. A child may not raise her hand again if, after being called on to respond, the teacher said angrily her answer was wrong. That one episode can have an impact on subsequent lessons.

Semantic Memory Semantic memory is detached from personal experience. It is an impersonal basis of your repertoire of knowledge.

Semantic memory allows for the retention of facts and holds information learned in words. Semantic memories are acquired by rote, aided by our ability to generalize and categorize information. Language depends largely on semantic memory. In order to have a universal system to communicate, we need a system of recall for impersonal knowledge—knowledge such as the meaning of words, grammar rules, syntax, and so on. This body of knowledge resides in semantic memory.

Most of our educational experiences have involved semantic memories. Semantic memories are formed while reading a textbook or listening to a lecture. If the new information is to be learned, it must be connected to previously learned information and sent to working memory. Working memory will continue to sift and sort the old and new information. Through prior knowledge and interest, the learner will be able to incorporate the new information with previously learned information to form long-term memories. Associations, comparisons, and similarities stimulate semantic memory.

Emotional Memory Emotional memory exerts a powerful influence on thought processes. Emotional memory registers and retains positive and negative occurrences if they are repeated. If the child has difficulty learning something, she will oftentimes experience a negative emotion. Lack of confidence is often associated with feelings of being incapable of learning. Those feelings are common in students who have not learned how to read. They become frustrated and, if left to draw solely upon their own motivation, they cannot sustain a commitment to learning (Coles 1998). For those students, a transformation of emotions and self-perception is necessary for literacy achievement.

Numerous studies have demonstrated a connection between anxiety and academic performance. The more anxious a person is, the poorer his or her academic performance (LeDoux 1996). Students' perceptions of teachers' emotions are also important. Research (Greenspan 1997) has shown that children as young as five years can interpret a teacher's expression of anger or disgust that the student had not tried hard enough. Children who repeatedly read or sense disapproval in the teacher's or parent's response to an error will not put themselves in the circumstance again.

One child, when asked why she did not want to try to learn to read, said that when she read to her father, he would yell when she did not know the words. If she was having special reading lessons, her father would make her read to him and the yelling would start again. Negative emotional memories prevented her from attempting to try to learn to read. Many individuals will remember their mistakes longer than their successes. Some individuals can give a concise, clear, one-hour talk and will remember the thirty seconds when they forgot where they were or fumbled the words. For some individuals that thirty seconds will prevent them from ever speaking in front of a group again.

Emotions affect short-term, working memory, and long-term memory. Negative emotions conveyed from the amygdala and parts of the limbic system can impair the activity of the prefrontal cortex, the area involved in working memory. That is why when we are emotionally upset, we experience difficulty thinking straight and why continued emotional upset can create deficits in a child's intellectual abilities, crippling the capacity to learn. Positive emotions can facilitate working memory, which is critical to long-term memory. A child's capacity to think and problem-solve is heavily dependent on positive affective experience with others.

Social Interaction, Experience, and Memory

Experience is a major factor in developing an infant's ability to reason and make sense of or comprehend what she hears and sees in the environment. Social interaction through language is the means through which this cognitive ability is developed. Language researchers (Bruner 1973; Lindfors 1999) have shown that a toddler's vocabulary is strongly correlated with the amount of talk between mother and child.

Information gained through language embedded in an emotional context seems to stimulate neural circuitry more powerfully than does information alone. The child will more readily learn the concept of the word *more* if it refers to the happy prospect of more milk, or the concept of *later* if it is used in connection to waiting for a trip to the playground. Happy and sad emotions contribute to vocabulary development and memory. If abstract words such as *more* or *later* were presented outside of a meaningful context, in isolation from things the baby cares and wants to know about, they would not be remembered. Feelings, concepts, and language begin to be linked in this way to form memories at age seven months (Gopnik, Meltzoff, and Kuhl 1999).

Infants cannot tell parents what they have learned because they do not have control of the necessary language to do so. They do, however, have a memory of what they know and the ability to demonstrate their knowledge. Especially when they are hungry, children know what they want and do not want to eat. Parents read the intonation of a child's voice or cry to interpret the child's wishes.

We continue to form memories in a similar way throughout life. Adults form memories much more readily if there is emotional content. Most adults can easily recall their wedding day and the birth of a child. If my father had not stepped in to help me with trigonometry, I probably would have had to drop the class. Who knows how that negative experience would have changed my educational life?

Joseph LeDoux (1996) believes that continued emotional distress can create deficits in a child's intellectual abilities, crippling the capacity to learn. That is why it is so important to look for and support the child's approximations or partially right responding and show him how to complete the processing. Without the will to learn, the child will not learn to read and write.

Learning and Remembering

In order to learn you need to do three things: (1) remember previously learned information; (2) retrieve that information from your memory bank; and (3) incorporate the old information into new information. Those three steps are the learning process. Recent discoveries in neuroscience have enabled researchers to gather more precise information about the brain's memory mechanisms and how they interact to facilitate learning. This research suggests four fundamental principles about learning and remembering (Figure 4–5).

Principle One: Learning and Memory Processes Exist in a Circular Relationship

As discussed in Chapter 1, when you learn, information in the environment is picked up by your five senses and then sent to your brain for processing. Those perceptions eventually become memories that will affect future learning.

For example, a child can look at a group of words on a page, but in order to read, she must engage her brain to attend to and focus on one word after the other. If she cannot do this task, the teacher will demonstrate the process of one-to-one matching by taking the child's hand and controlling the movement of her finger as she points and reads each word in a left-to-right serial order. This coordinated act of matching what she says to what she points to and sees will facilitate directional learning.

As the child gains more experience, confidence, and pleasure in accomplishing this action, she will begin to develop expertise. She will eventually be able to read one line of text, matching the text to the words read, without the need to consciously attend to every step of the act (e.g., using her finger to point to each word) as was required when she first learned the skill. Left-to-right visual scanning on one line of text will be automatic. And through repeated experiences, the child develops a memory of one-to-one matching that will affect future learning. If the child

Emergent readers are attending to print one word after the other.

does not have a positive experience while learning left-to-right directional scanning, she is less likely to develop this memory trace.

Principle Two: Individuals Recall the Same Event Differently

The formation and recall of memories are affected and influenced by an individual's mood, surroundings (people, places, and things), and the time the memory is formed or retrieved. Thus the same event can be remembered differently by different people.

The September 11 terrorist attack on the World Trade Center, for example, was remembered differently by different individuals. During the news coverage on that day, people living in New York City had a different perspective on the impact of that attack on people's lives than did those of us who watched the airplane crashing into the twin towers on television. New Yorkers who suspected that a loved one was missing distributed pictures of their friend or family member. Their recall of the event was filled with strong emotions. Wives, husbands, and family members

---

1. Learning and memory processes exist in a circular relationship.
2. Individuals recall the same event differently.
3. Memories change as individuals change.
4. Emotion is the heart of learning and memory.

Figure 4–5. *Fundamental Principles About Learning and Remembering*

of the deceased viewed the event differently than those who did not know anyone who had lost their life. One person isn't necessarily right and the other wrong when they recall this tragedy. They just see things differently depending on their personal situation, circumstance, and the emotions that were evoked when the tragedy occurred.

Principle Three: Memories Change as Individuals Change

New experiences change our attitudes, what we remember, and how we remember. The role of new experiences is important for all learners and teachers to understand. If children have a bad learning experience for whatever reason, they may decide not to put themselves in the same circumstance again.

Craig was having great difficulty learning to read and told his mother that he was flunking first grade because he was the worst reader in the dummy group. He explained that when he had to read aloud, his teacher told him he made too many mistakes and he didn't know why he made them. He decided to stop trying to read because nobody could help him. The mother acknowledged Craig's feelings, saying she understood how upset he was and to show her support she made an appointment to see his classroom teacher the next day so that he could get some help. As a result of their visit, Craig was placed in the Reading Recovery program.

For the first four days in the program, Craig refused to talk or engage in any activity. He listened to the stories the teacher read, but made few comments. On the fifth day the teacher broke through the wall Craig had built around himself. She read a story about a lost kitten. Craig reacted to the story because he had a lost kitten several years ago. With the RR teacher's help, Craig wrote a story about his experience. Craig and his RR teacher continued writing "Finding Craig's Lost Kitten" for seven days. Not only did he compose and write the story (with help), but Craig also read it easily to family members and to his classroom teacher.

Craig's mother and his RR and classroom teachers praised him daily, commenting on his reading and writing skills and how he had grown as a reader and writer. As Craig became more proficient reading books and writing stories, his memories of making mistakes while reading aloud in the reading group faded. Six weeks after his

mother and the classroom teacher met to discuss Craig's reading problems, he was moved to the middle reading group.

Craig's mother and teachers acknowledged his reading difficulties, conveyed their intentions to get him help, and regularly praised his improved reading and writing behaviors and efforts. When children receive concrete specific praise for their accomplishments, they begin to see the connections between their actions and adults' responses. Children's past memories of failure are then replaced with memories of success because they were taught how to change their behaviors and given credit for their accomplishments.

Principle Four: Emotion Is the Heart of Learning and Memory

This principle impacts on the other three and applies to all learners—infants, children, adolescents, and adults. Recent advances in neuroscience (Greenspan 1997; Levine 2002) leave no doubt that emotion is the heart of learning and remembering. The difference in Craig's disposition, attitude, interest, and motivation to participate in the RR lessons was likely due to the emotional responses he had to remembering the loss of his kitten. He had a story to tell and an interest in sharing it. Craig's reading experiences demonstrate how getting emotionally involved with a situation, whether it is a positive or negative one, creates a strong memory of the experience.

Individuals are ultimately responsible for how they learn and what they learn. Individuals construct their own understandings, their ways of thinking and acting on the environment. In order to become an independent and motivated learner, individuals must take charge of their learning. Taking charge of one's learning means that the person has become self-regulated.

Self-Regulation

A major premise of Vygotsky's theory of the zone of proximal development (see Chapter 3) is that higher psychological functions (problem solving, reasoning, decision making) occur when the individual is self-regulated. Self-regulation is the result of social interaction, such as parent-child or teacher-student, mediated through cultural tools, such as language and symbols (Wertsch 1998). Self-regulation is defined as the child's capacity to plan, guide, and monitor his behavior from within—his flexibility—according to changing circumstances (Diaz, Neal, and Amaya-Williams 1990). Two major concepts inherent in this definition are critical to understanding how emotion and cognition interact to direct the learning process: (1) capacity and (2) plan.

Capacity

The word *capacity* combines two separate but interrelated concepts: will and skill. According to *Webster's New World Dictionary* (Neufeldt 1988) *will* is defined as "choosing to act, a desire, volunteering to participate, and it is associated with pleasure, controlling your own actions, energy, and enthusiasm." This is the affective side of human development. From a neurophysiological perspective these properties are registered and reside in brain structures that are associated with emotional development.

The word *skill* is defined as "expertise that comes from instruction, training, acquired ability, or proficiency." Skill refers to the development of knowledge, understanding, and sound judgment. From a neurophysiological perspective these properties are registered and reside in brain structures that are associated with cognitive development.

Will and skill are two sides of the same coin. One depends on the other. If the child does not have the will to learn, there is no interest, no motivation, no focused attention, and few opportunities for the child to develop higher-order reasoning. Developing specific skills are equally important. The child must develop some fundamental cognitive skills in order to make continuous progress. For example, the child must develop the skill to distinguish the features of specific letters (lines, circles, squiggles), to recognize similarities and differences among letters, to determine features of a letter that other letters have in common, and provide a label (letter name) for specific letters, in order to organize them into a specific sequence to make up a word.

For some children, these skills are not going to emerge easily, not because they do not have enough neurons or brain power, but because they have had fewer early childhood literacy experiences to develop a working network of neurons to complete the task. Time has not run out for such children. It is possible, with expert teaching, to provide learning opportunities that enable students who enter school with a low repertoire of literacy skills to become proficient readers and writers in a relatively short amount of time. But to accomplish this goal, teachers must first address the affective side of learning.

Plan

The word *plan* in the definition of self-regulation refers to what the child does when she stops and does not know what to do. Every child has a plan. The child's next move at time of difficulty will provide you a clue as to what it is. Does she

◆ look to you for help?
◆ ask to leave the room?
◆ get a tissue to blow her nose?
◆ look up into the air?
◆ cry or yawn?
◆ put her head on the desk, saying her head hurts?
◆ get angry and quit?
◆ say she cannot think because she is having a bad hair day?
◆ lay on the floor or crawl under the table?

All of the above are behaviors I have observed. In each case the child's plan suggested avoidance, helplessness, frustration. The plan is an emotional or affective response to the situation.

Some children's plans are more cognitive. The child may:

◆ reread
◆ look at the first letter
◆ search the picture
◆ look at the end of the word or look for chunks
◆ look for a word she knows in the word she is stuck on
◆ try to think of a word that would make sense

Any of these plans alone will be insufficient and inefficient; the plan the child uses will help the teacher interpret her capacity (will and skill) to learn. Diversion means, "let me get out of this situation" and denotes little will to try. If the teacher assists the child in developing various strategic ways to problem-solve, she will acquire many different ways to attempt to resolve conflict. If the child demonstrates that she is using only one plan (reread and look at the first letter), she is on shaky ground. That plan will not serve her well, especially when the texts are more challenging. The child will not succeed and she will know it. And when the child encounters failure over and over again, the will to continue is jeopardized. Teachers should ask themselves:

◆ What is the child's plan?
◆ Does she have multiple plans?
◆ Does she have different plans to guide and monitor her behavior flexibly when the text, language structure, and/or format change?

When the teacher teaches the child how to use multiple strategies for reading and writing text and sees to it that she is successful in her attempts, the child will learn how to learn. The will to learn is *charged*. Success builds emotional support, confidence, and a willingness to try—a can-do attitude. That attitude motivates the child to continue to work with you and, in the process, become self-regulated when circumstances change.

Conclusion

The brain makes frequently used neural connections stronger by pruning connections that are not used. Learning experiences determine which connections will be strengthened and which will be pruned; connections that are activated most frequently get preserved and are stored in long-term memory, to be used for learning something new. Emotions, the brain's primary architect, facilitate this process.

In order to learn, individuals need more than being emotionally involved. They need to know what (the facts) and develop how (the skills). Multiple memory systems (procedural or automatic, emotional, semantic, and episodic) work together to store the facts and skills in many integrated regions of the brain, not in one specific area. Thus, learning depends on an effective combination of the emotional, factual, and skill knowledge we acquire and use over time.

The plasticity of the brain enables students who once had difficulty learning to become readers and writers. The downside of the brain's great plasticity is that it is acutely vulnerable to emotional stress and trauma. Experience may alter the behavior of an adult, which was apparent in my experience in high school trigonometry class, but it literally provides the organizational framework for the brain of the child. If the brain's organization reflects its experience and the experience of the child is fear, anxiety, and stress, then the neurochemical responses to these emotions become the most powerful architects of the brain. If you have experiences that are overwhelming and have them again and again, the structure of the brain changes.

Teachers may have to struggle with children from time to time to get them to overcome doubts about themselves, to try harder to understand the facts, and to develop the skills to learn how to read and write. It's a risk that many teachers are taking every day. But only by taking it will teachers have the thrill of seeing excitement in a child's face when she puts down the new book she has just read and says in a thrilled, surprised voice, "That was a great story and I read that whole book by myself." Real self-esteem grows from mastery of genuine challenges.

Educational Implications: Emotion, Memory, and Learning

Recent neurological research proves that emotions are central to learning. They impact what children learn, how they learn it, and how they feel about themselves while engaged in the learning process. Children who have positive learning experiences are happy and feel successful and supported. Children who have negative experiences are dejected and feel like failures and alone. Craig told his mother that he felt helpless and alone because he could not read as well as other children in his classroom and, as a result of telling her, his problems were resolved. Some children, especially older students, do not confide in parents or teachers that they feel hopeless, helpless, and worthless in school.

Parents and teachers can make *the* difference in children's educational experiences, for better or worse. The following five recommendations are provided to facilitate positive emotional learning environments.

◆ First, no human being can learn material presented in a form that is too difficult. Make it easy for children to learn by determining what they can do easily and building on these strengths. For example, if a child can write one letter in her name, use that one letter to show her how to form the other letters. Given tasks beyond their capacity, children lose confidence, the will to learn, and self-respect. They become defeated. It is the quality of experience and instruction, not the child's brain, that determines success or failure. In designing learning activities, make sure that children have a reasonable chance for success either from their own attempts or with support from the adult.

◆ Second, remind children of what they know and provide emotional support, encouragement, and positive feedback for their imperfect attempts and partially right responses. These actions will reassure children that they are on the right track and making progress. They also show that parents and teachers have high expectations for children to learn.

◆ Third, strive to understand and hear what children's words and actions are revealing. This will help guard against dismissing their thinking and feelings, which will eventually push the child away from wanting to work with the adult. It also means that teachers and parents must be willing to be honest with children and not pretend that they are making good progress when they are not. In order to effectively reach children and teach them, parents and teachers must be willing to confirm and acknowledge what they inevitably hear and see without devaluing or dismissing it.

◆ Fourth, emotional factors play a determining role in what children attend to and remember. Emotion drives attention, and attention drives learning, problem solving, and remembering. It adds impetus to children's attention system and keeps them engaged. Provide opportunities for children to take the per-spective of another child in the classroom, a family member, or a story character. This will introduce children to the affective side of the people in their lives or characters in stories and help them become sensitive to others' feelings.

◆ Finally, the mind learns through experiencing life in context and in relationship to everything else previously learned and remembered, and it is our emotions that mediate this learning context. Since emotional factors play the determining role in what is important to the child, parents and teachers will be wise to learn what interests children and to use those interests to engage children's minds.

We cannot prevent or stop the synergy of the emotional, cognitive, and social forces while learning; but as teachers and parents, we can create learning environments that facilitate a positive synergy. Dr. Stanley Greenspan (1991) quotes Melvin Konner, a physician and anthropologist who has studied the emotional and cognitive development of children:

> Consistently losing does not promote self-esteem, no matter how impervious to reality you may be. So every educational program needs to make a choice. You can get short-term gains in self-esteem and continue to lose ground; or you try this theory: that self-esteem can come from making a great effort, from facing uncertainty and overcoming obstacles that we are not sure we can meet, from doing our level best. (213)

 Find Article or book

SECTION TWO

Creating Literacy Environments to Help <u>All</u> Students Achieve Their Full Potential

The growth and development of a child's mind presented in Section 1 is supported by social-cultural theory, postulated by Vygotsky (1978) and Luria (1976). A basic premise and assumption underlying their theories of learning is that all uniquely human, higher forms of thinking, such as focused and controlled attention to tasks, identifying and solving problems, memory strategies, reflecting on experiences and ideas, and emotional growth and development, are deeply affected by children's social experiences.

Vygotsky emphasized that to understand children's development and learning potential, it is necessary to examine and understand the environment

and social context that adults create for them. Section 2 takes an in-depth look at how expert teachers in Reading Recovery, learning disabilities, and special education design social situations that catapult students from being nonreaders and writers to proficient readers and writers.

Close examination of videotaped lessons reveals characteristics of teacher-student interactions that facilitate and foster struggling students' cognitive and emotional growth and development. The three chapters in this section illustrate, through example, how expert teachers work with students who find learning most difficult and teach them how to read and write. Their understandings and actions provide insights into the social, affective, and cognitive processes that enable struggling learners to become actively engaged in literacy learning and that prevent them from even beginning unproductive activities. Every teacher and parent who has experienced frustration attempting to teach a struggling child to learn how to read and write should find the ideas and suggestions presented in the following chapters applicable to many situations and contexts, regardless of the age or grade level of the student.

In Chapter 5, I describe how best to work with reluctant, unmotivated students. Teachers' and parents' responsiveness to and understanding of unmotivated students' perceptions are critical to promoting student involvement and achievement. This chapter provides concrete examples of affective and cognitive teacher responses and actions that enhance and support children's ownership of literacy learning and alleviate feelings of anger, anxiety, passivity, and despair.

In Chapter 6, I provide detailed descriptions, examples, and practical advice on how to successfully teach "the hardest-to-teach RR students" to read and write. The children most at risk of reading failure have a difficult time developing a working system of strategies that enable them to learn how to learn and remember how to use those strategies to operate on increasingly more difficult text. The teacher is critical to improving student learning. The teachers' attitude and how they feel, act, and react can guarantee students' success and failure. This chapter examines variables that make the difference and how expert RR teachers create environments that facilitate self-directed student learning.

In Chapter 7, I focus on teaching students classified as learning disabled (LD) and/or diagnosed with attention deficit (hyperactivity) disorder AD(H)D. Historical and theoretical perspectives in the learning disability field are reviewed, with particular emphasis on the characteristics of students considered LD and/or AD(H)D. Factors that may contribute to LD and AD(H)D and suggestions for creating a learning environment that promotes success are provided. Specific techniques are provided by expert RR, learning disability, and classroom teachers who have successfully taught students considered LD and AD(H)D how to read and write.

Chapter 5

Teaching Reluctant, Unmotivated Students

Teachers are well aware of the fact that motivation is important for learning and that everything they do has a motivational influence on students. How teachers present the information, ask questions, select materials and tasks, interact with students, and provide students with opportunities to work in groups or alone impact motivation. Students act and react to what teachers do and say, and these interactions influence how comfortable they feel in the classroom.

Yet, in spite of this tremendous influence teachers have on motivation, there is generally little understanding of the nature of motivation and how to enhance it. In this chapter I: (1) define and discuss motivation; (2) briefly review seminal and current theories of motivation; (3) discuss the relationship between attention, motivation, and emotion; (4) identify conditions that support and develop motivation; (5) describe one child's transition from being a reluctant, unmotivated student to an intrinsically motivated learner; and (6) provide suggestions that will help parents and teachers create situations that support and motivate children to thrive and enjoy learning.

What Is Motivation?

The word *motivation* comes from the Latin word *movere*, which means "to set in motion." The root of motivation is *motive*, defined in *Webster's New World Dictionary* (Neufeldt 1988) as "inner drive, impulse, incentive, goal to be reached, and intention that causes a person to act in a certain way." Inherent in the definitions of *movere* and *motive* is that motivation is an internal state of mind that an individual must activate himself. Thus, motivation is self-generated and happens *within* the child; it is not done *to* the child.

Anyone who has watched an infant or toddler play knows that motivation is self-generated. Young children are naturally motivated to engage in a goal-directed activity; for example, Kenny's interest in playing with the buttons (discussed in Chapter 1). He was motivated to become an active participant in the activity, contributing to the creation of his own thought processes by collaborating with me. As Ken and I manipulated the buttons together, our communication developed. But it was his self-generated and self-directed motivation that initiated and expanded the activity throughout the first year of his life.

When a parent or teacher asks, "How can I motivate a child or student to learn or do something?" the answer is, "You can't!" You may succeed in getting the child motivated temporarily, through coercion or with a threat or promise of an immediate reward, but it will be at the expense of helping the child to develop long-term motivation, which is self-initiated. There have been theories that motivation is internally rooted and they were well explained and understood by their authors. Today we have more information on how the brain engages and processes information to expand and further explain these theories.

Theories of Motivation

For the last seventy-five years, psychologists have conducted studies on human behavior and proposed several different theories of motivation. Sigmund Freud (1947) thought infants are born with basic biological instincts that motivate them to behave in certain ways. Parents and teachers were supposed to help children control and direct these drives. B. F. Skinner (1968) proposed that infants start off with a blank slate on which experiences gradually condition certain behavior. According to the behaviorist point of view, motivation and learning could be controlled by managing behavior through external rewards and incentives such as prizes, grades, and money. Humanistic psychologists, such as Abraham Maslow (1954) and Carl Rogers (1961), suggested that infants begin life with a propensity for growth and self-actualization, and that motivation is an unfolding of an infant's basic needs, which significant people and events in their environment either support or hinder.

During the last twenty-five years, psychologists have extended or refined the three basic theories of motivation postulated by Freud, behaviorist psychologists, and humanistic psychologists, and versions of two general theories of motivation have emerged: cognitive and sociocognitive. Psychologists who hold a cognitive view (Dweck 1998; Weiner 1992) argue that motivation is based on an *individual's* learned beliefs about his worth and abilities, goals and expectations for success or failure, and the positive or negative feelings that result from self-evaluation. Thus, children's learned beliefs, goals, expectations, and feelings of self-worth influence the level and degree that they are motivated to learn.

Sociocognitive theorists (Deci 1980; Deci and Ryan 1985; Nicholls 1983) emphasize the importance of external and internal social and contextual factors that impact motivation. External factors, such as social and emotional support from significant others, and external rewards, such as recognition for accomplishments, support motivation (external motivation). At the core of motivation is the individual. Internal factors, such as beliefs and personal learning goals, motivate individuals to learn.

Individuals who hold a sociocognitive perspective of motivation place greater emphasis on the child's internal, natural inclinations than on the parent's or teacher's expectation and values. Edward Deci (1980) makes this point when he argues that individuals are born with a basic human need, desire, and motivation for self-determination; to feel competent and in charge of their actions. Furthermore, these basic human needs do not have to be developed; they exist in an undeveloped form at birth, and once they are allowed to unfold, individuals will be intrinsically motivated. Two types of motivation emerge from the cognition and sociocognitive theories of motivation—intrinsic and extrinsic.

Intrinsic Motivation

Intrinsic motivation refers to the internal desire of an individual to become involved in an activity and reflects the genuine inclinations of the child. An intrinsically motivated child will choose to read a book because he wants to read it, not because the teacher or parent told him to read it. Dr. Gabor Mate (1999), a physician and psychotherapist who specializes in working with unmotivated children, describes intrinsic motivation as follows:

> True motivation is knowing that I do what I do, not because someone else wants me to do it, or because I believe someone will respect or like me for doing it. What I do satisfies me regardless of what others may think. As long as I am doing no harm . . . I will honor my preferences and inclinations, even if others will feel disappointed in me. (204)

Mate points out that this true form of motivation reflects the genuine inclinations and feelings of the child, not the values or expectations of teachers or parents. He believes that, in many cases, parents and teachers do not support or give credit to the child's searching for knowledge and show a lack of faith in the child and in nature. In order to enhance and promote naturally and instinctively motivated students, therefore, parents and teachers must provide opportunities and experiences that enable children to reveal, know, understand, and use their knowledge, skills, inner strengths, inclinations, desires, and competencies.

Extrinsic Motivation

Extrinsic motivation refers to an individual's involvement in an activity because an incentive or reward external to the activity has been offered. An extrinsically motivated child will choose to read a book or complete homework because he will get five stickers when he has finished or not be allowed to watch TV if he does not finish. Another frequently used tactic to motivate children is threatening to call the parent or some other authority figure if they do not get their work done. "If you do not turn in your homework tomorrow, I will call your parents for a conference." Mate (1999) argues that trying to motivate children by coaxing or pressuring them does not promote growth of children's self-generated motivation.

Researchers studying motivation (Deci 1980; Deci and Ryan 1985; Nicholls 1983) generally agree on three points. First, motivation is an inherent natural capacity to learn that needs to be elicited from within an individual rather than established from outside an individual. Second, teachers and parents must become aware that the long-term learning goal is to promote the development of motivation that arises for the child's own nature and inclinations. Third, children must be intrinsically motivated to become self-regulated, independent, lifelong learners.

Extrinsic and Intrinsic Motivation and Learning or Teaching

Although the motivation literature points out that intrinsic motivation is critical to student learning, the U.S. education system is organized and administered in a way that supports and promotes extrinsic motivation. For instance, many parents and teachers believe that external rewards such as stickers, money for good grades, and bribes ("You can have a new bike if you get on all A's") are the best way to motivate children. The bribing approach to motivation has also consumed some educational communities. In one school I visited students who read twenty-five books during the month of September were invited to a pizza party. In another classroom, as soon as children had finished reading one book, they got to pick something out of the surprise box. The more books read, the more trips to the surprise box. Pizza Hut, McDonald's, and local public libraries in this community organize contests that give prizes and food to children who read the most books in the summer.

These well-intentioned, quick-fix approaches to motivation communicate the message that there should be a tangible reward for doing schoolwork or behaving appropriately. While these techniques may work in the short run, they will undermine the development of intrinsic motivation. Bribes, rewards, or threats as a means to motivate students are counterproductive and used at the expense of promoting personal self-esteem and satisfaction with a challenge successfully met.

Internal and external motivation do not necessarily reinforce one another. Extrinsic rewards can interfere with intrinsic motivation by turning an intrinsically attractive activity, such as reading for pleasure, into a means to an external goal, such as getting a pizza. One teacher reported that she disliked the school's policy to provide prizes for the children who read the most books because it prevented children from reading for enjoyment. For children who found reading pleasurable, the reward actually diminished their enthusiasm to read. They read books that they were not really interested in quickly and put them aside so that they could pick up another quick-read book and "get the pizza." Prior to the contest, these same children enjoyed reading more challenging children's literature and sometimes read the same book several times and discussed it with friends.

Motivation and Attention

It is difficult to separate motivation from attention. Although motivation is not attention per se, it is a process intrinsically linked to attention. As described in Chapter 2, the young child initially must learn how to focus attention on a specific task, but the shift from external control to internal control is dependent on motivation. When Ken asked me to find the button that did not belong in the pile of white buttons, he was intrinsically motivated to organize and implement the activity. Prior to that, I controlled the activity and he took part. Vygotsky (1978) recognized the importance and critical role motivation plays in attention.

> If we ignore the child's needs and the incentives which are effective in getting him to act, we will never be able to understand his advance from one developmental stage to the next (reference to the zone of proximal development), because every advance is connected with a marked change in motives, inclinations, and incentives. (92)

Developmental changes in attention and motivation are also dependent on social interactions, particularly the type of feedback the parent or teacher provides. Positive feedback supports and maintains the child's attention to the task at hand; negative feedback hinders and oftentimes prevents the child from attending. Parents and teachers who praise children for little successes are more likely to keep the child motivated and attending, which will support further learning.

As children get older, they are more likely to become intrinsically motivated by the activity itself. Additionally, as the child's knowledge and awareness expands and motivations change, the development of voluntary control contributes to increasing independence of attention. The phenomena of the widespread reading of Harry Potter, Nancy Drew, and the Hardy Boys books suggest that if peers are recommending and discussing books, students are motivated to read. Additionally, when the teacher reads aloud and encourages book talks, students are more likely to read a book. Motivation is critical in determining the circumstances in which attention becomes more directed.

Motivation and Emotion

Just as you cannot disconnect motivation from attention, you cannot separate motivation from emotion. Ratey (2001) suggests that motivation directs attention and determines how much energy and attention the brain directs to the task. How motivation and emotion are intertwined become clear when we examine brain structures involved in the process.

The cingulate gyrus, discussed in Chapter 2 and illustrated (see Figure 2–4), is the main link between motivation and emotion. The cingulate gyrus assesses motivational aspects of the environment and compares them with memory systems in order to prioritize incoming stimuli or information from the environment. The limbic system is also involved in motivation; specifically, the thalamus and basal gangalia, which are discussed in Chapter 4 and illustrated in Figure 4–3.

Two-year-old Mikey is intrinsically motivated to write his story.

These two substructures interact to perceive and assess the different motivational influences in the environment and hold the various motivations in working memory to compare with conflicting goals. This complex working system of brain structures motivates individuals to make choices, inhibit some information, focus on other information, and seek rewards. The working system enables individuals to attain goals that initially seemed out of reach, something I learned firsthand one day at school.

During the third week of school, I challenged the thirteen boys (ages ten to twelve) in my transitional second-grade class to walk in a straight line down the hall to the rest room without yelling, slugging, or pushing each other while I stayed in the room. This was quite a challenge for boys who were known for their aggressive, disorderly behavior. They prided themselves on upsetting the principal and other teachers in the school and on harassing students, even those who were older. As they started down the hall, I had reservations, especially since they wanted to know what they would get in return if they met the challenge. I would not tell them because I had not decided what I would do if they accomplished the feat.

They also enjoyed the challenge and had a reasonable chance for success if each boy controlled his own actions while walking down the hall and going to the bathroom. To my surprise (and that of the other teachers on the first floor) they were orderly, mannerly, and quiet. When they returned smiling and congratulating themselves, I asked what they thought they should receive as a reward. Willis said, "We got it already." I asked him what it was and he said, "The surprised look on Mrs. Campella's face when she saw that it was the thirteen of us walking down the hall."

From a physiological perspective, my challenge to the boys caused their limbic system to overreact, which turned on the motivational machinery in the prefrontal cortex. They chose to show the teachers in the building and me that they could walk down the hall in an orderly manner. In doing so, they had to inhibit their normal tendencies and reactions that usually emerged when left on their own. These thirteen boys had accomplished something most teachers and students thought impossible and their reward was a form of retaliation to those who thought the "un-

ruly gang of boys," a nickname given to them by the teachers in the building, could behave.

These boys had few successes, both academically and personally. Since they were not accustomed to success, they enjoyed mastering this "not-so-difficult" task. They were intrinsically motivated to try the walk, and the reward (payoff) was not money or food but the thrill and satisfaction of seeing the teachers who thought so little of them look surprised. The most effective payoff took the form of internal (intrinsic) satisfaction rather than external (extrinsic) reward. That walk down the hall was our first step in developing a rapport, which lasted for over a two-year period. The second year I requested to be their teacher again, which surprised the teachers and administrators even more.

Conditions That Support the Development of Motivation

Psychologists have varied perspectives on motivation (see Deci and Ryan 1985; Dweck 1998; Guthrie and Wigfield 1997; Ratey 2001; Weiner 1992), but they converge on one point: children must have time and space to do their own mental growing, which requires intrinsic motivation. Parents and teachers are invaluable assistants, but the child is the creator, with an instinctive need to learn, to seek out and master the right challenges. Adults who try to take over and impose demands or tasks too difficult for the child to learn run the risk of damaging the child's will, leaving him with little or no motivation to learn. Educational psychologists, psychiatrists, and physicians generally agree that three conditions are required to promote the development of internal motivation: attachment, autonomy, and challenge.

Attachment
According to Mate (1999), intrinsic motivation requires a secure attachment relationship with a parent. Without feeling connected in some way with the adult, preschool children will be too anxious to focus attention on a meaningful exploration of the environment around them. And by school age, these same children will automatically be guided by what they perceive to be the values and opinions of others. Children who do not have a strong attachment to a parent cannot develop intrinsic motivation.

Matthew is a prime example of a child who experienced learning difficulties in kindergarten and continued the same pattern of behavior in first grade. The school psychologist believed that Matthew was too busy dealing with the pressures of trying to do what parents and teachers wanted and expected him to do while simultaneously working overtime to gain their acceptance.

Matthew's teacher described him as a handful and always in trouble. The psychologist's report indicated he was impulsive, sensitive, anxious, angry, and lacking confidence. Matthew's parents said he was full of energy but unmotivated, had frequent outbursts of rage, and was difficult to discipline. His mother told the following story to illustrate.

Matthew was sitting at the kitchen table doing homework. He had to write his name in his best handwriting five times because his teacher said his writing was sloppy. Matthew moved his pencil quickly and made large vertical strokes on the paper. Noting how sloppy the letters looked, he angrily tried to erase the letters and tore the paper. He got up from the kitchen table, stomped out of the room, and returned with another piece of paper. He started over again but was too upset and could not remember how to write a capital *H* in his last name. He asked his mother for help. She showed him how to make the letter. He quickly made large vertical lines to form the letter *H*, and the paper tore again. After another ten minutes of frustration, Matthew got up from the kitchen table and announced, "I'm finished."

His mother looked at the paper and said, "No, you are not, this is sloppy and you did not spell your name correctly. Do it again." He started to cry and stamp his feet. "It's too hard." His mother reminded Matthew that he was beginning first grade and both his teacher and parents expected him to be able to easily write his first and last name. She told him to sit there until he had a neatly written paper to turn in.

Matthew started crying and yelling back, "I can't do it." Hearing this comment, his mom's anger rose exponentially. The more insistent her tone, the less cooperative Matthew became. She finally yelled, "Get it done or else." Matthew yelled back, "NO!" His mom told him to go to his room and not to come out until he was calm enough to sit down and do his homework. Time out was the most frequently used approach to discipline Matthew. Matthew stomped out of the kitchen, slamming the door behind him. After one hour of "time out" spent in his room, Matthew was permitted to come back to the kitchen table to work on his homework, but his anger had become rage. Matthew's anxiety resulting from his inability to write his name and his outburst of anger as he was sent to his room will diminish his capacity to develop self-regulation (see discussion in Chapter 4).

Mate (1999) argues that using the time-out approach to discipline children interferes with a critical factor in developing motivation—attachment. When Matthew is sent to his room, he is banished from contact with the parent. His mother wants to help him learn the difference between appropriate and inappropriate behavior. What he learns, however, is "If you do not do what I want you to do, I will send you away and sever our relationship. I only want you around when you do what I want you to do."

Time out can achieve a short-term, immediate goal but have negative long-term impact. Mate (1999) suggests a better way to help Matthew get his homework done and preserve attachment. As soon as he begins the homework, Mom sits down next to him to make sure he is remembering how to form the letters in his last name correctly. If she sees a problem, she immediately helps him so that he has a good model to guide his behavior. Once she is sure Matthew is on the right track and can successfully complete the task, Mom stays in the kitchen and continues to work. She does not hover over him, watching his every move.

In this scenario, the parent-to-child attachment is reinforced and solidified, leaving further room for emotional development. Matthew knows that his mother supports him and has demonstrated her basic faith that he can get the job done. Matthew, free of anxiety about a break in attachment with his mother, will gradually become more conscious and, in the process, gain much needed self-confidence.

Autonomy

The second condition that supports the development of motivation is autonomy. Autonomy is a strong sense of self and a feeling of ownership. Children who have chosen a course of action to take are intrinsically motivated. Autonomous people want the pleasure of feeling successful.

Deci and Ryan (1985) argue that the degree to which individuals have a perceived choice is a critical factor in how they will respond to a parent, teacher, and situation. Some of the factors that affect children's perceived choices are their own expectations; the teacher's expectations; the contexts the teacher creates, including the tasks, materials, and rewards; and the amount of choice children have in a learning situation (Bruning, Schraw, and Ronning 1995).

Children who develop autonomy take personal responsibility and learn from their mistakes, suggesting that experiencing some failure isn't all bad. If parents continue to help children with homework so that they are not forced to face unpleasant consequences, they will have an exaggerated or unrealistic notion of their capabilities and experience more difficulty facing problems in later years.

Autonomy also requires that parents and teachers provide a supportive, calm, consistent structure that includes setting limits and boundaries so that children and teachers know when and where the autonomy of one individual ends and the other's begins. For example, the teacher is responsible for making decisions on a choice of book for the child to read for instruction, but the child can select from among many suitable books those he wishes to read independently. Mate (1999) points out that attachment must always be attended to once the teacher and parents set limits and boundaries.

Children lacking autonomy are most often extrinsically motivated, working mainly in order to attain a reward or avoid punishment. They doubt their own ability and attribute both success and failure to luck or blame others for their shortfalls. "I really didn't deserve the 100 percent on my math test, I was just lucky." "The teacher didn't give me a chance." "She doesn't like me and that's why I did not get a good grade."

Children lacking autonomy feel anxious if the desired outcome is not achieved; for instance, if I do not get 100 percent on the spelling text, my mother will not like me. In other words, it is the achievement, not the child, that the parent values. Since they think praise and reward are the goal of doing something, they will tend over time to get by with the least amount of effort necessary to receive a reward or praise. Deci (1995) argues that parents and teachers can support a child's autonomy when they encourage self-initiation, experimentation, and responsibility, and do not pressure children.

Challenge

The third condition for the development of motivation is challenge. Most psychologists believe that appropriate levels of challenge and complexity can stimulate curiosity, which, in turn, motivates children to learn. Other researchers point out that when children are motivated to accept new challenges, they develop belief in their capabilities to learn and behave in an appropriate way, which is called *self-efficacy* (Bandura 1997; Fullerton 2001). They also develop self-worth or self-esteem, which is viewed as a reflection of self-efficacy (Ruddell and Unrau 1997). Conversely, when teachers go through the motions and distance themselves from students; that is, when they act like robots going through a lesson, they ultimately reduce the degree of challenge and motivation.

Teachers can promote motivation if they consider the degree of challenge and offer specific useful feedback to support problem solving. Motivation feeds on reinforcement. If the child learns that it feels good to try hard and succeed and that the teacher will provide help when needed, he will strive to do more. If on the other hand, he develops feelings that his own efforts are not effective or even necessary, he may lose that important drive to succeed.

Uncertainty, errors, struggle, and failure to reach a goal will inspire continued effort only if there is a reasonable chance that the child will succeed (Greenspan 1997). Furthermore, those who have persevered and succeeded are more willing to take another risk. Working hard, surmounting challenges, and ultimately succeeding build intrinsic motivation. Children who are not challenged become bored, disinterested, and unmotivated.

Teachers and parents have tremendous influence and power to cultivate the notion that learning is inherently interesting and fun. Providing children with ongoing opportunities to expand their understanding and skills will increase motivation and confidence and help students learn to take constructive intellectual risks. When our children enter high school, college, and eventually the workforce, they will need sufficient motivation

Expert teachers support children's attempts to read and write and show joy in their success.

to work independently and enjoy the challenge of lifelong learning.

Becoming Motivated to Learn How to Read and Write: One Child's Journey

Motivation is arguably the most critical ingredient for long-term success in learning to read and write. But how do teachers create situations to promote and support it, especially when the children they are expected to teach are described as unmotivated or disinterested and the students themselves have the attitude that it is a waste of time to try to teach them, that they are too dumb? One child who fits this description is Matthew.

Matthew's First Three Weeks in First Grade

Matthew was excited about going to first grade. He was anxious to see his old friends, but expressed concern about the "school" part. The first week of school was good—he played with his friends and was picked to be the line leader. He could also write his name! Then came the

second week when the class started learning the letters of the alphabet. Many of his classmates knew all the letters with their corresponding sounds and some knew how to combine them to read. The teacher gave his classmates what she called "easy" books and some of his friends could read them. Matthew could not read any words. He did not know what was going on. He couldn't remember the name of the letters on the page or tell the sound a letter made. He came home from school one day and asked his mother if she knew the name of the stupid man who invented the sounds for the letters.

By the third week, the work at school grew harder. Matthew's friends started to notice that he never said anything during reading. His best friend asked if he knew the letters. Matthew said he did . . . but he didn't. He started to look out the window a lot, which seemed to upset his teacher. She moved him to another seat so he wasn't next to the window anymore. Matthew's teacher was always asking him to pay attention. When his classmates were reading the little books, Matthew went to the bathroom.

In the fourth week of school he took a letter test and was asked to read and write some words. He came home and told his mother he flunked. He started to get headaches and stomachaches. His mother made him go to school anyway. Matthew started getting into fights on the playground. His mother learned that the kids were calling him stupid. Matthew was miserable. The teacher called his parents and set up a conference.

The classroom teacher told his parents that Matthew's behavior had deteriorated every week. The first few days he seemed happy and participated in class activities. During the second week his behavior started to change. The teacher said that he no longer volunteered to participate in any class activities. He slumped in his chair and did not want to pass papers. She estimated that

Matthew's attention span was about three minutes long. When she read to the children, he was easily distracted and had a difficult time sitting still. He was disinterested in books she read to the class. When she asked him how he enjoyed a story, he shrugged his shoulders. Matthew would draw a picture rather than attempt to write anything.

The teacher shared Matthew's scores on the Observation Survey of Early Literacy Achievement (Clay 1993a). He recognized eight letters and he wrote his name, MTH. Matthew's teacher knew he could write his name, but when she asked why he didn't write it, he said, "Why bother?" Matthew had given up on himself and it was only the fourth week of school. His teacher recommended that he be placed in Reading Recovery (RR) because "he was the very lowest student in the class and probably learning disabled."

Matthew's Next Five Weeks in School

After about five weeks in Reading Recovery, Matthew's classroom teacher noticed a major shift in his behavior. This once fidgety, overactive, unmotivated, disengaged child, who seemed reluctant to talk in class, was beginning to settle down and become more task oriented and was communicating with his teacher and classmates. He listened to the stories the teacher read in class and was willing to discuss why he liked or did not like them. Matthew wanted to share and write about personal experiences. He reacted to stories read in class and wrote some of his own.

Matthew's parents noticed a change in his attitude and behavior at home as well. He didn't have any more headaches or stomachaches. They did not have to drag him out of bed to get ready for school. He read his RR easy books to them every night. He asked his mother and father to read him a bedtime story. His disposition had changed as well. He was more willing to do chores and homework. Most important, he could do the homework without their help. His parents and classroom teacher wanted to know why there was such a dramatic, positive change in his attitude, motivation, and behavior. The classroom teacher said it started after several weeks in RR so they asked me, his RR teacher, what I thought might have changed his attitude and behavior.

I said that I did not do anything *to* Matthew. I engaged him in such a way that he showed me what he already knew about reading and writing and how to work together on appropriate levels

of difficulty. Once Matthew realized that I would help him if he had difficulty, he started to make more attempts to read and write, which motivated him to try more. I admitted that during the first week, Matthew and I had one-sided conversations walking from his classroom to the RR room, but I knew he was listening because he smiled when I said something he thought was funny. After looking at the lesson records, I identified three experiences during the first six weeks of RR that seemed to impact his behavior.

The first event took place as we were walking down the hall and I asked Matthew for some help. The second event occurred after I selected I particular book for him to read. The third event took place when I prevented him from making a letter backward. These three events were turning points in our relationship and dramatically improved Matthew's level of motivation and commitment to become my partner in learning. Through these experiences, I learned three important lessons about working with children who appear unwilling and unmotivated to learn how to read and write. A description of each event and rationale for the recommendation follow.

Working Effectively with Unmotivated Students

1. Demonstrate that you are genuinely interested in the child—in what he thinks, what he does, what he feels, and what he cares about.

The first week we worked together was difficult. As soon as he sat down, Matthew put his head on the table and reluctantly sat up only after being told. His body language suggested he was bored and not interested in reading and writing. Matthew also used many different avoidance tactics. He routinely asked to go the bathroom and get a drink of water. He dropped his pencil on the floor and left his chair to retrieve it. He fell off his chair and crawled under the table. Matthew sighed loudly many times throughout the session and repeatedly blew his nose. I started to wonder how long it would take to change his attitude and behavior. That question was answered on the seventh day we worked together.

As we walked down the hall, I asked Matthew a question that became a turning point in our relationship. "What should I get my fifteen-year-old son, Ken, for his birthday?" The first words out of his mouth were, "You want some ideas from me? You think I can help?" I was surprised that he answered in this way but reassured him that he was the best person to ask because he was a boy and he had an older brother. Matthew's face lit up. He had several ideas, but the best gift he could think of was a puppy.

When we reached the RR room, Matthew went in and sat down without first putting his head on the table. He immediately picked up one of the little books I had waiting for him without being told. When I asked him to start reading, he did so without hesitation or trying any avoidance tactics. After reading several little books, I asked him why he thought a puppy would be a good gift for Ken. Matthew volunteered many reasons for getting a dog for Ken and also revealed experiences he had had with his dog, Max.

◆ A puppy is alive and always happy to see you.
◆ A puppy jumps on you when you come home from school.
◆ Puppies don't grumble and are always willing to play.
◆ You can teach a puppy tricks.
◆ Puppies like to go for a walk and chase other dogs.
◆ They don't crab at you.
◆ Puppies don't get mad when you make a mistake.
◆ Puppies' ears lay on top of the snow.
◆ My dog Max gets the paper every day.
◆ On Sunday I have to help Max bring in the paper because it is too heavy.
◆ I put a cowboy hat on my dog, Max.

Matthew knew I was sincere when I asked his advice. His reasons for getting Ken a dog were personal and revealed Matthew's past experiences and feelings. These reasons were included in a book we wrote together, *Why Everyone Needs a Dog* by Matthew Hunter.

When teachers engage in genuine, relevant, ongoing conversations focusing on the child's interests and share their own interests, they create environments that build trust and facilitate communication. Children need to view teachers as thinking, feeling, human beings, not robots. Those conversations we had while walking down the hall opened the door to the happy part of Matthew's life. He was able to put what was happening in the classroom out of his mind for a while.

The first several weeks of the school year are critical to establishing a positive working relationship with students. During this time the children and teacher begin to form their first perceptions of each other, which set the tone of the teacher-student relationship for the rest of the year. Getting off to a good start plays a major role in establishing the trust that will support and motivate children to work with (not against) the teacher. As discussed in Chapter 3, once the child is willing to work with the teacher, the skills needed to read and write can be taught.

The first two weeks in RR is called "roaming around the known" (Clay 1993b). It is a relaxing, fun, stress-free, thirty-minute period for teachers and children to get to know each other and for the teacher to observe how the child is responding to reading and writing texts. Teachers select readable texts that they are sure the child can read at about 90 percent accuracy. They collaborate with the child to write a simple story in his own words and about his own experiences, which he will be able to read later.

Through these experiences, children reveal what they know about letters, words, and sentences. This information reveals children's zone of actual development (discussed in Chapter 3) and provides a firm foundation on which the teacher can build future lessons. Children develop confidence in their ability to read and write and oftentimes discover things that they did not realize they knew. This lesson was learned the last day Matthew and I were "roaming around the known." He wanted to write, "I put a cowboy hat on my dog Max" (Figure 5–1).

TEACHER: How are we going to start the sentence?
MATTHEW: I can write the first letter *I*.
TEACHER: Do you want to try to write *put*?
MATTHEW: No, you do it.
TEACHER: OK [writes *put*] Your turn.
MATTHEW: I can write *a*. You write *cowboy*.
TEACHER: How about the next word?
MATTHEW: *Hat*? I'll try. [says *hat* and then writes the word] Am I right?
TEACHER: Do you think that word looks like *hat*?
MATTHEW: Yeah and it almost looks like my name. Take the *h* off and put a *M* and it spells my name. I can write *hat*. It's a miracle.
TEACHER: It really isn't a miracle, Matthew. You know much more about writing and reading

Figure 5–1. *Collaborative Writing During Roaming Around the Known*

than you think you know. As we work together, we will discover all kinds of things that you already know about letters and words.

MATTHEW: I can write *on* and *my*.

TEACHER: Good—go ahead. You don't need help at all! Can you finish the sentence?

MATTHEW: I have trouble with *d*'s. You write *dog*. I know how to write *Max*.

TEACHER: Yes you do! Excellent work, Matthew. Read the whole sentence.

MATTHEW: [confidently reads the sentence without help]

Matthew revealed that he could use the first part of his name to figure out how to write *hat*. He thought it was a miracle that he could write *hat*, but was reminded and reassured that he knew and could do much more than he thought possible. His confidence escalated and he immediately wrote *on* and *my* with no help. He knew he might have trouble making the letter *d* in *dog* but confidently said he would write *Max*. He read the entire sentence confidently and with pride.

The conversation we had while writing this sentence was pivotal to changing Matthew's attitude, interest, and feelings about working with me. In this interchange, I enthusiastically and genuinely acknowledged Matthew's problem solving and achievement. I thought he was beginning to develop a more secure attachment, which, as reported earlier in this chapter, is critical to the development of intrinsic motivation and self-regulation. This attachment was further developed as I started to learn more about Matthew's life. I learned

- ◆ that Matthew enjoys camping with his family;
- ◆ how many pets he has and how he helps to take care of them;
- ◆ what he enjoys in school and the names of special friends he plays with every day;
- ◆ what kind of books he likes to read and why he likes them;
- ◆ what his family does on the weekend and what chores he helps with around the house;
- ◆ how many brothers, sisters, and cousins he has, and their names;
- ◆ what he does with his grandpa when he visits him by himself;
- ◆ what sports he plays and which sports he likes to watch on TV.

I did not ask twenty questions to get this information, nor did Matthew and his mother complete a questionnaire. I learned about his interests in daily, unplanned, informal conversations walking to and from the lesson, while we were getting ready to begin the lesson, after reading or writing a story, and as we put things away after the lesson.

I valued his opinion, cared about him as a person, and was willing to share my personal life with him. Matthew started to feel valued and important . . . powerful feelings to motivate a child and strengthen a weakened self-image. The process of helping a reluctant, unmotivated child feel safe enough to risk being wrong takes time and energy. The relationship becomes much smoother and less frustrating if teachers show that they like the children and enjoy their company, have high expectations for their success, and have some understanding of their individual likes and dislikes. Mate (1999) points out that to focus on and give his full attention to material or a task with the mind fully engaged, a child must be highly motivated and interested. The second recommendation addresses this point.

2. Select books and encourage students to write stories that reflect their interests and their level of achievement.

Carefully selecting texts that are within children's instructional level and that you think they will be interested in shows children that you really care about their interests. Using children's interests and background knowledge makes it much easier for them to read and comprehend the text. Notice in Figure 5–2 how Matthew is drawn into a conversation during the introduction of a new book.

I selected a book that Matthew could relate to and enjoy. The opening remarks engaged him immediately because he and Pat had similar experiences. He could relate to the excitement that Pat felt when she received her new puppy. Matthew immediately started to look through the book without prompting, suggesting he was motivated to read the story. He had an emotional commitment and motivation to learn what happened. He learned how to assume the main character's perspective when asked what he would do in a similar situation. This comment provided a feed-forward mechanism (see Bruner's and Clay's theories discussed in Chapter 2) that enabled him to predict the plot and anticipate the words and language structure of the text. This introduction took approximately one minute. He was highly motivated to start reading.

Matthew's incidental comments while reading the story showed that he was comprehending what had happened so far and anticipating what would come next (Figure 5–3). He read the text with 93 percent accuracy, which is well within his instructional level or zone of proximal development. His understanding of the story led to most self-corrections. After he read page 12, the comment "Oh, no" suggested he had a good idea about what might happen next (inferencing). The closing comment, "That was a good idea," suggested he agreed with Pat's solution to the problem. Matthew's comprehension increased as he turned every page.

According to Marie Clay (2001),

We probably want to reserve the terms "comprehension" and "understanding" for some overarching processes but at least the word-by-word decision-making (as in parsing) marks out a path towards comprehension. A comparable situation arises as a writer composes. Sequential decision-making depends on tentative understanding of the message so far, while allowing the language user to change direction en route. Early effective reading and writing of continuous

---

Pat's New Puppy by Helen Learning

TEACHER: Matthew, I chose a new book that I think you will really like. It's called *Pat's New Puppy*. It's a story about a little girl who gets a new puppy. She is so excited about the puppy. The story is about all the things Pat and her new puppy do. How did you feel when your parents brought Max home?

MATTHEW: I was excited too when I got Max. [immediately starts looking at the pictures in the book] Here she is putting the puppy in a wagon.

TEACHER: Yes, you're right. What letter would you expect to see at the beginning of *wagon*?

MATTHEW: A *w*—here is *wagon*. [locates the word *wagon* in the text]

TEACHER: What happened while they were on the ride?

MATTHEW: [turning the page and looking at the pictures] The puppy jumped out?

TEACHER: What would you do if Max jumped out of your wagon?

MATTHEW: I would run after him and get him back in the wagon.

TEACHER: Start reading the story and see if Pat does the same thing.

Figure 5–2. *Book Introduction and First Reading of the New Book*

Pat's New Puppy

	text	Matthew's Comments
p. 2	Pat got a new puppy.	
p. 3	The puppy was brown and white.	"Just like Max"
p. 4	The puppy had big feet and a long tail.	
p. 5	Pat named the puppy Happy.	"That's a good name."
p. 6	Pat put Happy in her wagon.	
p. 7	She took him for a ride.	
p. 8	Happy jumped out of the wagon.	
	He ran into the park.	"Oh no, he might get lost. She better chase after him."
p. 9	Pat ran after Happy.	
p. 10	Happy ran through the yellow flowers.	
p. 11	He got mud on his feet.	
p. 12	Happy saw a big dog.	"Oh No."
p. 13	The big dog barked at Happy.	
p. 14	Happy ran away fast.	
p. 15	He ran to Pat.	"That big dog is getting close."
p. 16	Pat carried her puppy home.	"That was a good idea."

Figure 5–3. *Matthew's First Reading of the New Book*

texts places a high demand on understanding groupings of words in the message read or written so far. (106–107)

The conversation immediately following the first reading showed that Matthew understood what happened (Figure 5–4). The conversation started with a follow-up of something I overheard Matthew say. It was a genuine question. "What was a good idea?" Matthew showed empathy for Pat's predicament and agreed with her decision to pick Happy up, but he also understood that he might not have had to pick Max up because Max was bigger. Again Matthew is able to make inferences while reading the story, which is a more complex form of comprehension.

Matthew demonstrated the second factor essential to helping students develop intrinsic motivation: autonomy. He was in charge of and responsible for the decisions made while reading. He found his own errors and provided a rationale for why he self-corrected without prompting. I stepped in only when necessary to reinforce his problem solving and self-corrections. Matthew was

TEACHER: Matthew, I heard you say that was a good idea. What was a good idea?

MATTHEW: That she picked Happy up because if she put him back in the wagon, the big dog might get Happy.

TEACHER: Is that what you would have done if a big dog chased Max?

MATTHEW: Yea I sure would, but Max is bigger than Happy so it might not be as much a problem.

TEACHER: I was very proud of the way you were thinking of the story and figuring out what the words said. Let's go back to page 5. The first time you read this you said . . .

MATTHEW: I know, I said Pat knew the puppy, but that wasn't the real thing that happened. She named the puppy Happy, so that was an easy fix.

TEACHER: Yes, it was a good thing that you were thinking about the story. Does that word looked like *named*? Does "she named the puppy Happy" sound right?

MATTHEW: Yes.

TEACHER: Can you find another place that you took a closer look at the words?

MATTHEW: [pointing to page 16] Here on the last page.

TEACHER: What happened on the last page?

MATTHEW: Well, she took Happy home but the word isn't *took* because it has a *t* at the beginning and really she carried Happy home and that word looks like *carried.*

TEACHER: You are exactly right and you figured that out by yourself. Aren't you proud of yourself? I am.

MATTHEW: Yeah, I am too.

Figure 5–4. *Conversation Following Matthew's Reading of the New Book*

becoming an intrinsically motivated, self-regulated, independent learner on most occasions. However, when he met difficulty and could not do it right the first time, he lost control and started to hit his head and call himself stupid. These actions were reminiscent of his behavior sitting at the kitchen table trying to write his name. I had to help him learn how to control outbursts of frustration after making mistakes, which is addressed in the third recommendation.

3. Anticipate the students' problems and prevent inappropriate behavior from occurring.

It is not always easy to anticipate children's processing before they start to read and write. However, it is possible to make an educated guess about what children may do based on past experiences. In order to prevent a habituated pattern of behavior from occurring, teachers must help children learn how to engage in a new pattern of behavior to replace the old behavior. For example, Matthew routinely wrote the lower case *d* backward. I would watch him closely, and as soon as he was going to start writing the semicircle on the wrong side of the vertical line I intervened, taking his arm and hand through the appropriate movements while verbally describing the movement. I knew Matthew's tendencies well and could anticipate a move that might launch an inappropriate behavior. I stopped the inappropriate behavior from occurring and continued to do this until Matthew managed without guidance.

Why? Because the more often an inappropriate response is repeated, in Matthew's case making a lower case *d* backward, the more difficult it becomes to unlearn. Matthew was a quick responder, labeled impulsive by the school psychologist and classroom teacher. If I did not catch him in time to stop the inappropriate movement, Matthew would become upset and make holes in the paper. He was mad at himself for not remembering how to make the *d*, which created a downward spiral of emotions and affected his memory, preventing him from retrieving previously acquired information. For example, he would not be able to remember how to write high-frequency words he knew because he was too upset to recall the information. The emotions took control of his mind and memory. Fullerton (2001) describes a similar experience working with another unmotivated child.

Research reported by Clay (2001) and Greenspan (1997) shows that for some children, getting off course or track causes a downward spiral that is very hard to stop and reverse. Saying "You can do it" is not enough. As was discussed in Chapter 4, there is a strong relationship between emotion and cognition. Matthew's emotional response to a mistake was so strong that he had difficulty recalling previously acquired skills, which prevented him from attending to the remainder of the lesson.

Conclusion

Vygotsky (1978) used the term *zone of proximal development* (ZPD) to refer to changes in individuals' cognitive development, differentiating between a person's actual developmental level as determined by independent problem solving (zone of actual development) and the level of potential development as determined through problem solving with guidance. Matthew demonstrated that the ZPD could also refer to changes in an individual's emotional development, which includes motivation, effort, ability, and efficacy. Matthew's new view of himself and the resulting views of his parents and classroom teacher facilitated further changes in Matthew's attitude about himself as a learner and improved his motivation to learn.

Wood (1998) suggests that how the child views himself as a social being is a crucial determiner of his motivation. "Motivation and de-motivation for learning are not simply manifestations of individual cognition but consequences of a complex interaction between the person and the social" (286). Fullerton (2001) reminds us that "self-perceived competence and control, goal attainment, and engagement all relate to learners' self-efficacy and motivations and are critical considerations in relation to self-regulation" (65).

Parents, caregivers, and teachers have a tremendous influence on children's cognitive and emotional development. Through their efforts, fear of failure may be changed to self-confidence, motivation may rise from low to high; insecurity may become self-assurance; self-

Old	New
Fearful of failure	Feeling successful
Unmotivated	Highly motivated
Easily defeated	Determined
Insecure	Self-assured
Self-hating	Self-confident
Extrinsically motivated	Intrinsically motivated
Negative	Positive

Figure 5–5. *Changing Emotional States of Mind*

hatred can change into self-esteem; and extrinsic motivation can turn into intrinsic motivation as children's overall attitudes become positive (Figure 5–5).

These transformations can occur through parents' and teachers' scaffolding and guidance as children acquire new emotional responses that motivate them to achieve, to become tenacious, and to sustain their attention, motivation, and tenacity when tasks become more difficult. The following ideas can help parents and teachers motivate children.

Educational Implications: Motivating Reluctant Readers

There are nine important factors that influence student motivation and that relate to the decisions teachers make about how they interact with children and how they organize the learning environment. Implementing these factors will expand children's perceptions and have a positive impact on their motivation and achievement.

◆ Create a warm, supportive interpersonal relationship with children. In order to establish this relationship, it is essential to find out what is special about each child and learn to accept and appreciate their uniqueness. For example, Bobby, a child who is discussed in Chapter 7, was an expert in major-league baseball. He watched baseball games with his father and grandfather from June through September every year. Through his interest in baseball, I was able to begin to build a relationship with Bobby. We routinely discussed team members' batting averages, which team was leading the league in the number of wins, and speculated on which players would go to the All-Star Game that year. Whenever possible, I selected books about baseball for Bobby to read, and baseball became the topic of many stories that he composed and wrote. Teachers who become personally involved with children will show their enjoyment while working with them.

◆ Show a personal interest in children's lives by demonstrating genuine interest, caring, commitment, and concern. Ask children how they are doing and how their school day is going. Share some of your experiences, likes, and dislikes with them. Teachers familiar with children's interests and concerns are more likely to create a safe, trusting, and supportive context for learning and to demonstrate a concern for and commitment to students' achievement.

◆ Create learning situations and activities in which children are interested and can meet with success. Select challenging books that children can relate to and enjoy and that are well within their range of reading ability. Allow them to have personal choice and encourage them to express what they think and how they feel about the stories. Children are more likely to become motivated and involved in an activity when it means something to them.

◆ Structure the environment to ensure children's success. Make expectations for behavior clear and set boundaries so children can control their behavior and achieve success. Teachers need to develop appropriate and realistic expectations for children and move them along a continuum at a pace the children can manage. Examples of how to set boundaries and expectations for children's reading, writing, and classroom behaviors are discussed in Chapters 6, 7, and 8.

◆ Provide opportunities for children to take risks without fear of failure. Reassure children that they will be helped when they need it and encourage them while they are trying to problem-solve. Part of children's motivation to achieve is related to their perceived role as struggling readers and writers. Teachers should attempt to modify or change children's expectations by placing them in situations requiring different types of behav-

ior, such as trying to figure out one word on a page and then positively reinforcing their attempts or partially right responses.

◆ Value and praise children's efforts. Praising specific behavior when warranted will motivate children to continue to problem-solve. Young children view effort and ability similarly, so praise can enhance their perceptions of their competence and motivate them to persevere. Always praise genuine progress and tie it to a specific action. For example, after a student corrected an error the teacher might say, "You did a very good job of looking closely at that word and checking the first letter, Michael. You realized that the word had to be *sat* instead of *cat* to make sense and sound right in the story."

◆ Introduce tasks and books in such as way as to challenge and entice children to become involved. Teachers who appear negative or disinterested in the lesson—for example, sighing often or rush through a lesson—are sending a message that they are bored, not interested in what they are doing, and going through the motions to get the lesson over. This kind of behavior has a negative impact on children's motivation to attend and continue to work.

◆ Expect children to succeed. High expectations for children's achievement are related to teachers' attitudes and beliefs about themselves and their ability to effectively teach. Teachers', parents', and caregivers' expectations of children's ability can make a major difference in children's perceptions of themselves as capable or incapable of learning.

◆ Teachers' beliefs about motivation impact children's motivation. Teachers who believe that students will have little inclination to learn unless they are encouraged though external incentives such as stickers are more likely to control the learning activity and emphasize getting the job done. Teachers who believe that children are naturally curious and that learning is a process of self-discovery (internal motivation) are more likely to establish shared responsibility and a partnership with children during the learning process. These teachers will follow students' leads and give them choice in activities. What teachers, parents, and caregivers do and say impacts young children's learning and belief in themselves and their abilities for a lifetime.

Chapter 6

Teaching Hard-to-Teach Students

What is a hard-to-teach student? I have asked that question for the last ten years in my developmental and corrective reading graduate courses. My students teach kindergarten through grade twelve; they are classroom teachers, reading teachers, and learning disability teachers. Typical responses to the question focused on emotional and behavior problems. For example, the hardest-to-teach students were inattentive, hyperactive, disobedient, aggressive, uncontrollable, and distant. They were also considered learning or reading disabled, hyperactive, and in some cases, dyslexic. When learning problems were mentioned, cultural differences, poor home environment, lack of basic skills, or neurological problems were given as plausible causes for the problem. Underlying the teachers' responses was the assumption that students who cannot read and write have something wrong with them. They had a deficit, disability, or dysfunction.

When asked what they have done to help students who were hard to teach, I saw blank faces and shrugging shoulders. Many responded that their job was to either control the situation through behavior management techniques or remove the student from the classroom so that the rest of their classmates could learn. It wasn't that the teachers in my classes did not care, but they felt helpless when confronted with hard-to-teach students. They had received little training to work with them.

Finding out how best to work with hard-to-teach students is the focus of this chapter. In this chapter I: (1) describe hard-to-teach students; (2) discuss the knowledge and skills needed to work with them; (3) identify hard-to-teach students' major processing problems; (4) describe, through examples, how expert teachers facilitate their emotional and cognitive development and growth; and (5) draw implications for parents and teachers who work with children considered hard to teach.

Behaviors of Hard-to-Teach Students

For the last several years, I have asked groups of Reading Recovery (RR) teachers to describe the behaviors of the hard-to-teach students they have taught. Although their responses were similar to the graduate students in that they focused on emotional and disruptive behaviors, they also mentioned that hard-to-teach students had difficulty learning letters, learning how to read in a left-to-right direction across a line of print, writing their name, and remembering previously learned information. Also, few RR teachers suggested that there was something wrong with the child. Instead they wanted to know what they were doing or not doing to help the child learn how to read and write.

The RR teachers believed that hard-to-teach students had a difficulty rather than a deficit. Reading difficulties suggest that children who are struggling have a *difference* rather than a disability, which implies that it can be altered with good teaching. This assumption is supported by leading authorities in beginning reading instruction, who argue convincingly that the key to amelioration of reading problems is early one-to-one intervention in first grade (Adams 1990; Clay 1991; Snow, Burns, and Griffin 1998).

Why did the two groups of teachers express different attitudes or beliefs about working with hard-to-teach students? Certainly they were correct in saying that oftentimes hard-to-teach students display signs of emotional or behavior problems that interfere with learning. I believe the major difference between the two groups of teachers, however, was the amount of knowledge they had acquired and the skills they had developed to teach their students. Because graduate students have had few, if any, courses specifically designed to learn how to teach struggling readers, ignoring their behavior or removing them from the classroom were the only options that came to mind.

Reading Recovery teachers, on the other hand, had participated in yearlong graduate-level course work (thirty hours of graduate credit) specifically designed to teach them how to observe, diagnose, and design individualized intervention programs to facilitate hard-to-teach students' learning. They concurrently take the graduate-level courses and teach four RR students daily in a one-to-one setting. Therefore, RR teachers attributed reading difficulties to a learned rather than an innate difference, which they believed could be changed and dramatically improved with the right kind of instruction. Reading Recovery, a short-term intervention program, was founded on this belief (Clay 1979, 1993b).

No matter how much training or experience teachers have had, working with the hardest-to-teach or -accelerate RR students is always puzzling. Clay (1993b) comments,

> In general, when the child is hard to accelerate he is finding some part or parts of the reading process difficult. Oftentimes he has learned to do something, which is interfering with his progress, and he may have learned it from the way you have been teaching. (57)

Who better to share their knowledge and insights into how best to meet the needs of the hard-to-teach children than RR teachers who have successfully taught them how to read and write? I analyzed videotaped lessons of ten expert RR teachers to document ways in which they manage distracting and nonproductive behavior while helping students learn part or parts of the reading and writing process they found most difficult.

Observing and Assessing Reading Achievement

Efficient and effective measures have been developed by Clay (1993a) to assess students' current levels of understanding based on a set of real-world reading and writing tasks, which are then used to inform instruction. Students who are experiencing reading difficulty at the beginning of grade 1 are administered six assessments from *An Observation Survey of Early Literacy Achievement* (Clay 1993a). Once it is determined that a child's literacy knowledge and skill are within the bottom 20 percent of her class, she becomes a candidate to receive RR.

The RR program relies heavily on the teachers' ability to observe and support changes in students' processing and progress over time. Using daily running records (Clay 1993b) of the child reading yesterday's new book, teachers capture children's processing and how they monitor, problem-solve, and self-correct while reading continuous text. By analyzing running records, the teachers are able to see where children are from moment to moment and how they use their developing competencies to acquire more complex reasoning and skills every day.

The running record is analyzed daily throughout the child's program to determine how struggling readers perceive, process, and interpret information. Running records enable the teacher to interpret how the child's brain is organizing assemblies of neurons to make new connections, through revisiting and repeating what has been read previously, and strengthening (myelinating) existing networks that are already organized. These daily assessments reveal what information children think is relevant, what they use, and how they use it. Processing data collected on running records is used daily to inform teachers' thinking and practice.

Expert Teachers' Knowledge and Skills

Effective RR teachers have acquired six fundamental understandings about how children learn to guide their instruction.

1. No two children learn the same way. Children have many different cultural, social, and school experiences from which to organize and structure their brains.

2. Every individual has emotional and cognitive responses and reactions to learning.

3. The cognitive and emotional dimensions of learning are two sides of the same coin. One depends on the other. If children are distraught, there is no interest, no motivation, no focused attention, and they will not engage in the thinking and learning process.

4. Until steps are taken to address and improve the affective side of the learning context, it is unlikely that hard-to-teach students will make accelerated progress.

5. New emotional responses and skills must be taught to replace destructive, nonproductive behaviors.

6. Positive social and emotional environments must be created before students will trust enough to engage in the learning process.

When the teachers' instruction is grounded in these six understandings, children's increasing self-esteem, interest, and motivation make for more opportunities to engage in the learning process. These six fundamental understandings underpin how expert teachers think and act. But it is an understanding of the affective and cognitive dimensions of learning that impact how they teach.

The Affective Dimensions of Teaching and Learning

Throughout this book I have provided physiological evidence that learning is strongly influenced by emotion and that emotion plays a critical role in the learning process. The stronger the emotion connected with an experience, the stronger that memory of the experience. Neurotransmitters in the brain are signaling the importance of the information, which strengthens and increases retention. If the emotion is a positive one, learning increases. Recall Kenny's playing with the buttons and the calendar trick. Although he does not remember the button jar, the positive emotions he experienced enabled him to learn a great deal. Ken does remember the great pleasure he derived from "doing the calendar trick" for friends and neighbors.

On the other hand, emotions can have a negative impact on learning. If an individual perceives the learning environment as threatening or is afraid of making a mistake for fear of embarrassment or humiliation, learning decreases. My experiences at the blackboard during trigonometry classes make this point clearly. The dual role emotion can play in learning has huge implications for teaching, especially when working with hard-to-teach students.

The psychology section of every major bookstore has many shelves of self-help, how-to books: how to improve and control emotional responses, how to work with individuals who are emotionally disturbed, how to repair a marriage void of emotions, how to cope with your own and others' emotions, etc., etc., etc. There are also best-selling books that increase our understanding of emotion, such as Goleman's (1995) *Emotional Intelligence* and LeDoux's (1996) *The Emotional Brain*.

To my knowledge, no one has published a book or written an article listing the behaviors that classroom or reading teachers have observed while teaching students considered difficult to teach. I have been gathering information on this topic for several years from teachers in my graduate classes and from RR teachers who work daily with difficult-to-teach students. Although these teachers gave a range of responses, they identified the behaviors listed in Figure 6–1 most often.

It was not difficult for the teachers to generate the list of student behaviors, but it was difficult for them to decide what to do about them. Emotional and disruptive behaviors interfere with teaching the children and with their reading progress. Clay (1991) reminds us, "learning to read requires a great deal of personal initiative and a willingness to take risks which the insecure child is unwilling to take. It is easier for him to apply to the new learning tasks of school his old emotional reactions of withdrawing or attacking, distorting or ignoring and so by applying old habits to the new situation, causing himself to fail again" (42). Expert teachers create a learning context that builds on students' emotional and cognitive strengths.

Cognitive Dimensions of Teaching and Learning

Reading is a cognitive activity, that is, it requires problem solving, choosing among alternative sources of information, and making meaning. Clay (1991) defines reading as "a message-getting, problem-solving activity which increases in power and flexibility the more it is practiced" (6). She goes on to say,

> Within the directional constraints of the printer's code, language and visual perceptual responses are purposefully directed by the reader in some integrated way to the problem of extracting meaning from cues in a text, in sequence, so that the reader brings a maximum of understanding to the author's message. (6)

Cognitive development includes development in the areas of perception, attention, and memory, all of which have been discussed in the first section of this book. As with all cognitive abilities, these three areas change and develop over time. Moreover, individual differences in these areas of development affect children's learning. The cognitive dimensions of becoming literate are com-

avoidance	temperamental (easily upset)
tired (yawns loudly)	withdrawn/shy
angry (bangs on table)	hyperactive (in constant motion)
destructive (throws books; tears paper)	not motivated
clumsy	tries to control ("If you do this, I'll do that.")
resists authority ("You can't make me.")	fragile (cries easily)
arrogant ("I know that already.")	afraid to make a mistake
easily distracted	uneasy
passive	not interested in anything teacher does/says
slow-moving	quits
won't initiate	stares at pages, out window, at chalkboard
lacks responsibility (won't bring books back)	reluctant (afraid to try easy tasks)
apologetic ("It's all my fault.")	aggressive (throws things)
unwilling to risk	poor self-image ("I'm stupid.")
mood swings (laughs and cries same day)	fidgety
gets mad at self; hits head	screams at teacher
lays head on desk	looks at floor, out window, up in air
fakes being ill	throws head back and arms over head
defensive ("You aren't helping me.")	argues ("I said the word is *going* not *go*.")

Figure 6–1. *Emotional and Behavior Problems of Hard-to-Teach Students*

plex and ever changing, especially when working with a hard-to-teach student.

Expert Teachers' Decision Making and Practice

Expert teachers learn how to select from among the various procedures and techniques offered in *Reading Recovery: A Guidebook for Teachers in Training* (Clay 1993b) those that are most likely to meet the idiosyncratic strengths and needs of the student. In order to select the most appropriate techniques the teacher must

- observe the idiosyncratic way the child interacts while reading and writing;
- describe the child's reading and writing strengths behaviorally and specifically;
- analyze the behaviors in relation to the entire complex processing system needed to read and write;
- think about problem behaviors in relation to cognitive and emotional development;
- determine when problem behaviors occur and how often they are repeated throughout the lesson;
- think about what the teacher does or does not do in response to the child's affective and cognitive processing;
- think about what the child does in response to the teacher's actions and verbal and nonverbal responses;
- decide which affective behaviors to address and/or prevent;
- prioritize actions and responses and determine what needs to be done first;
- decide under what circumstances, when, and how to intervene;
- determine the affective and cognitive behavioral indicators to watch for to suggest children are gaining control and becoming self-regulated;
- record on the lesson record what children do and say in response to the teacher's actions.

The quality of interactions between the teacher and child will determine success or failure. When a child is not making accelerated progress, Clay (1993b) suggests that the teacher take a closer look at what she has been doing, "because invariably the child is finding some part or parts of the reading (and writing) process difficult . . . or some important aspect of the reading process has not received attention" (57).

Videotaped analyses of the children featured in this book revealed that the hardest-to-teach students had great difficulty acquiring the fundamental early learning behaviors that are prerequisites to becoming a reader and writer:

- learning to look at print
- learning how words work
- learning about direction
- learning to hear and record sounds in words
- remembering

These early literacy behaviors are related to the development of visual and auditory perception. In order to develop visual perception, the neural networks of the brain must be organized in such a way that children can focus on and attend to the visual features of print. Children must be taught how to look, what to look at, and what to look for. The most difficult-to-teach children have great difficulty acquiring visual and auditory perception skills.

In addition to having processing difficulties that are cognitive in nature, hard-to-teach children develop emotional and behavior problems that interfere with learning. The following section discusses each of the five processing problems and how expert teachers helped children overcome the problem while meeting their emotional needs and redirecting behaviors that interfered with learning.

Learning to Look at Print

Learning to look at print requires that children visually attend to the features of letters. They must learn which way the letters have to look in order to be *n* or *r*; *d* or *b*. Learning how to attach lines, circles, dots, and tails in just the right places and just the right ways requires much abstract processing and places a high demand on memory.

As children learn letters they begin to discern the distinctive features that distinguish one letter from another. Learning how to see a letter symbol as a distinct entity and how to discriminate one letter from another requires visual discrimination skills.

Patty was a shy, insecure little girl who cried easily. She did not attend kindergarten and had few opportunities to interact with books and writing materials. Patty entered first grade without knowing how to write even one letter. She had some ideas, but they were not helpful. The following interaction between Patty and her teacher reveals how the teacher supported Patty's emotional development while teaching her how to write her name.

TEACHER: Patty let me show you how to write the first letter of your name.

PATTY: I don't want to know how to write my name.

TEACHER: You have such a beautiful name, it would be wonderful if you could write it.

PATTY: Why?

TEACHER: Because then people you might not know too well will be able to read your name and know who that pretty girl is in the room.

PATTY: My name has too many lines. It's too hard to make them. I tried once.

TEACHER: I will take your arm and hand and show you exactly what to do.

PATTY: Will I make a mistake?

TEACHER: Absolutely, not. I promise.

PATTY: OK, show me.

The teacher takes Patty's hand and together they move the pencil to make a capital *P* while saying aloud, "Down, up, and around."

In this vignette the teacher is addressing Patty's emotional and cognitive needs. She is reaching out to this shy, withdrawn child by letting her know she is pretty and that she has a beautiful name that others would like to know. This statement should boost her self-image. The teacher is also attending to Patty's insecurity and unwillingness to take a risk by reassuring her that she would not let her make a mistake.

At the same time, the teacher is helping Patty learn how to write her name. By taking the child's hand to organize and demonstrate the action sequence, she is simultaneously engaging the neurons in her brain in such a way that the child will begin to form a memory trace of the action. Through much practice (a) modeling the movement action sequence to make the *P* in Patty's name, (b) providing a verbal description of the movement while forming the *P*, and (c) writing the letter in a letter book to represent a visual model of *P*, Patty learned how to make the first letter and remaining letters in her name. She also practiced the action sequence in sand, on the white board, and on the chalkboard, which provided many opportunities to organize the network

of neurons needed to make the letter *P*. Through repetition the action sequence will become myelinated and a memory will begin to form that will help with recall.

Learning How Words Work

Eventually Patty will be able to know and write the letters, but then she will have another visual processing challenge. She must learn how to extend her knowledge of letters and learn how words work. For example, she must learn how to make connections between letters, sounds, and letter names and use this information to work with letters that are embedded in words. One expedient and efficient way to help children learn how words work is to engage them in the action of making and breaking words using magnet letters. They learn to attach names to letters and relate sounds to these written symbols. This is not an easy process for some children to learn.

Charles had difficulty standing and sitting still. He was constantly in motion, stretching his arms over his head, moving from side to side, and occasionally pushing things off the table. He yawned often and was disengaged, frequently appearing disinterested in the activity. His teacher knew that to keep Charles attentive, he had to be actively involved in the task. In the following vignette, Charles not only learns how words work, but also learns how to initiate and control his behavior.

TEACHER: Here is a word you know, Charles. [selects the correct magnet letters and places them at eye level on the chalkboard to make *go*, a word Charles knows] What is that word, Charles?

CHARLES: *go*

TEACHER: Show me the first part of *go*. [Charles correctly points to the *g*] Check it with your finger. [Charles looks at the teacher] Say that word slowly and run your finger under it. That's what I mean by checking it.

CHARLES: *g* [while running his finger under it so that when he made the sound of *g* his finger was under *g* and when he said *o* his finger was under *o*]

TEACHER: You are so good at this. Excellent checking. Let's try another one. Here is a word you know. [makes *me* with magnet letters] What is that word?

CHARLES: *Me.*

TEACHER: [taking out a *b* and showing it to Charles] If I took off the *m* and put this letter here [pointing to the first letter and substituting a *b* for *m*] what word would I be making?

CHARLES: *He.*

TEACHER: Oh, you're so close. Are you checking and looking? [Charles is moving away from the board.] Stand close to the board, so you can see what you are doing. [gently moves Charles closer to the board] Let me try another way. [takes off the *b* and replaces it with an *h*] Now what word did I make?

CHARLES: *He.*

TEACHER: Good job, you really know how to do this. You can think about a word you know and that will help you figure out a word you don't know. Here is a word you know. [makes the word *dad*] If I give you this letter [gives Charles a *m*] can you make a new word?

CHARLES: [makes the word *mad*] *Mad.*

TEACHER: Run your finger under it. Now change it back to *dad*, real quick.

CHARLES: [quickly changes *mad* to *dad* and runs his finger under each letter while saying] *Dad.*

TEACHER: Oh, Charles, lovely. Ah, ah, you changed the first part and made a new word! Let me see, now I'll give you another letter and see if you can change the first part. [gives Charles an *s*]

CHARLES: It says *sad.*

TEACHER: Exactly. Check it with your finger, Charles. [Charles runs his finger under the word and says *sad*.]

CHARLES: I just said it [*sad*] right away. I didn't even know it!

TEACHER: You are really good. I am so impressed!

CHARLES: Give me another one.

TEACHER: OK, change *sad* back to *mad*. You are so right. Golly, you are good at this! Because you know *dad* you can figure out *mad*, which is a new word.

CHARLES: Yeah, I can do it. [takes the initiative and shows the teacher how he can make *dad*, *mad*, and *sad* with the magnet letters] Here is *dad* and here is *mad* and here is *sad*. [Each time he makes a word, Charles says the word and checks it.]

TEACHER: Exactly.

The movement of letters is a constructive process that helped Charles to visually discriminate among two and three letters in a word and begin to understand how letters are placed in a particular sequence to make new words. The task was made easy because the teacher taught the process using words Charles knew. She was careful to make sure she used specific language to direct his actions. For example, when she asked Charles to check the word to make sure it said what he thought it did, he gave her a questioning glance. She immediately picked up on this nonverbal action and said, "say the word you just made slowly and run your finger under it." She then demonstrated the process, ending with the comment, "That's what I mean by checking it." Too often teachers assume that children know what they mean and the children do not have an understanding.

Starting with a known word freed Charles' brain to attend to the order and sequence of letters and sounds to make new words. Charles was able to successfully use the eye and hand coordination required to complete the task. Once done, he was able to look at the word, say it slowly, and run his finger under the word while reading it. This pattern of actions became a consistent, routine program. Manipulating the letters strengthened his eye and hand coordination and also facilitated the formation of a memory trace. Charles was acquiring a program of action to help him use known words (*dad*); construct a new word (*sad*); and, throughout the process, organize and myelinate the neural structures in his brain to see, produce, and recall previously learned information.

There was also a shift in Charles' attentiveness and behavior. On one occasion Charles said the word was *he* instead of *be*, and the teacher commented, "Oh, you're so close." He seemed to understand that he was wrong and withdrew from the board suggesting his motivation had slipped. The teacher gently moved him closer to the board. She immediately gave him another word that she knew he could successfully analyze (*me*) and Charles once again became attentive.

The teacher commented, "I was constantly working on Charles' engagement and attention, more so than most students. He was pretty successful completing an auditory-visual analysis but visual-auditory was a challenge. When he came up with *sad* it was a huge deal. Keeping the known visible and going quickly from that to the new word really seemed to help him."

The teacher's direct, consistent, calm interest and joy in Charles' success kindled his interest in exploring how words work and helped him organize and control his attention. The ecstatic exchange between them when he realized that he could make and read a word that he never read before (*sad*) motivated Charles to continue to manipulate the letters and make new words. Throughout their conversation, the teacher was positive, encouraging, and truly excited about Charles' accomplishments and he knew it.

Repeated positive experiences develop strong connections between neurons in the brain to form positive memories that last a lifetime. Such experiences also provide hard-to-teach children such as Patty and Charles with a sense of security and a can-do attitude. They learned what to expect from reading and writing and how to use that knowledge to understand and effectively work in the literate environment around them.

Learning About Direction

Learning about direction is an act of perception in the brain that enables children to attend to print in a left-to-right serial order consistent with written English language (Clay 1991). Controlling directional processing involves the coordination of a network of neural structures that enables children to

◆ move their eyes from left to right across a line of print;
◆ focus on the left page before a right page;
◆ start at the top of the page and read downward;
◆ read across a line of print and, when they get to the end, return to the beginning of the next line at the left side. (Clay 1991)

Locating Responses

In addition to the four complex early learning processes mentioned above, children must also learn how to attend to each word while reading a line of print. The processing challenge is to locate words in a line of print (left-to-right directional scanning) by attending to, focusing on, and pointing to one word after another (Clay 1991).

Expert teachers withdraw support as children develop competence in controlling directional movement.

Hard-to-teach children initially learn to control the movement of their eyes by using their fingers to point to one word after the other in a line of print. The teacher controls the sequence of action by first taking the child's pointing finger and moving it across the line of print, matching what the child points to, sees, and says. Through repeated coordination and one-to-one correspondence of seeing, pointing, and saying behaviors, the action sequence in the brain becomes more stable and memorable.

Beginning readers must develop assemblies of neurons organized to match words in speech to each word in print. Eventually the neural networks of the brain that control left-to-right visual scanning patterns and that involve children matching what they point to, see, and say, become organized and myelinated. When this occurs, the child's eyes alone can process word-by-word across a line of print without support of the child's finger, which initially served as a guide or external mediator to monitor and direct eye movements.

Collin had a very difficult time learning the left-to-right directional constraints required to read and write. His extensive vocabulary, prior knowledge, and good memory for text gave him the erroneous idea that reading was looking at the pictures and inventing text. Collin was also in the habit of getting his way. He disliked having someone tell him what to do and routinely negotiated with the teacher on what he would and would not do and when he was finished with a task. His aggressive behavior, coupled with outbursts of anger and many different kinds of avoidance tactics, were the norm in most lessons. The vignette in Figure 6–2 shows how the teacher managed Collin's behavior while helping him learn what it means to match units of speech (words) to words in print.

Collin could easily "read" this text by looking at the pictures. His excellent memory enabled him to read the first seven pages of this repetitive book easily, without having to think much about the words in the text. When he read page 8 he invented the text, which in his opinion was better than Joy Cowley's version. The teacher realized after Collin's outburst that he did not understand what she meant when she asked him, "Did that match?" She immediately demonstrated what she meant by taking his finger and pointing with him as they read the page.

The teacher also attended to Collin's emotional needs. First, she did not react to his angry outburst. It was pointless to get into a power struggle with this child. She also realized that Collin was right. She had assumed that Collin knew what she meant when she said, "Did that match?" Second, she provided a rationale for why he should read the words on the page instead of inventing the text. This action communicated the reason for her request and showed that she was

---

Down to Town by Joy Cowley, Level I

Page	Collin reads
2.	The sheep go down.
3.	The cows go down.
4.	The horses go down.
5.	The dogs go down.
6.	The ducks go down
7.	The farmers go down.
8.	to town to eat their supper with the people.
	to town.

TEACHER: Did that match, Collin?

COLLIN: [in an angry voice] Matching! Matching! You're always talking about matching. I don't know if it matched!

TEACHER: Let me show you what I mean. Let's look at page 8. How many words are on this page?

COLLIN: Two.

TEACHER: You're right. Put your finger under the first word. What does it say?

COLLIN: To. I know that word, you don't have to ask me.

TEACHER: Put your finger under the next word. What does that say?

COLLIN: Town.

TEACHER: Yes, that word is *town*. Point to each word and read what the book says.

COLLIN: To town.

TEACHER: Good. You matched what you said with the words on the page. When I say, did that match? I am asking you to read the exact word you pointed to.

COLLIN: I get it, but my ending to the book is better.

TEACHER: Yes, you had a good ending to the story, but my job is to teach you how to read and that means you have to read what the author said in the book.

COLLIN: Sometimes what the author said does not make much sense.

TEACHER: Sometimes you are right about that.

Figure 6–2. *First Reading of the New Book*

not the "authoritarian figure" demanding compliance. The teacher is establishing an atmosphere of mutual respect and trust. The unstated message is "I want you to succeed and pointing to each word as you read will help you." Third, Collin learned what the teacher expected and what was expected of him. Setting limits is critical to changing disruptive behaviors. Finally, the teacher explained that she had a job to do, which was to teach him to read. Again, the unstated implication is that it was Collin's job to point to and read each word on the page, not to make up the words.

The interaction between Collin and his teacher set boundaries and expectations for future lessons. This is a good first step in helping a hard-to-teach, aggressive, outspoken child to see another individual's point of view. The expert teacher in this vignette was teaching Collin to take responsibility for his own learning and behavior in a positive, supportive way. She had many different kinds of opportunities to help Collin manage his behavior and replace disruptive behaviors that impede learning with behaviors that support learning, as you will see in later chapters of this book.

Learning to Hear and Record Sounds in Words

Clay (1991, 1993b, 1998) has shown that children's early writing efforts reflect their close attention to the written language in their environment and that writing plays a significant role in early reading progress. In reading, children must use some visual information to confirm the author's message; thus, the child must conduct a visual-to-auditory analysis. In writing, children must produce visual forms (letters) to represent the sounds in the words they are writing; thus, the child must conduct an auditory-to-visual analysis. In order to complete both actions, children must organize and direct their attention to a specific part or parts of a word and analyze the word in detail and in an appropriate sequence.

Writing is a powerful way to teach reading, and it also provides teachers with valuable insights into what children are attending to in print and how they are processing the information. For example, are children attending to

- the form and features of letters so that they distinguish one letter from another?
- sequence or order of letters to make up a word?
- sequence of sounds to make up a word?
- the initial letter or ending of the word?
- letter groups or chunks of information at the beginning, middle, or end of the word?

Writing helps children organize and engage their neural networks to visually analyze print. The processing challenge is first to hear the sound segments (syllables), then to hear the order of sounds in spoken words, then to analyze the sequence of sounds in the new words children want to write—that is, to complete an auditory-to-visual analysis. In order to accomplish the action sequence, children must coordinate the movements of their eyes as they visually scan the word with the movement patterns of their hands as they produce it (Clay 2001). Before children learn how to develop the program of action required to hear and record sounds in words, they must be able to hear larger chunks of sound, or syllables, in words. The following vignette shows how difficult it is for some children to acquire this ability.

According to his first-grade classroom teacher, Kevin was not interested in learning anything. He would reluctantly join the class on the rug to hear a story. Instead of listening to the story, Kevin would disturb the other children until the teacher sent him back to his seat. He seemed

Expert teachers determine if children can hear the sequence of sounds in words.

to enjoy leaving the group and would smile as he sat down at his desk. During writing time he would scribble on his paper and then turn it in. The teacher was very frustrated with his behavior and felt he always seemed "to get his way." Her major question was "How am I going to teach him when he doesn't want to learn?" Since he was the lowest performing child in the class, he was placed in RR. Kevin resisted working with the RR teacher throughout "roaming around the known."

During the first week of RR lessons, it became clear that Kevin had difficulty hearing the sounds in his name. He could not hear the difference between *Kevin*, *king*, and *kingdom*. The teacher asked him to clap once for each chunk of sound he heard. For each word he clapped one time. The RR teacher understood that before Kevin would be able to hear sounds to write the words in a sentence, she had to teach him the task of slowly articulating a word so that he could hear the parts in a word. This was a much easier task than hearing single sounds in a word. Teaching Kevin to hear chunks of sounds, or syllables, in words became a turning point in their relationship.

TEACHER: Kevin, help me clap your name. [says his name and makes two claps]

KEVIN: I don't want to clap. I want to hit the desk. Kevin. [one pound on the desk]

TEACHER: [taking Kevin's hands in her own] Let me show you how to clap your name. [Together they clapped *Kevin* several times.] There are two claps.

KEVIN: [withdrawing his hands from the teachers] Let me do it alone. Kevin. [one clap]

TEACHER: How many times did you clap?

KEVIN: Two.

TEACHER: Are you sure? Try it again.

KEVIN: Yea I'm sure [claps once]

TEACHER: Let me help you. [tries to take Kevin's hands]

KEVIN: I don't need your help. I can do it. Do you think I am stupid? I've been clapping all my life.

TEACHER: Stupid? Absolutely NOT. You are very bright. I know that because you can explain things so well.

KEVIN: What do you mean? Everyone knows how to talk.

TEACHER: I agree, everyone knows how to talk, but you have a special gift of being able to tell good stories. Like the story you told me

when we first met about playing T-ball. Now it is time to learn how to write your words down on paper so that I can read the T-ball story. I know I would like to read it and I bet the other children in your class would like to read it too.

KEVIN: Do you think so?

TEACHER: Yes, I am sure of it. But first I want to help you learn how to hear the sounds in words you want to write. The first step in learning to write words down is hearing those sounds. That is why I asked you to clap your name, Kevin.

KEVIN: OK, so teach me.

TEACHER: Let's start with your name. Give me your hands and together we will clap your name. Let me know when you can hear two parts in *Kevin* and then you can try clapping yourself. [Together they clap *Kevin* several times.]

KEVIN: OK, I'm ready. [claps the two parts of his name]

TEACHER: You have learned that Kevin has two parts so fast. It took a few minutes. You're ready to move on to the name cards.

KEVIN: Good.

TEACHER: [takes out picture cards of a cat and a dog] Clap what animal you see on this card.

KEVIN: Cat. [claps once]

TEACHER: Do it again. [Kevin says "cat" and claps once.] How many parts did you hear in the word *cat*?

KEVIN: One part.

TEACHER: You are learning this so fast. Try this card. [shows him a picture of a dog]

KEVIN: Dog. One part. But if it is a puppy, there are two claps. Pup–py.

TEACHER: I knew you were smart. You figured that out all by yourself. Puppy does have two parts just like your . . . ?

KEVIN: My name. Give me another picture.

TEACHER: Are you ready for a harder one? [shows him a picture of a basketball]

KEVIN: [proudly] Basketball. Two claps.

TEACHER: Say "basketball" again slowly.

KEVIN: Basket-ball [two claps]

TEACHER: [taking his hands] Bas-ket-ball. How many parts in *basketball*?

KEVIN: Three parts.

TEACHER: Kevin, you are absolutely right. Try it again by yourself. Say "basketball" slowly and clap the parts.

KEVIN: Bas-ket-ball.

TEACHER: You have done a tremendous job today Kevin. [extends her hand to shake his hand] Congratulations, you will be writing that T-ball story very soon.

KEVIN: [shaking her hand] I know.

Early on in the lesson, the teacher ignored the pounding on the desk and immediately took Kevin's hands to demonstrate what he was expected to do in a positive manner. It was important that Kevin know what he was supposed to do (clap the sounds in his name) and that the teacher set limits on his participation so that he felt successful and still in control. Kevin wanted to try clapping his name by himself but he was not successful. The teacher did not have to say he was wrong, Kevin knew it and again resisted her helping him clap his name.

The turning point in their conversation came when the teacher conveyed her high expectations for Kevin's ability in an emotionally supportive way. She convinced him that he was capable of doing great things because he was a good storyteller. Kevin was initially defensive ("everyone knows how to talk") but his defensive attitude changed when she expressed how much she enjoyed the T-ball story and that she thought the children in the classroom would enjoy reading it.

The teacher conveyed to Kevin that she admired him, which changed his tone and attitude immediately. She then provided a reason for clapping the syllables in words (he could learn how to write his T-ball story). She invited him to learn how to clap the syllables in words. Kevin was interested in learning to clap the syllables because it would enable him to do something that was personally relevant and that mattered to his teacher. Kevin was ready to learn, and, as discussed in Chapter 5, motivation is critical to learning.

Once he became fully engaged in the task, Kevin learned quickly. Knowing the routine ("say the word slowly and clap the syllables") was critical to building his sense of security. He was responsible for letting the teacher know when he learned how to clap a two-syllable word. Taking responsibility for his learning was critical to helping Kevin become self-regulated. She also had a helpful and encouraging tone and way of praising Kevin's efforts.

In one lesson, Kevin learned to analyze words into syllables, articulate the speech sounds of those chunks, and coordinate the movement of his hands to clap the sound segments of one- and two-syllable words. More important, Kevin discovered something on his own, that is, the distinction between one-syllable (*dog*) and two-syllable (*puppy*) words. After five days he had learned to coordinate what he was saying with the motor action required to clap the sound segments of three- and four-syllable words. None of this would have happened without a change in Kevin's attitude and his interest in working with this teacher. The emotional power of this warm, supportive environment strengthened his disposition and his resolve to work in a collaborative way with the RR teacher.

Developing Strategies for Remembering

When asked what characterizes a hard-to-teach child from other RR students, teachers almost always respond that children cannot remember what they have learned from day to day. The student's processing challenge is to call up strategies for remembering such as letter name, letter sound, or word that begins with a specific letter.

The expert teachers agreed that once they insisted that children learn how to coordinate and integrate the action patterns of what they see and say with the motor activity of their hands, the students developed ways for remembering. And when the children were struggling, if they were asked to write the word, they could recall it. Furthermore, children who had difficulty completing a visual-to-auditory analysis, taking words apart "on the run" while reading, were able to analyze the sequence of letters in the word when asked to think about how they would write it.

Alex was one of those children who needed the kind of analysis required to write words (auditory to visual) in order to read them. He was a shy and withdrawn child who did not participate often in class. He had many experiences listening to stories at home and in kindergarten, but he seemed reluctant to share his ideas with others. He had a large vocabulary, good sense of story structure, and strong memory for text and thus relied on his knowledge of text structure and making sense to read. Alex became frustrated with himself and also with the authors he read because he had difficulty matching his language to the print in the books. Once he learned how to monitor his errors, he frequently commented, "It should say . . ." or "It would be better if it said . . . here." His mother reported that he had difficulty learning and recalling letters as a preschooler. He would learn a few, but as more were added to the repertoire, he would mix the newer one with the ones she thought he knew.

Alex also had difficulty calling up strategies for remembering. For example, when he came to an unknown word, he could not recall a word that began with the letter or what sound the letter made. Alex's strong sense of story and oral language overrode the text. It was much easier for Alex to complete an auditory-to-visual analysis to write a word than to complete a visual-to-auditory analysis to read a word.

The transcript in Figure 6–3 shows Alex reading *School*. Alex easily read the word *the* on page 8 of *School*. After reading the text, he also easily spelled the word *the* when his teacher place the magnet letters on the board. As illustrated in the transcript, his own language initially overrode the word *the* as he read yesterday's new book. After his independent reading and with help from the teacher, Alex found and corrected his error, but had difficulty reading the word *the* while the teacher was taking a running record.

Alex's teacher had to give him a consistent way or approach to study words so that he could develop strategies for remembering. Moreover, she had to continue to reinforce this sequence of actions throughout Alex's program. The program of action to help Alex develop strategies for remembering required movement (writing, moving magnet letters to make and break the word *the*) in order to help him organize and control attention. Through practice and repetition, the action sequence moves from short-term to long-term memory. Movement also plays a critical role in initiating and sustaining the processing. With much effort, Alex gradually learned how to use what he knew about words and letters to read. Alex passed the state-mandated fourth-grade proficiency tests. His mother reports that he loves to read. He is entering the sixth grade.

The relationship between writing activities and skills needed to read is discussed in detail elsewhere (see Clay 1998, 2001). The links between directing one's attention and behavior to carrying out a sequence of movement needed to write words has been explained well by Luria (1973) and is reported by Clay (1975). This movement pattern also develops a memory trace. The more the action sequence is repeated, the more myelin is produced and the stronger and faster a memory of that action sequence will be formed. The neurophysiology of this complex action sequence and the role of movement in directing and maintaining one's attention is discussed in Chapter 2.

Highly specialized and coordinated movement patterns *must be taught*; for example, those used to: (a) learn to look at print to form and to recognize and use letters to make words and sentences; (b) learn about direction and coordinate the movement of speech patterns for the spoken words with left-to-right visual processing while reading a line of print; and (c) learn to hear chunks of sounds (syllables) and the sequence of sounds while reading and writing stories. Mastery of these action sequences is typically difficult for hard-to-teach (or hard-to-accelerate) students. The importance of early acquisition of such skills is critical to learning how to read and write.

Neuroscientists studying the fluctuations in levels of the neurotransmitter serotonin have found that serotonin inhibits quick motor responses and enhances relaxation that leads to smoothly coordinated and controlled movements (Pert 1997). Recall Matthew's quick actions while sitting at the kitchen table trying to write and then erase his name discussed in Chapter 5. He erased the letter so hard and fast that he tore the paper. Because effective movement is central to reading and writing, it is not surprising that when children are able to make a letter correctly or read a line of print without teacher's support, serotonin levels increase and they experience a burst of self-esteem. Matthew demonstrated this phenomenon. The expert teachers were able to address both the cognitive and emotional dimensions of these hard-to-teach students, resulting in positive outcomes.

Conclusion

Children who have the most difficulty learning to read have not learned how to control these complex sets of early strategies and relate one to another. Nor have they learned strategies to recall and use previously learned knowledge and information. Interestingly, the teachers of seventy-two

My School by Catherine Peters

p. 2   ✔ ✔ ✔ ✔
          This is my school.

p. 3   ✔ ✔ ✔ ✔
          This is my teacher.

p. 4   ✔ ✔ ✔ ✔
          This is my class.

p. 5   ✔ ✔ ✔ ✔
          This is my principal.

p. 6   ✔ ✔ ✔   ✔
          This is our playground.

p. 7   ✔ ✔ ✔ ✔
          This is my friend.

                my/our

p. 8   ✔ ✔   ✔   ✔
          This is the school bus.

p. 9   ✔ ✔ ✔ ✔ ✔ ✔
          It is time to go home.

TEACHER: [pointing to page 8] Read this page again and look very carefully at all the words you know.

ALEX: [pointing to each word] This is my [waits] our [waits] school bus.

TEACHER: That is very smart of you. When I asked you to read the sentence again to check all the words you know, you noticed that this word [points to *the*] isn't *my*. This is a word you know.

ALEX: Yea, I know that word.

TEACHER: What's that word?

ALEX: *The*.

TEACHER: That was very smart of you to check that word and know that isn't *my*. Come to the board. [places three letters on the board] Can you make *the* with magnet letters Alex?

ALEX: Sure it's easy. [rearranges the magnet letters to make *the*]

TEACHER: It is easy but we want to practice making it so that when you see the word *the* in your book you won't hesitate and be able to read quickly. Take a good look at that word now that it is all together. Do you know how *the* looks?

ALEX: *The*, yea.

TEACHER: I'm going to put enough letters on the board so that you can make *the* three times.

ALEX: [looks at the magnet letters and begins to make *the*]

TEACHER: I'm glad that you started with the first letter and that you used both hands. Each time you make the word take a good look at it, and say the word out loud as you run your finger under each letter of the word. Can you make all three words?

ALEX: [completes the routine the teacher established] That was easy.

TEACHER: Do you know how the word *the* looks?

ALEX: Yes, I'm sure.

TEACHER: I'm going to write the word *the* on the blackboard. [says *the* slowly while writing the word] Trace the letters that make *the* and say *the* as you trace them.

ALEX: [begins to trace *the*, but runs out of breath]

TEACHER: Good, try tracing *the* again. You must go faster or you will run out of breath.

ALEX: [traces the word *the* while reading it]

TEACHER: You can write it by yourself now.

ALEX: [begins to write the letter *t*]

TEACHER: I'm glad you started at the top to make the *t*. What word did you make?

ALEX: *The*.

TEACHER: Are you sure? Write *the* again.

ALEX: [quickly writes *the* two more times] *The, the*.

TEACHER: [gets the book and finds the sentence "This is the school bus."] Find *the* on this page.

ALEX: [locates *the*] Here it is.

TEACHER: Now write the word *the* and make it with magnet letters.

ALEX: [writes *the* on the chalkboard and runs his finger under the word while saying it, makes *the* with magnet letters, and locates *the* in the book]

TEACHER: Can you read *the* in your book now?

ALEX: Yeah.

Figure 6–3. *Running Record of Yesterday's New Book*

RR children who experienced difficulty learning to read discussed in Chapter 2 (Lyons 1995) had the same areas of difficulty.

It has been my experience that when RR teachers are asked to describe behaviors of hard-to-teach students the list includes affective responses that are emotional in nature and responses that suggest cognitive processing problems. Both kinds of observable behaviors interfere with children's ability to "integrate the complex network of working systems that will enable them to lift literacy performance on increasingly difficult texts, until they become silent readers with self-extending systems for reading and writing" (Clay 2001, 2).

Furthermore, as the first section of this book illustrates, it is not possible to separate emotion and cognition. In fact, emotion is the brain's primary architect (Greenspan 1997), and it can impede or support a child while she is constructing the complex network of brain systems required to read and write. The hard-to-teach children in this chapter—Patty, Charles, Collin, Kevin, and Alex—struggled to learn to read and write. It wasn't until they developed self-confidence and the belief that they could learn that hard-to-teach children begin to gain self-esteem.

Self-esteem has to do with children's self-evaluations as well as their affective reactions to these judgments. The expert RR teachers understood that to increase children's self-esteem, they must work simultaneously on the affective and cognitive dimensions of learning. In order to foster intellectual and affective development, a certain kind of interpersonal context must be created. The teacher must establish an atmosphere in which mutual respect is continually practiced. The examples in this chapter illustrate how teachers can create a learning context that supports children's emotional and cognitive development.

Educational Implications: Working Effectively with Hard-to-Teach (and Reach) Students

Every teacher at one time or another has tried to teach a "hard-to-teach" student to read and write and become frustrated because they were not successful. Some teachers stop trying when they do not experience success the first few times working with a hard-to-teach student. Other teachers try harder to teach the material the same way over and over again. Those who succeed in helping hard-to-teach students learn to read and write have personal characteristics and a broad base of knowledge and skills from which to operate. The following set of implications are based on my observations of teachers working with hard-to-teach students over the past ten years. I have classified the implications in three categories: communication, attitude, and teaching stance.

1. Communication, both verbal and nonverbal, has a tremendous impact on how hard-to-teach children relate and respond to teachers. Children read and respond to adults' nonverbal and verbal actions and words, and their responses and behavior usually mirror adults' responses and behavior. Therefore, try not to react emotionally to children's behavior. Calm teachers and parents are more likely to have calmer children. Be honest, available, consistent, and responsive to the children so that there are no surprises and they know that you are listening and what to expect. Adults should never assume that they know what children mean. Watch for their actions to show you what they understand. Show respect and trust in children's abilities. Without trust and respect communication suffers.

2. Every human being has an attitude about learning and teaching, which is communicated by what they say and do. Teachers who are particularly effective working with hard-to-teach students have a can-do attitude and show excitement and pride when children learn something they initially found challenging. They think about their practice as a work in progress because every hard-to-teach student will teach them something new and important about the learning and teaching process. As a result of this attitude, they take special interest in knowing children and their environment well enough to try to take the child's perspective as they work with them. That is exactly what Collin's teacher did while working with Collin (see discussion in this chapter).

3. Teaching is complex work and it becomes even more complex when working with students considered hard to teach. Teachers who are especially effective in teaching hard-to-

teach children have a particular teaching stance or approach to instruction and the act (or art) of teaching. There are several specific actions expert teachers take while interacting with hard-to-teach students.

◆ They engage in the process of continual learning, studying how a certain child attempts to put the pieces together as she reads and writes. They enjoy the challenge of this inquiry.

◆ They enjoy the challenge trying to figure out what children are trying to do.

◆ They reveal alternative problem-solving strategies or ways of thinking to help children solve problems while reading and writing.

◆ They teach children how to devise a plan of action. Developing a plan reduces children's anxiety. For example, if using the initial letter to solve words does not help, what else could you do? The more plans (or strategies) children have in their repertoire of knowledge, the less anxiety they will experience and the more successful they will become.

◆ They always work from and with children's strengths and honor and recognize their partially right responses and approximations.

◆ They never convey that children cannot do something. When children are experiencing difficulty, they find another way to teach them.

◆ They don't let children continue to struggle. Hard-to-teach children are easily discouraged.

◆ They give children responsibility for specific tasks and teach them how to accept them. For example, they make it clear what task is the teachers' responsibility and what task is the child's responsibility and then make sure that they both take care of their responsibilities.

◆ They don't tell how to complete a task or action but rather reveal through demonstration.

◆ When children work really hard, they notice and comment on their tenacity.

Effective teachers establish a balance between providing hard-to-teach children with opportunities to learn and at the same time reassuring them that the teacher's job is to take care of them and teach them. Effective teachers know how to keep the intricate balance between the emotional and cognitive sides of learning and teaching intact.

Chapter 7

Teaching LD and AD(H)D Students

Most children learn to read and write with relative ease and accomplish this feat by the end of first grade. These children become self-regulated early on and learn from their own attempts to read and write. For other children, however, this is not the case. These children generally fall into two groups.

The first group includes the lowest-achieving 20 percent of children in any first grade in a school. As discussed in Chapter 6, these children have reading *difficulties*, and they require specialized individual daily instruction by a well-trained teacher to read as well as the average students in the classroom. Patty, Charles, Collin, Kevin, and Alex, described in the last chapter, fell into the lowest 20 percent of first-grade children in their respective schools. What made these children unique is that they were the very lowest achieving of the bottom 20 percent of students in their school and considered by the expert teachers as the hardest to teach. Despite the fact that these five children entered first grade with the lowest literacy knowledge and repertoire of skills, they made accelerated progress and were all reading as well as the average students in their respective classrooms by the end of first grade.

The second group of children who find learning to read and write difficult are classified learning disabled (LD). Some of the LD students may also have an attention deficit disorder (ADD) and/or have this disorder with hyperactivity (AD(H)D). These children may be in first grade until space becomes available for learning disability placement. Three of the first-grade children described in this chapter fell into this group. Bobby was classified LD and AD(H)D, Collin (whom you met in the last chapter) was classified LD and received both LD service and occupational/physical therapy, and Tommy was considered developmentally handicapped (DH). Two twelve-year-old LD students who were placed in a transitional second-grade classroom are also the focus of this chapter.

Though it was not easy, the expert teachers featured in this book taught the five children how to read and write in less than five months. They had not only developed the knowledge, skills, and tenacity to accomplish this remarkable task, they were able to convince the children, classroom teachers, and parents that five labeled children could learn to read and write as well as their classmates. In this chapter, I (1) provide an overview of the learning disabilities field and attention deficit disorder; (2) discuss the emotional and cognitive behaviors of students labeled LD and AD(H)D; (3) discuss critical teacher and student interactions that help them learn to read and write; and (4) provide recommendations for teaching "labeled" children to read and write.

Learning Disabilities

Three terms are generally used interchangeably to discuss children who have reading difficulty: *learning disability* (LD), *reading disability* (RD), and *dyslexia*. There are as many definitions and interpretations of these terms as the number of people who use them. For example, dyslexia is a label oftentimes used for seriously disabled readers whose disability occurs as the result of a neurological defect that is either genetic or induced by minimal, nonobservable brain trauma (Ellis 1984). But, as Goldberg, Shiffman, and Bender (1983) and Vellutino (1979) point out, many of the same neurological hypotheses used to describe dyslexia have been offered to explain students labeled learning disabled and reading disabled. Some authorities in the learning disability field (Ysseldyke and Algozzine 1983; Clay 1987; Coles 1987, 1998) argue that the term *learning disability* defies definition. Today there is still no universal agreement among physicians, psychologists, or teachers on how to classify and diagnose the constellation of problems that fall under the umbrella term *learning disability*.

Since there are no hard and fast rules about how to define learning disability, state department and school district policies for identifica-

tion and classification vary widely (Lyons 1995b). The terms and definitions have one thing in common, however, and that is the assumption that students have something wrong with them, a deficit that may be organic in nature. The deficit is generally the result of underlying abilities such as perceptual, language, or memory problems (Spear-Swerling and Sternberg 1996).

Learning Disability Assessment

Documentation of a student's learning disability is crucial to his being entitled to receive specialized services, accommodations, or treatment. Evidence of a learning disability is dependent on what tests are used for diagnosis and how school psychologists interpret the results. Large-scale studies of the underlying abilities tests administered to determine if students are LD revealed that the tests lacked reliability and validity; for example, the text may reveal that a child has an auditory or visual perception problem today and it will not be evident one month later (Coles 1987, 1998; Vellutino 1979). Moreover, a student who is labeled LD in one school district may move to another school district within the state during the same year, receive LD testing, and not qualify for services (Lyons 1994a; Lyons and Beaver 1995).

Batteries of standardized assessments identify various factors that may be contributing to the reading problems. The factors are frequently referred to as correlates of reading disability because the presence of difficulties in any of these areas is correlated with poor reading performance. Generally speaking, psychologists consider four factors when discussing reading and learning disabilities: (1) physical development, (2) cognitive development, (3) language development, and (4) social and emotional development. When one or more of these factors is strongly lacking, the student is considered at risk for school failure (Snow, Burns, and Griffin 1998). However, there is no research that shows that the presence of a high correlation among the factors ensures causality (Coles 1987, 1998). In some cases, difficulties in these areas may account for or contribute to a reading problem, but in other cases they will be ruled out as playing a meaningful role in the reading disability.

Furthermore, while acknowledging the role of social and emotional development in learning to read is commendable, there is little evidence that classroom and special education teachers are accommodating this need (Allington 2001). But one thing is certain. Once diagnosed learning disabled, most children have the "deficit" for life, and there is little chance that the problem will be corrected permanently. Moreover, the longer students struggle, the more compounded the reading problem, and the further behind their classmates they fall (Johnston and Allington 1991; Snow, Burns, and Griffin 1998).

Learning Disability Services

Most educators believe that the best way to work with children considered reading disabled or learning disabled is to administer a specific battery of standardized tests to pinpoint the reading problem. Once the processing problems are identified (e.g., phonemic awareness, comprehension, word recognition, vocabulary), teachers are required to focus instruction in the target areas. Oftentimes consumable commercial kits designed to remediate targeted deficits are purchased for teachers to use.

Proponents of standardized tests argue that the tests improve teaching and learning. I believe the opposite is true. Standardized tests have a negative impact on students' learning and do not improve teaching. Since state-mandated standardized tests have been administered to students (including children labeled learning disabled) in elementary and middle schools in Ohio, there have been dramatic changes in teachers' practice.

Classroom teachers have been required to change their instruction in significant ways so that students will score well on state-mandated standardized tests, even if their own goals are undermined. Teaching to the standardized test is the norm. Moreover, teachers and parents report that the increased pressure to score well enough to pass the test and the fear of failure overwhelms some children, especially children considered learning or reading disabled, and leads to anxiety, sleeping problems, depression, and illness. Physicians also report increased symptoms of anxiety as well during "testing months."

This adverse impact on parents, teachers, and children is not surprising. As reported in Chapter 4, anxiety is a full-body physiological and psychological response to a stressful situation. The higher the stakes, the more anxious the children, parents, and teachers.

Attention Deficit (Hyperactivity) Disorder

Attention deficit disorder (ADD) is a special education category used to classify students with cognitive and emotional problems of distractibility (inattention) and poor impulse control, with or without hyperactivity (AD(H)D), that interfere with learning. The hyperactivity involved in AD(H)D may stem from difficulties in restraining impulses (Mate 1999). It is believed heredity plays a factor in ADD, and may be due to some form of neurological dysfunction related to incomplete development of pathways in the cerebral cortex and between the cortex and lower regions of the brain (Mate 1999). Attention deficit (hyperactivity) disorder also needs to be understood in sociological terms; that is, the student's difficulty in responding to the expectations and environmental demands of home, school, and community (Weaver 1994).

Unlike a learning disability, which is identified by using standardized tests, physicians, parents, and teachers diagnose AD(H)D through observation in naturalistic settings. The observers document the degree to which the individuals are able to cope with the demands of everyday life that occur within and outside of the classroom (Weaver 1994). Matthew, the unmotivated child discussed in Chapter 5, was diagnosed as having AD(H)D. Today he is a productive, self-employed adult who has a tremendous amount of energy and stamina. He has not outgrown the disorder but has learned to accept and cope with it.

Gabe Mate, a physician and psychotherapist, and his three children have all been diagnosed as having attention deficit disorder. Mate (1999) argues that the first step to helping children with AD(H)D is to discard the medical model and the notion that medication is the answer. He suggests that instead of controlling students' behavior, which is counterproductive, the focus should be on supporting children's active involvement in successful learning, which in turn improves their behavior in school. Some of the techniques used by Matthew's parents and teachers, discussed in Chapter 5, have helped AD(H)D children learn to cope with their condition and alleviate or circumvent learning difficulties.

The sociocultural perspective postulated by Vygotsky (1978) emphasizes the importance of positive teacher and student interactions within the learning environment. This perspective views the learner in context, taking into account the learner's strengths, not weaknesses. Teachers who hold a sociocultural perspective support the social, emotional, and cognitive dimensions of learning and provide the kind of experiences children need to construct new understandings and develop the skills necessary to become proficient readers and writers. Effective teachers know how to shape the learning environment to promote students' strengths, meet their needs, and, by observing their responses, direct their actions and reactions. The expert RR and learning disability teachers featured in this chapter have acquired these abilities.

Stories of Successful Students

The classroom teachers, parents, and even the students thought it couldn't be done. The idea that three children who were thought to be LD, AD(H)D, and developmentally handicapped (DH) could learn to read as well as the average children in first grade by the end of the year seemed impossible. The RR teachers, on the other hand, believed they could do it, and they did. They had the essential insights and skills to plan and implement an intervention program to support the emotional and learning needs of these AD(H)D, learning disabled, and developmentally handicapped children.

Bobby's Story

Bobby was diagnosed learning disabled (LD) by a school psychologist and an interdisciplinary team of district-level professionals prior to grade one. Physicians at Children's Hospital diagnosed him as having an attention deficit disorder (ADD) with hyperactivity (H). At the end of kindergarten Bobby was the lowest performing student in his class. His kindergarten teacher recommended retention so that he would have time to mature, but his parents objected because he was already bigger than the rest of the children in the class.

Bobby hated coming back after the summer vacation to start first grade and he didn't mind if everyone at home or in school knew it. Scores on the Observation Survey of Literacy Achievement (Clay 1993a), administered during the first two

weeks of school, placed Bobby as the lowest achieving of the 110 first-grade students in his school (Figure 7–1).

The second week of school Bobby was waiting in line with his first-grade classmates to go to the restroom when suddenly, without warning, he punched a little girl in the stomach. The little girl fell to the floor crying and Bobby was sent to the principal's office for the second time that day. It was his fifth trip to the principal's office since school had started two weeks prior. He was suspended for three days. Last year Bobby was considered the worst-behaved child in kindergarten and it was not likely that his reputation was going to change now that he was in first grade.

Creating a Positive and Emotionally Stable Environment

Bobby started RR the first day back after his suspension. He was angry and did not want to come to the dummy class "down the hall." The first week they worked together was a struggle for both the RR teacher and Bobby. The teacher selected books she thought he would be interested in but he pushed them off the table. She tried to find out what he liked to do but Bobby did not want to share anything about himself.

He had a very difficult time sitting in his chair and attending to the story the teacher read. He appeared upset that he could not write his name and resisted the teacher helping him. He wanted to write his name "his way," which were two jerky lines on the paper. Bobby kept talking about what others were doing to him and blamed others for his suspension from school. He did not seem to realize that it was his behavior that caused the problems. He had no friends. The other children feared him. Bobby's tall, overweight body and out-of-control, explosive behavior intimidated the children in his class.

After one week of failing to build rapport, the teacher knew she needed to change what she was doing or Bobby would become accustomed to being uncooperative. His preoccupation with negative school experiences seemed to be his biggest barrier to learning. She knew she had to redirect his anger by creating experiences in which he felt some control and success. On Monday of the second week they worked together, she asked Bobby, if he could start school all over again, what would he do? Bobby, with support from his teacher, wrote the following story: "I would make friends.

Measure	Bobby	Total Possible
Letter Identification	2	54
Children are asked to identify 54 characters, upper- and lowercase.		
Ohio Word Test	0	20
Children read a list of high-frequency words.		
Concepts About Print	0	24
Examiner reads a short book and children show what they have learned about the way spoken language is put into print.		
Writing Vocabulary	0	unlimited
Children write as many words as they can in 10 minutes.		
Hearing and Recording Sounds in Words	0	37
Examiner reads a short sentence and child writes the words.		
Text Reading	B	1–24
Children read a series of increasingly more difficult texts they have not seen before. Tester records reading behavior on running records to determine the highest level the child can read with 90% accuracy. Levels range from B (lowest) followed by A, 1, 2, 3, etc.		

Figure 7–1. *Bobby's Fall Observation Survey of Early Literacy Achievement*

I would learn to read and write" (Figure 7–2). The teacher said she would help him make the story come true and if he was willing, they could start today. Bobby was willing. Writing those two sentences was the first step in changing his attitude and relationship with his teacher.

Once Bobby stopped being defensive, he started to share his feelings and interests. Through shared writing activities and conversations around books they read, the teacher gained a better understanding of what Bobby needed to learn in order to control his anger and manage his behavior. She realized that this unhappy child wanted to feel he belonged.

Bobby knew that he mattered to his RR teacher because she was going to help him reach his goal of learning to read and write. He also gained an understanding that he could make a difference in his learning. Bobby and the teacher were partners . . . members of the same team. He was ready to be a full participant in the thirty minutes they worked together. Bobby regained the will and motivation to learn, which is fundamental to all learning.

Building a Responsive Learning Environment

Prior to entering school, Bobby had few opportunities to write. He avoided drawing and writing activities in kindergarten. Close observation of writing behaviors revealed that Bobby did not know how to hold a pencil, where to place the paper on the table, or where to begin writing on the page. The classroom teacher commented that even when he had a model to look at, Bobby could not write the letters in his name. Bobby recognized a few letters by name, but he had many confusions. For example, he could not distinguish between *B* and *D*, *n* and *r*, *p* and *y*. Bobby's strength was that he was willing to learn, so the teacher began teaching through demonstration.

Demonstrating the Process The teacher showed Bobby how to make a *B* by holding his right hand and guiding his movement in the air while verbally describing the action. For example, to make the *B* in *Bobby,* the teacher said: "Down, up, and around to the middle of the line and around again to the end of the line." This action helped

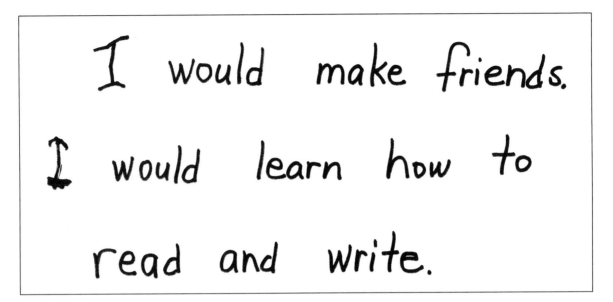

Figure 7–2. *Bobby and the Teacher's Shared Writing About Starting School Over*

him to identify the first letter in his name by movement. When he finished writing the letter, he had to name it, and the name of the letter had to be *B* not *D*.

Initially, it was difficult for Bobby to talk and write at the same time. He relied on the oral feedback to guide his movements while making the letter. The teacher provided the oral feedback and description of the sequence of movements for Bobby, and he did the writing. After several days, Bobby tried to make the *B* by himself. This was not an easy task because of his quick responding and impulsive behavior. His movements were awkward, fast, and jerky. The teacher was attempting to slow him down and guide his movement when Bobby erupted.

BOBBY: [pushing the teacher away] Let me do it by myself.

TEACHER: OK, what are you going to say while you are making the *B*?

BOBBY: Down, up, around. [making the vertical stick of his name]

TEACHER: Were you going around when you said around?

BOBBY: No, my words are too fast and this board is too slow. I can't do it because the blackboard stinks.

TEACHER: We can fix that. Try making the letter *B* on the white board.

BOBBY: Down, up, and around. [coordinates the movement with his words and makes a *D*]

TEACHER: Was it easier to make the letter on the white board?

BOBBY: Yes, but I forgot to say the right words. I made a *D* not *B*. *B* is down up around and around, two arounds for two bumps.

TEACHER: Congratulations, you made a great discovery without my help. You are on your way to becoming a good writer!

Bobby smiled at his teacher and they shook hands. He was pleased with himself. Writing on the white board helped him to understand and feel the sensation of a fluid stroke. And once he became more fluid it became easier to match the words with the movement pattern.

Facilitating Emotional and Cognitive Development and Growth Through Writing

Two key components of the learning process were working together to facilitate Bobby's cognitive development: movement and speech. The movement involved in writing letters was key to keeping Bobby attentive and engaged. Verbal directions guided his processing and helped him to remember how to form a letter and recall the letter name.

Whenever a new letter was introduced, Bobby practiced the verbal description of the movement in the air, in sand, in shaving cream, or on the blackboard with a water pen. As he gained control of a few letters and their names,

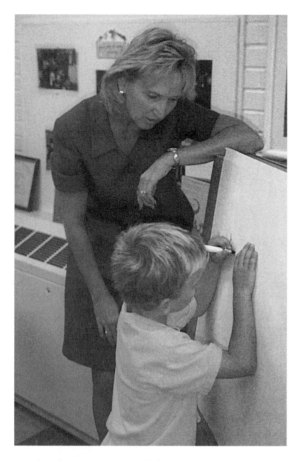

Verbal directions help children remember how to form a letter.

Bobby learned how to use what he knew to form other letters. For example, he learned to form a lowercase *b* in three days because he already had learned to write the uppercase *B*. The verbal direction for lowercase *b*, "down, up half way, around, and down" was similar to that used for the uppercase *B*. As discussed by Clay (1993b), Bobby was learning to remember how to form the letter in three ways: (1) through movement, (2) through verbal description to control the movement, and (3) through visual form. When he forgot how to write his name, he would begin to say aloud, "down up and around and around," which triggered his memory, and he could write *B*.

Clay (1991) reminds us that in the act of writing, the child must attend very closely to the features of letters. As discussed in Chapter 1, writing activates the child's RAS (Unit I); the occipital lobes (eyes), temporal lobes (ears), and parietal lobes (motor), all housed in Unit II and working simultaneously in an integrated way; and the frontal lobes (Unit III), which organize and direct the working networks of the brain (Luria 1973).

The teacher arranged for over learning and lots of repetition in different mediums, which enabled the assemblies of neurons in the brain to myelinate. Throughout the process, Bobby's frontal lobes (Unit III) organized and directed his program of action for learning, storing, and recalling letters.

Bobby did not like saying the words to guide his pencil every time he made the *B*, even though it helped him. The teacher explained that saying the words reminded him how to form the letters and to distinguish one letter from another just like it helped him to notice he made a *D* instead of a *B*. She also let him know that soon he would no longer need to say the words. Bobby agreed to continue using the words "until he was ready to stop."

This teacher understood the functional development of private speech and its role in developing Bobby's capacity to become self-regulated. As discussed in Chapter 3, self-control is a developmentally earlier and simpler form of behavioral organization in which the child merely copies and then complies with an adult command in the teacher's absence (Diaz, Neal, and Amaya-Williams 1990).

The teacher and student interactions around letter formation supports Vygotsky's (1978) and Luria's (1976) work suggesting that through speech, children develop the capacity to control their own actions. Initially, the teacher directed Bobby's actions using consistent language that was specific to the actions required to form and name the letter *B*. Bobby used private speech to coordinate his hand, eyes, and mouth and to guide, regulate, and control his actions while forming letters without help from the teacher.

The teacher watched Bobby interacting with print to determine if he was becoming impatient or frustrated. If she noticed the slightest bit of frustration, the teacher intervened to prevent his frustration from escalating. When Bobby had difficulty, they talked about how he felt and what he could do about it. He decided the best way for him to "control his madness was the same way he learned to make the letters . . . talk to himself." The teacher thought this was a great idea and she would help him remember whenever necessary.

The RR teacher found that the most effective way to keep Bobby attentive and on task was to change activities, move to another location, and, if possible, provide opportunities for him to manipulate objects. For example, he might move from the table to write on the blackboard with chalk or a water pen and move to the white board to write with a felt-tipped pen. During the same lesson he might stand at the magnetic board and sort letters or construct words using magnet letters and move to the salt tray to write words and letters in salt. When encountering reading or writing difficulty, Bobby found that talking to himself enabled him to find solutions to the problem quicker and regain composure to direct his actions.

Vygotsky (1978) believed that eventually, private speech splits off from teacher-directed, socially communicative speech as a child develops a new cognitive skill and is then transformed into inner speech, which is a tool for individual problem solving, planning, and self-regulation. Inner speech helped Bobby develop the self-regulation and independence he needed to build a self-extending system of behavior, which enabled him to learn more every time he read and wrote.

Reflecting on Bobby's Emotional and Cognitive Development

The teacher confessed that collaborating with Bobby was not easy. There were many moments when she had to remind herself to remain positive and calm. As she reflected on the four and one-half months they worked together, the teacher discussed emotional and cognitive barriers Bobby and she had to work through in order to maintain and strengthen their partnership.

Gaining Bobby's trust was the first step in developing a good working relationship. Trust started to build from the moment they wrote the story about starting school all over again. It was difficult for him to put into words how he felt. She believed attaching words to his feelings helped Bobby develop some emotional skills that enabled him to take a different perspective. For example, they were able to write about how the little girl felt when someone bigger pushed her to the floor, which was the incident that got him suspended.

The RR teacher had to continuously work on improving Bobby's inattentive and impulsive behaviors. The following are inattentive behaviors Bobby showed most often:

◆ easily distracted . . . noise from the lights humming, playground noise bothered him.

◆ couldn't sit still in the chair . . . his feet, arms, head were in constant motion.
◆ difficulty staying on task . . . He wanted to jump from one thing to another. For example, he would start making the first letter of his name and then wanted to sit down and read a story.
◆ difficulty completing an activity . . . He wanted to write part of a sentence during writing and finish the next day.
◆ avoidance . . . Initially Bobby tried to get out of writing. It was to hard to move the pencil.

At the same time Bobby was impulsive. The impulsive behaviors included:

◆ easily frustrated . . . especially when he couldn't remember which way to go when he was at the end of a line of text.
◆ impatient . . . Bobby did not want a book introduction, he wanted to get started reading right away.
◆ easily overwhelmed . . . The teacher had to make sure the task was doable or he would become irritated and quit.
◆ needed immediate gratification . . . Bobby would quit after the first attempt if he could not figure something out right away.
◆ difficulty persevering . . . If the first thing he tried did not work, he did not try anything else. He looked to the teacher for help.

The teacher concluded that when compared to other RR students she had taught, it took Bobby three times as long to develop a program of action to form and recognize letters quickly and learn how to attend and control impulsive actions. Bobby's story demonstrates that attention—the ability to focus the mind—is critical to learning and a prerequisite to motivation, memory, and self-regulated learning. He was released from RR in February reading as well as the average students in his class. Today Bobby is a sophomore in college.

Collin's Story

Collin had an extensive vocabulary, much prior knowledge to bring to the reading and writing experiences, and a very good memory for text. He expressed himself well and seemed interested in telling others everything he knew. Although

Collin and Bobby displayed similar behaviors, Collin was more aggressive, demonstrative, angry, and argumentative. He repeatedly argued with the teacher, banged his hand on the table to make a point, threw back his head expressing disgust and exasperation, and thought he was right most of the time. When he became frustrated, Collin would oftentimes quit trying.

Creating a Positive and Emotionally Stable Environment

The RR teacher knew that she had to create a positive working environment in which to teach. Furthermore, she had to teach Collin that the disruptive behaviors were interfering with his learning progress. Managing anger constructively is an important developmental task for some children, especially when they have spent several years practicing explosive, uncontrolled anger. Early childhood experts (Katz 1977; Paley 1981) believe that one of the best ways children learn anger management is by observing how adults express, discuss, manage, and control their anger.

The RR teacher did several things to manage her own anger and Collin's uncontrolled outbursts. First, she did not respond to his frequent disruptions when he made an error. Instead she conveyed that she understood his frustration while reassuring him that she would help him figure out what to do next. This action helped him to channel his actions to resolve problems.

Second, she identified situations that may trigger an angry response and prevented these situations from occurring. In some cases, she stopped taking a running record because Collin's voice and body language indicated he was becoming frustrated and angry with himself. When he made an error, he had a difficult time composing himself to continue reading even when the reading was easy. As soon as the teacher sensed that Collin was becoming anxious and upset, she intervened. As was discussed in Section 1 of this book, when children are angry or anxious their emotions take over, impeding further learning. Wise teachers prevent the downward spiral from occurring.

According to Katz and Gottman (1991), children who are developing competence in the regulation of emotions are able to: (1) inhibit inappropriate behavior related to strong positive or negative emotion and (2) soothe themselves or calm themselves down when they become highly aroused emotionally. It was very difficult for Collin to develop these two capacities; however, by the end of his RR program the number of angry, impulsive outbursts was reduced. This was probably due to the teacher's heightened awareness and sensitivity to potentially volatile situations and her resistance to letting him get his own way.

Building a Responsive Learning Environment

A critical factor in broadening children's positive emotional responses to learning is the teacher's attitude that children are capable of learning how to tackle new and possibly difficult material. The teacher had high expectations for Collin's ability to learn how to read and write and for her ability to create a learning context that would facilitate his progress. She also understood that she must use Collin's strengths when introducing new concepts and tasks and work within his zone of proximal development. She also had to *teach* him, which required a delicate balance between challenging his thinking and helping him manage his behavior. The interaction shown in Figure 7–3 illustrates how she accomplished this task.

Several times in this conversation the RR teacher conveyed confidence in Collin's ability to problem-solve and at the same time reduced his anxiety and frustration. For example, when Collin hit his hand on the desk and screamed "SWAT, SWAT," the teacher tried to calm him down by putting her hand on his arm and saying, "OK OK, you're working, you're working." This action reassured him and at the same time encouraged him to keep trying. He was probably mad at himself for not getting it right the first time, and the teacher conveyed an understanding of his reaction to the predicament.

The teacher also supported his efforts and offered help, "Let's look at it together." She helped him understand how to read *she's* by covering up the final *s* and then asked him to add the *s* at the end of *she*. When this occurred Collin's anxiety level was reduced and he easily read *she's*, which boosted his confidence. If the teacher had rushed in and told him the word, she may have undermined an opportunity for Collin to regain a positive learning disposition. He did not quit, but continued to read the text.

Text:	*Sleeping Out* **by Joy Cowley**
p. 7	What's that going zzzz-zzzz?
p. 8	It's Mom. She's gone to sleep.
COLLIN:	It, it said Mom. [hesitation]
TEACHER:	It's.
COLLIN:	It's . . . It's Mom. [hesitation looking at *she's*] SWAT, SWAT [loud voice while banging hand on desk] SWAT! [very loud, angry voice]
TEACHER:	OK, OK, you're working, you're working. Let's look at it together.
TEACHER:	What else does it say? [covers up the 's on *she's*]
COLLIN:	It says She, She.
TEACHER:	Good, that is *she*. Now add the *s* on *she*.
COLLIN:	She's . . . She's going to sleep.
TEACHER:	Good and what has she done?
COLLIN:	She's going to sleep.
TEACHER:	It makes sense to say she's going to sleep, but check this word. [points to *gone*]
COLLIN:	Going to sleep.
TEACHER:	[turning to page 7, "What's that going zzzz-zzzz?"] Show me *going* on this page.
COLLIN:	[points to *going*]
TEACHER:	Yes, look at *going*, you know how to write *ing*, don't you? [turns to page 8] Show me *going* on this page.
COLLIN:	[takes a close look at *gone*]
TEACHER:	[points to *gone*] Does this say *going*?
COLLIN:	NO. [bangs hand on desk]
TEACHER:	Good checking, that's right, it says *gone*. She's already gone to sleep, she's already snoring.
COLLIN:	[banging hand on desk while throwing head back] THAT DOESN'T MAKE ANY SENSE! THAT DOESN'T MAKE ANY SENSE!
TEACHER:	[calm voice] Yes, it does. Here, let me read you the last two pages. [reads from page 7] "What's that going zzzz-zzzz?" [reads from page 8] "It's Mom. She's gone to sleep."
COLLIN:	No, it says *going*.
TEACHER:	[turns to page 8] Show me *gone* on this page.
COLLIN:	[points to *gone*]
TEACHER:	Yes, that word is *gone*. [pats Collin on the back and smiles at him. Collin looks away. He gets up from the table and moves to the blackboard.]

Figure 7–3. *Teacher and Student Interaction Following Reading of the New Book*

Facilitating Emotional and Cognitive Development and Growth

Although the concept of scaffolding is most often used in discussion of adults' roles in supporting children's cognitive development through interaction and encouragement as they work on emerging skills (Vygotsky 1978; Wertsch 1985), the concept is equally useful in reflecting on young children's emotional development. The teacher tried to help Collin understand that the phrase "gone to sleep" makes sense in the story by reading the last two pages to him. Even though he resisted her suggestion that the word was *gone*, not *going*, she did not let him off the hook by giving in to his reasoning. The teacher's final statement, "show me *gone* on this page" made two points: First, it demonstrated to the teacher that Collin knew the word *gone* and could locate it on the page. Second, Collin learned that "gone to sleep" did make sense and that his teacher was not going to give in to his whining, angry demands to be right. The following day, Collin read the last two pages of *Sleeping Out* correctly.

Collin's opposition to the teacher's insistence that he read the sentence "gone to sleep" correctly is an example of counterwill. According to Mate (1999) counterwill is an automatic resistance by an individual with an incomplete sense of self that is the reflexive and unthinking opposition to the will of another. Collin showed many signs of counterwill early in his RR program. His resistance to the teacher's interventions arose from his fear of being controlled. As he became more confident in his ability to read and write, his counterwill dissipated. However, this disposition did not continue in the classroom. When he began to feel threatened or thought that somebody was controlling his actions, Collin's counterwill emerged again. His opposition to authority figures continued throughout elementary school.

Reflecting on Collin's Emotional and Cognitive Development

Collin was an emotionally responsive, excitable, interesting, intelligent child. When interested in a story or what he was writing, Collin expressed strong positive emotions. Within a one-to-one environment his impulsive behaviors and tendency to act out feelings in the moment were accepted by the teacher and curtailed when they interfered with his learning. Limits were set for him in such a way as to safely contain disruptive behaviors, while at the same time allowing for emotional responses.

Once in a classroom setting, however, Collin had difficulty modifying and controlling his emotions and did not show his classroom teacher how well he could read and write. As shown in Figure 7–4 on page 120, Collin was not too interested in writing in his journal in the classroom. Collin's classroom journal entry on January 10 does not show much improvement, despite the fact that he was making considerable writing progress in Reading Recovery (see Figure 7–5 on page 121). The RR teacher was surprised to learn that the classroom teacher saw no improvement in Collin's classroom writing. Then she saw what he wrote on January 10 in the RR lesson (see Figure 7–6 on page 122).

When questioned about the difference between the two writing samples, Collin told his RR teacher, "Gail [the classroom teacher] gives me a break."

While there may be times when it is appropriate for the teacher to follow the child's lead, the RR teacher understood that she must retain her role to set limits. She set limits that were firm and neutral but at the same time accepting. She acknowledged Collin's viewpoint and place in the learning situation. She listened attentively to his expressions of joy, sorrow, hope, and interest in what he was reading and writing. The stories he wrote every day were colorful and interesting. Effective limit setting is done within a supportive, nonthreatening relationship, which Collin and his teacher had established.

Despite his ability to read and write as well as the average students in his class, Collin's LD classification continued and he received LD and physical occupational therapy and attended speech classes. His interpersonal and social skills, frequent outbursts of anger, and compulsive and inattentive behavior interfered with his learning progress in the classroom. Today, Collin is a third-year student at a private high school.

Tommy's Story

According to most teachers, Tommy was the "biggest behavior problem" in the school. He picked on younger children and bullied older students. He did not relate well to adults. Tommy never looked an adult in the eye. When asked a question he would respond with short answers in a muffled voice. The lack of eye contact built an unseen wall around Tommy that few peers or adults tried to penetrate.

His intense distractibility in the classroom prevented him from maintaining social interactions. Tommy's inability to initiate and sustain positive social interactions with peers and teachers, coupled with his failure to complete most classroom activities, was strong enough evidence for school authorities to recommend that he be placed in the school for developmentally handicapped (mildly retarded) students at the beginning of first grade, but space was not available.

Tommy entered first grade knowing thirty-three letters by name and hearing two sounds (*b* and *t*). He had poor motor skills and could not write his name. Tommy did not recognize any high-frequency words and had the lowest possible

Figure 7–4. *Collin's Classroom Journal Writing in October*

score reading an easy text. Classroom teachers, learning disability teachers, and administrators commented that "if Tommy can learn to read and write, Reading Recovery really works."

Tommy's RR teacher decided that if the RR program were going to be adopted by the school district, she had to teach Tommy how to read and write. She believed that "through the right learning experiences, Tommy could learn how to read." She "just had to find the right way to teach him."

Tommy believed that he could not learn; her first goal was to change his viewpoint.

Creating a Positive and Emotionally Stable Environment

The RR teacher was well aware of Tommy's reputation as a troublemaker with few social skills and low literacy knowledge. She knew she had to change the antisocial nature of his behavior with peers and adults. One of his teacher's major chal-

tris is a toastor

(toaster was copied)

Figure 7–5. *Collin's Classroom Journal Writing in January (RR Lesson 17)*

lenges was to create a satisfying social relationship for both of them so that they could work in a positive and constructive way together.

The teacher understood that in order for Tommy to learn how to read and write, she needed to set boundaries that he could not estab-lish for himself. She found that the structure of the RR thirty-minute lesson played a major role in helping him to develop the emotional and social stability that he needed.

The consistent daily schedule and routine of the lesson conveyed that someone was in charge

Figure 7–6. *Collin's Reading Recovery Writing in January—Lesson 17*

who would take responsibility for making sure he was in a safe, predictable place where his basic needs to learn to read and write would be met. Knowing that he could rely on certain things each day, such as the same teacher and the repeated occurrence of specific activities (e.g., rereading familiar stories, letter work, writing, and the introduction of a new book) seemed to relax Tommy, and he was able to invest attention and energy into learning. Tommy liked the security of the structured RR lesson. He knew exactly what to do, when activities would change, and what he was expected to do.

He was also easily distracted and upset when the letters and words in text he was reading were different. For example, he could not read a page when *l* in the word *little* looked like an *I*. In order to minimize distraction and disruption of the lesson, the teacher changed the letters in a story before he read the book so that he would not become too distracted to continue reading.

Characters in books who communicate in "speech bubbles" also disturbed him. When he saw dialogue between two characters written in a "speech bubble," Tommy would become confused and lose track of what he was to be looking at. The RR teacher said he was obsessive about the print layout and form. He would become upset with the

authors of the book because "all little books were to have certain things that looked the same and there should be no circles with talk inside."

As the teacher developed a consistent way of interacting with Tommy, he began to feel comfortable and confident in his environment, which supported more risk taking. The teacher was able to slowly decrease the amount of structure he required. For example, he did not engage in letter work every day. She did not change the print symbols in the books to accommodate his inability to read them nor did she avoid books with speech bubbles. By the middle of his program, Tommy read text with speech bubbles easily without hesitation or comments.

Building a Responsive Learning Environment

After working with Tommy for several weeks, the teacher noticed that he did not have a clear understanding or concept of a letter or word. She also observed that he could read a known word, but did not know the corresponding sounds of each letter in the word. For example he could read *to*, but did not know the sound of the *t* and *o* in the word. The RR teacher took an inventory of the words Tommy could read and asked him the corresponding sound of each letter in the word.

He knew eight sounds. Knowing Tommy's attention and response level was heightened when the learning context was structured, she developed a routine program of action to help him learn the corresponding sounds to letters in known words.

TEACHER: Come to the board and read this word Tommy. [*to* is written on the board]
TOMMY: To.
TEACHER: Show me the first letter in the word.
TOMMY: [points to *t*]
TEACHER: What letter is that?
TOMMY: A *t*.
TEACHER: What sound do you hear in *t*?
TOMMY: [says the corresponding sound]
TEACHER: What letter makes that sound?
TOMMY: *T*.
TEACHER: What is that word?
TOMMY: *To*.
TEACHER: Do you think you can figure out what this word is? [writes *took* on the board]
TOMMY: Took. Just like *book* but you make the *t* sound and get *took*. That's easy.
TEACHER: Did you know that word?
TOMMY: No, but I knew how to figure it out.
TEACHER: I am so proud of you, Tommy. You are an excellent problem solver. Reading is problem solving and making sense of what you are read.
TOMMY: I'm going to like reading. I'm good at it.

Tommy and his teacher had developed a collaborative relationship in which both were satisfied and successful. They were also able to experience and express honest genuine emotion in Tommy's newfound ability to use analogy to solve an unknown word.

Facilitating Emotional and Cognitive Growth Through Language and Structure

As exemplified in her conversation, the teacher used the same language to ask each question in the specified order. This program of action was used until Tommy was able to read the known word, provide a corresponding sound in sequence for each letter he read, and read the word. He had to learn how to work with known words until he was able to understand how individual letters correspond to specific sounds and how to analyze the sounds in a word in a left-to-right sound sequence. The repetition of that routine provided a memory trace of the action sequence and enabled

him to call up strategies for analyzing unknown words.

The prefrontal cortex (see Chapter 1) is involved in decision making and in the reflective processing of emotions. The prefrontal cortex monitors private speech, which gives direction to word solving. The program of action designed specifically to help Tommy learn how to use predictable letter-sound sequences to solve unknown words helped him to organize thoughts, decide priorities, and choose strategies for word solving (e.g., using a simple analogy to read *took*, rather than auditory-to-visual analysis). The prefrontal cortex provided guidance through self-monitoring and determining what is relevant to the task.

Without attending, focusing on relevant information, and self-monitoring, Tommy could not become a reader and writer. Research investigating young children classified as ADD suggests they have a problem of development labeled a "neurodevelopmental lag" rather than one of pathology (Mate 1999). Neuroimaging studies of ADD patients have shown smaller-than-normal structures and lower functioning in the prefrontal cortex of the brain and less production of dopamine, the neurotransmitter that facilitates individuals' ability to stay focused and that is necessary to develop self-regulatory behaviors. Moreover, the underdeveloped prefrontal cortex is reflected in the social-emotional skills of children diagnosed with ADD (Mate 1999). These findings suggest that if physicians, psychologists, and educators were to think about how to promote individuals' ability to become self-regulated, then it would be possible to provide the experiences necessary to support and grow neurons in the underdeveloped prefrontal cortex (Mate 1999).

Although Tommy was not diagnosed as having ADD, he had some of the social-emotional behaviors associated with the disorder. For example, he overreacted to emotional situations. In RR, he learned to use reflective, evaluative thought processes. Unfortunately, this behavior did not carry over into the classroom, where he remained quick to respond.

Reflecting on Tommy's Emotional and Cognitive Development

Tommy finished the RR program in February, reading as well as the average students in his class. By the end of first grade, he was reading at a second-grade level. Tommy never attended the school for developmentally handicapped children. His success in RR was the reason given for the district implementation of the program. The RR teacher said, "Tommy taught me that any child can learn how to read with the right instruction, and the teacher's job is to find how to teach him."

Tommy had few problems academically throughout elementary and middle school. He passed the fourth- and sixth-grade state proficiency tests. He works better in structured classroom settings. Unfortunately, Tommy continues to have problems getting along with peers and teachers. The middle school teachers said he is easily frustrated, lashes out, and bullies other students. He is often seen sitting in detention halls reading a book. Tommy is a freshman in high school.

Teaching in a Primary Learning Disability Classroom

My husband and I moved from Tacoma, Washington, to Connecticut in the middle of September. Since school had already started, I decided to submit applications to various school districts for substitute teaching. I was surprised to be offered a full-time position one week after school had been in session. I was the third teacher hired for the transitional second-grade learning disability position. During the first week of school, two teachers had resigned.

I arrived at Lincoln Elementary School at seven o'clock in the morning to meet the principal and arrange the classroom. The principal told me that the age range of the thirteen boys in the class was ten to twelve years, and several had juvenile records. Twelve of the thirteen boys were enrolled in Lincoln School last year and none had received passing grades. (These are the same boys mentioned in Chapter 5 who successfully walked to the bathroom without supervision.)

I asked the principal what he meant by a "transitional second-grade LD classroom." He told me that my class was created specifically for these thirteen boys because they were too old to be in second grade and the LD resource room was overcrowded. He also mentioned that the boys' reading, writing, and mathematics skills were far below other students in the LD classroom. The principal reassured me that the school

psychologist and he would do everything possible to help me "get through the year" and if I had any problems he would suspend the students involved. His final comment was that the boys were behavior problems and two were probably going to be moved to a class for emotionally disturbed children, so I would not have them all year.

The room was a mess. The floor was dirty and the tables and desks were pushed to one side of the room. The bulletin boards were empty and books were scattered on the floor. The principal said he would send the janitor immediately. When the janitor arrived, he told me that he had already cleaned up most of the mess. I washed the blackboards and arranged the books on the shelves while the janitor cleaned the floor. He helped me put my desk in the back of the room and arrange thirteen desks in a semicircle. I had ten minutes before school started.

The boys entered the room and did not sit down. They stood together talking loudly in the back of the room and continued talking through the pledge of allegiance to the flag. I knew if I was going to succeed in this classroom, I could not run to the principal's office for help. I had to deal with the situation. As I watched the boys I tried to figure out the ringleader of the group. I decided it was Willis. He was bigger than the others and my height.

I tapped him on the shoulder and asked him to please take his seat. Instead of sitting, he stood on the top of his desk. As soon as he did that the other boys followed. Soon there were thirteen boys walking in a circle on top of their desks, laughing and singing a rap song. I was horrified.

I went to the front of the room and told them I was the head of Motown Record Company and I was going to select a few of them for an audition. My job was to invite them to "come on down" for the audition. Their job was to stand still on their desks until it was their turn and I would help them down. The student closest to me was Karl. As I took his hand we both fell against the blackboard. He said something obscene and instead of reacting, I asked for his help. He looked surprised and then turned to the group and said, "Me and 'the teach' will help you down." Together Karl and I escorted each boy to a seat. The rest of the day we conducted the audition for Motown Records.

The boys were asked to share something about their school and home life. I heard things I cannot put in writing that were probably said to upset and shock me. I found out that these boys were street kids who lived by their wits and fists. They expressed little hope for leading a law-abiding life because the "big money" was made in drug dealing.

They had all attended remedial reading classes and had never been out of the low reading group. They were currently reading first-grade basal texts. The boys were self-diagnosed poor readers and writers. Furthermore, they believed school was a waste of time simply because they did not see the relevance of most learning tasks. The long history of remediation and failure to learn how to read and write helped to confirm teachers', administrators', and their own self-diagnosis that they were failures.

The boys placed little value in staying in school because they were never going to make it out of the ghetto. The twelve-year-olds in the group said they would drop out when they were sixteen so that they could make "big money." Eight boys had been retained once, two had too many absences to be credited for attending a school year, and the other three boys started school when they were seven years old. None of the boys had attended kindergarten.

When asked about their prior literacy experiences in school, the boys said they read baby books, did ditto stuff "for babies," and never wrote. I told them that things were going to change. They were not going to do dittos and they would not read any baby books. They would write books for each other to read and what they wrote would become their textbooks.

The look on their faces showed a lack of enthusiasm. Willis thought it was too much trouble to learn stuff that you are never going to use. The other boys nodded their heads in agreement. Karl spoke up and said, "Wouldn't you want to know if someone was ripping you off?" The others seemed to agree with him. I learned that day that Karl, not Willis, was the leader of the group.

I knew that if I was ever going to teach them how to read and write, I needed to change their attitudes about learning and convince them that learning to read and write was time well spent because it was their ticket out of the ghetto. I was thankful for the six years of teaching I had prior to taking this position and especially for the last two years that I had taught on a military base in Tacoma, Washington, during the Viet-

nam War. The year I taught third grade, four students lost their fathers. The U.S. military provided emotional support and advice for teachers during times of crisis. The best advice I received was to read to the children often; select books that dealt with problem solving, coping with fear and anxiety, survival, and self-esteem; and provide many opportunities for children to discuss and write about their feelings. Since I found myself once again teaching in an unstable emotionally charged classroom, I decided to use the same advice I had been given by the psychologists on the military base.

Creating a Positive and Emotionally Stable Environment

The first book I read to the class was *Bridge to Terabithia* by Katherine Paterson. In this story a grief-stricken, lonely, ten-year-old boy copes with the drowning of his best friend, Leslie, by building a bridge to Terabithia, a kingdom where he and his sister are able to have a better life. The boys in my class related to Jess, his sorrow at losing a best friend, and his desire to move forward to improve his life.

A well-written fantasy such as *Bridge to Terabithia* does not deny emotions or show emotional sentimentally. Katherine Paterson's in-depth description of characters allowed the "worldly, streetwise boys" to experience healthy emotional responses without fear of embarrassment. They loved fantasizing about another place where circumstances would be different. Their ideas and thoughts were similar to the third and fourth graders in Tacoma, Washington. Both groups of students were able to escape through the author's words and, in the process, develop a stronger sense of self and their role in making life better. Our conversations were about hope, the future, and the power of friendship and teamwork to escape circumstances beyond one's control.

Discussions about Jess and Leslie's experiences in *Bridge to Terabithia* helped these thirteen boys dream about what a better place to live might look like. They also began to realize that if they worked together they could create this new and improved place. Our classroom became this new world. The boys called it Marvella, which was short for marvelous. Just as in Terabithia, Marvella had rules we agreed to live by. As the oldest person in Marvella, I was in charge of enforcing these rules.

Rules of Marvella

◆ Respect yourself and others.
◆ Work cooperatively.
◆ Don't quit.
◆ Be fair and honest.

During the last hour of every day I read the students chapters from children's literature books. We discussed the positive and negative experiences of the characters in the story, issues, feelings, and solutions to problems the characters experienced. The children looked forward to the daily story hour, and it seemed to change their attitude about school. Our ongoing conversations helped to establish a more trusting, supportive, and satisfying climate in which to work, play, and belong. Reading to the boys was the most powerful way I found to gain their confidence and trust in this place we called Marvella.

Building a Responsive Learning Environment

My biggest hurdle was to create a learning context that was challenging, encouraged active involvement, and helped them feel successful. The boys had a difficult time articulating and demonstrating what they knew about reading and writing. I had to reveal through clear demonstrations the reading and writing process.

Demonstrating the Reading Process Reading aloud *Bridge to Terabithia* not only created a positive, emotionally stable environment in which the boys agreed to work together but also provided opportunities for me to demonstrate the reading and writing process. I would watch the students' reactions to the story, stop when I saw a questioning or thoughtful look on an individual's face, and ask him to share his thoughts. I also commented on the dialogue between Jess and Leslie and wondered aloud what they were thinking. I asked myself questions while reading, predicted what would come next, and anticipated the characters' next moves and the reactions of different characters to the problems that emerged.

By the end of the first week, some of the students started thinking aloud with me. Several boys related Jess' experiences to something in their personal lives. I explained to them that even though they were listening to me read, they were engaged in the reading process. They were doing what adult readers do, which is trying to understand what the author wrote. I knew they were

comprehending the story by the expressions on their faces and by the thinking they were doing to predict and anticipate the characters' next moves. I explained how they were developing powerful thinking strategies that would help them read and write their own texts. The boys seemed pleased that I thought they were successful learners and offered many comments to prove that they were thinking about the story.

When the book was completed, we discussed the many feelings of joy and sorrow Jess and Leslie experienced in their magical kingdom, Terabithia. One unexpected outcome of these lively conversations was Karl's idea that we build a bridge to our own magical kingdom, Marvella. The rest of the boys thought that this was a good idea.

Each boy drew a bridge to his ideal kingdom, a place where he could escape his life and that would have everything he ever wanted. Once the bridge and the magical kingdom were built (drawn), pairs of boys interviewed each other. One boy was the investigative reporter, who asked questions and listened to the responses. His partner was the author of the story, who tried to make his ideas clear through speech. The author had to make sure that his story was understood and the listener had to make sure he understood the story. Then their roles were reversed. The interviews stimulated thinking and caused others to react. They were powerful ways to show the boys how they were constructing stories by drawing on their oral language skills as well as their drawings, prior experiences, and knowledge of *Bridge to Terabithia* to make sense. They began to think about the audience and the purpose for writing a story and to see writing as a source of enjoyment for themselves and others. They expressed an interest in writing and were motivated to write their own Bridge to Marvella stories.

Demonstrating the Writing Process I asked for a volunteer to demonstrate the writing process. Karl immediately jumped up with his drawing, titled "Karl's Bridge to Marvella." I guided his retelling by asking a few questions and writing the answers on an overhead projector for the others to see (Figure 7–7).

With the class watching, I transformed our conversation into a story. The story contained a setting, two characters, a problem, several solutions to the problem, and an ending. Although it

TEACHER: Where does your story take place, Karl?

KARL: In Harlem.

TEACHER: Where in Harlem? In a house, or store, park?

KARL: In the alley behind the store.

TEACHER: Who are the characters in your story, Karl?

KARL: Michael, he is like Jess, he loses his friend. Sarah is Michael's girlfriend and she is always getting in trouble.

TEACHER: It sounds like there is a problem? What is the problem?

KARL: Sarah's Mom has to move again and she doesn't want to go. So she asks Michael to run away with her. Michael has $15.00 but he says they wouldn't be able to live very long. Sarah says she is going to run away alone then.

TEACHER: What does Michael do? Does he have any ideas about how to help Sarah?

KARL: Yeah, they could rob a store. Or he could use the money he has to buy a walkie talkie and no matter where Sarah moves they could talk to each other. Or they could each get a job sweeping floors and when they had enough money they could run away. He thought about an old house he had seen in the neighborhood and thought they could see if it would be a good place to live.

TEACHER: Karl, you just said four different solutions to the problem. What did Sarah think about these ideas?

KARL: She was afraid to rob a store. She liked getting the walkie talkies and she wanted to see the old house.

TEACHER: What happened?

KARL: They decided to go to the house but when they got there it was pretty bad, lots of rats and stuff, so they cleaned it up. Some nice man saw the work that they had done and gave them $100 for fixing up the house. They put the money in a pot for when they would run away together.

TEACHER: What happened then? Is that the end of the story?

KARL: They used the money to build a bridge to an island. The island had a beautiful house. They lived off the land and fished in the sea for food. They had lots of kids and no one bothered them forever.

Figure 7–7. *Karl's Oral Retelling of "A Bridge to Marvella"*

was a simple story, it was a lived experience, something Karl had faced the previous year, with a different ending. His friend Sarah and her family moved and he never heard from her again. Karl wondered where Sarah was living today. His story had a happy ending.

Through the writing demonstration, the boys appeared to gain some understanding about how to craft a story, retell it orally to another, and then write it on paper to be read by others. Karl's story was our first homemade library book. It provided a launching pad for future thought and served as a model for how to write personal narrative. It gave Karl and others in our class confidence in themselves as writers and became a catalyst for developing our classroom library books, which were copied and used in guided reading groups.

Throughout the next several weeks, I provided a demonstration of the writing process using different students' tape-recorded Bridge to Marvella stories. Initially I wrote most of the sentences, sharing aloud what I was thinking about when I wrote the words in the text. For example, when I was writing "Marvella," I said, "What letter does 'Marvella' begin with? It starts like *my* so it begins with an *M*. Should it be a capital *M* or a lowercase *m*? It is the name of a specific place so it should be a capital *M*."

As the children became more familiar with thinking about how to write letters, words, sentences, and paragraphs, they were able to coconstruct the text as we discussed the auditory-to-visual processing, format, structure of sentences, and so forth. Gradually some of the students learned to complete most of the writing and I did very little.

For the first month, I demonstrated the writing process to the entire group of boys. Individual differences in students' writing ability and skill levels emerged. Seven students did not need as much guidance as the others, so I commissioned them to work together to write books for our library on specific topics of their interest. These boys knew much more about the reading and writing process than they realized. The six remaining students were divided into two groups. These children needed much guided practice. Texts they wrote for our library were within their range of reading abilities and skills.

High standards were set for every book published. The boys began to see how their writing was valued and could influence their classmates. These thirteen boys learned to read through writing and they were motivated to read because they were the writers of the texts. The impact of writing on their reading achievement is described well by Clay (1998).

> In short, writing allows a slow analysis of detail in print; both reading and writing draw on the same sources of knowledge about letters, sounds, chunks, clusters, words, syntax (or grammar and sentence construction), the rules of discourse, and narrative structures and genre differences; gains in reading may enrich writing and vice versa; and dipping into a large pool of both reading and writing knowledge will help those with limited knowledge of the language, and may have cognitive advantages. (139)

In my view, the boys in my transitional second-grade LD classroom were excited and motivated to learn to read because their initial attempts to write their stories were accepted, acknowledged, and personally rewarding.

Facilitating the Boys' Emotional and Cognitive Growth

Although the term AD(H)D was not used to describe any of the thirteen boys in my classroom, I believe some of them, including Willis and Karl, demonstrated many of the classic characteristics of students having ADD and AD(H)D discussed in this chapter and elsewhere (Mate 1999; Weaver 1994). Yet, when compared to other students in the classroom, Karl and Willis showed the most emotional and cognitive growth and development. They also had very different temperaments and learning behaviors.

Karl loved to be the center of attention. He was always ready to help the other boys when they were having difficulty learning. When I had laryngitis and could not speak loudly, Karl devised signals for me to make so that the class could carry on without my voice. He was the one who noticed when Anthony was beginning to have an epileptic seizure. He closed the window when it started to thunder because Ishmal was afraid of storms. Karl was the class clown.

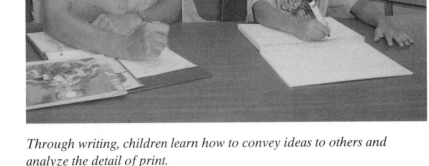

Through writing, children learn how to convey ideas to others and analyze the detail of print.

Children in the school, including his classmates, liked and respected Karl.

During lessons Karl interrupted to share personal anecdotes even when they were not on the topic of discussion. He could express himself orally very well and offered opinions on many topics. Karl became bored easily and would wander around the room aimlessly during work periods. He did not concentrate on tasks for a long period of time and seemed to have several projects going on at the same time. He had a difficult time completing tasks on time.

Karl was put in charge of our weekly symposium, a time when the students displayed their weekly work through writing, drama, art, song, or oral recitation. He was the master of ceremonies and organized the program. Teachers, parents, the principal, and other students in the school were invited to attend. Sometimes nobody came but that did not matter. The boys took great pride and pleasure in entertaining each other and sharing their work with an audience.

Willis was withdrawn, immature, and irresponsible. He was ready to leap into a situation without thinking about the consequences. For example, he would get into a fight even when he did not know what the children were fighting about. When Willis did not know how to read a word in the text, he threw his book on the floor. He lost control easily and became loud and demanding. Willis held a grudge when he did not get his way.

Initially, Willis had a difficult time understanding what to do to complete an assignment. He required very clear oral directions for the assignment; a written, step-by-step reminder; and someone to listen to his explanation of the assignment before he could get started. He needed consistency in directions and exact times when something was to begin and end. Upsetting the routine made him uneasy and angry.

To alleviate his anxiety, Willis become the classroom timekeeper. As the year progressed, he learned how to adjust times for specific activities when more or less time was needed to complete a task. By the end of the year, Willis was better able to manage changes in routine. He also developed confidence in his own ability to remember what to do without asking the teacher or other children for help.

Both boys had years of reading failure, no desire to learn how to read, and little expectation that they could become readers and writers. Their attitudes changed as soon as they learned how to put their thoughts down on paper. Through writing, they become more skilled and successful readers. As discussed previously, the act of writing engages the cognitive operations and skills involved in the arousal, attention, sensory motor, language, and memory processing systems necessary to become a reader.

Karl and Willis wrote more books than anyone else in the class. Karl enjoyed history, so he wrote about historical events and famous people. Willis liked science. His books were about the weather, electricity, magnetic fields, and animal habitats. They enjoyed writing short stories and writing daily in their journals. Through writing they developed momentum and motivation to learn.

Reflecting on the Students' Emotional and Cognitive Growth

The year I taught the boys from New Britain was my worst and best year of teaching. It took until Christmas to develop a positive, cooperative learning environment. By the end of the first year, most of the boys had improved their reading and writing skills, but they had not made enough progress to be placed in regular education classrooms. So I requested to have the same boys for a second year.

The second year I taught these boys was the most rewarding year in my professional career. They worked collaboratively in Marvella and most made substantial gains in reading and writing. Eight of the thirteen boys were placed in regular education classrooms. Willis and Karl went to fourth grade and six students were placed in third grade. The remaining five boys were assigned to the LD resource room. The transitional second-grade LD classroom was dissolved.

I continued to inquire about these students after we moved to Columbus, Ohio. Two of the thirteen boys died in middle school. One was shot in a gas station robbery and the other boy died of a drug overdose. Willis and Karl attended high school, but I do not know if they graduated. If they are alive today, Willis is thirty-two and Karl is thirty-three years old.

The boys from New Britain made a huge difference in how I think about learning, teaching, and the teaching profession. I realized for the first time the incredible impact (both positive and negative) teachers have on students' lives—academically, emotionally, and personally—for a lifetime.

Conclusion

This chapter shows how the learning context significantly impacts the behaviors and cognitive processes of students thought to be LD and AD(H)D. In addition to unwarranted labels, the five boys' experiences and attitudes were similar in the following ways:

1. Their negative attitudes about school and learning were shaped in the early years of schooling.
2. They were acutely aware of their learning problems and comparisons between themselves and others.
3. As they moved through the primary grades, they began to make judgments about their own abilities to read and write.
4. Feeling inadequate, they gave up and acted out in unacceptable and unpredictable ways.
5. They had difficulty getting along with their classmates.
6. Their social development had a profound effect on their academic progress.

The teachers who successfully taught these students to read and write also shared similar attitudes and expectations. They created a predictable environment that built security by letting the children know how people are likely to behave and events are likely to unfold. This environment provided the emotional stability that the students needed in order to get back on track and believe they could learn to read and write. The context was responsive to individual needs and helped the children feel accepted. This responsive context also helped the students come to understand that there are consequences to their actions and that they can make a difference in their academic and personal life.

Educational Implications for Teaching LD and AD(H)D Students

The term Attention Deficit Disorder (ADD) is used to describe children who are easily distracted and show poor impulse control, with or without

hyperactivity (AD(H)D). Children classified as AD(H)D reflect in many different ways a lack of self-regulation.

Individuals are not born self-regulated; rather, they acquire the ability to become self-regulated through experiences in their environment. Instead of looking for a medical answer to explain LD and AD(H)D, why not think about the possibility proposed by Mate (1999) that there is an underdeveloped prefrontal cortex that needs the right kind of experiences and environment to develop? The following recommendations are presented to create this nurturing environment. Although the recommendations are for teachers, they can be adapted for parents and caregivers.

◆ For many children and especially those that may be LD and AD(H)D, classroom activities can become overwhelming both psychologically and cognitively. Teachers should arrange for these children to sit near them or another student who can help when they become confused. If the LD and/or AD(H)D student could help in the selection of this buddy or partner, it is more likely that they will be able to manage the many activities that take place every day in the classroom. Teachers should also establish strong eye contact with the children whenever possible.

◆ Establish everyday routines to help children know what to expect for the day and post them in the room. Some children may need to have the classroom routine written down and in their pockets so that they can refer to it throughout the day. For particularly anxious children, alternative plans should be worked out with the teachers and classmates so that children do not become so upset that they can't think if plan A does not work out. For example, if for some reason a child becomes ill and the teacher has to take care of him, the remaining members of the class should know exactly what to do (plan B) in case of an emergency. For many children, a variation in the classroom routine is upsetting, but it is doubling upsetting for children who may be LD and/or have AD(H)D.

◆ Limit distractions and avoid disruptions whenever possible. LD and AD(H)D children are easily distracted, which interferes with their ability to attend. When they lose their focus it is very difficult for them to regroup and get back on track. If teachers can eliminate distractions, they will help children sustain their attention for longer periods of time.

◆ Develop a cueing system; for example, touching the student's shoulder, to remind them to attend. This action is not threatening and does not put children on the spot or embarrass them in front of others for not paying attention. It does remind them, however, that it is time to focus. Provide consistency in your responses to children's behaviors so that they understand what the cueing system means, how it works, and what they are expected to do.

◆ Structure a warm, calm, supportive, organized classroom and home environment. Without that, students who have attention problems are not likely to attend and sustain their attention for long periods of time. Teachers and parents who can maintain nonthreatening, warm, and stable relationships with the AD(H)D and LD students will find that children are less disruptive and have longer attention spans.

◆ Praise, encourage, and support students often for genuine accomplishments. This can be done verbally and by establishing private signals such as thumbs up when the student does something positive or well. These actions will establish and sustain teachers' and parents' relationship and attachment to children.

◆ Set time limits and attainable goals. Everyone needs to feel that they are accomplishing their goals. Children thought to be LD and AD(H)D are no exception. But these goals may need to be adjusted from time to time so that children can be successful and do not become discouraged and quit. When children experience failure it may be because the goals set for them by parents and teachers were not attainable at this point in time.

◆ Teachers and parents working with children who may be AD(H)D and/or LD should make an effort to learn all they can about these two different kinds of learning problems. They should also involve support teachers and parents who are working with these students so that the students are not getting mixed messages.

In my view, the children who are the focus of this chapter were not learning disabled (LD) but instructionally disabled (ID), and the expert teachers proved that point. Collin and Tommy may have been AD(H)D. The expert teachers, however, provided the right conditions and environment to facilitate their neural development, proving that neurological and psychological development is possible under the right conditions and circumstances. Furthermore, as Mate (1999) argues, this development is always possible—even in adulthood.

SECTION THREE

Understanding What Makes Teachers Expert

Two questions are generally asked when educators are talking about expert teachers and effective teaching practices: (1) What is an expert teacher? (2) How does one determine if a teacher is expert? In responding to the first question, most psychologists and teachers would likely say expert teachers *teach* a large majority of their students—including those who come from low socioeconomic populations and are considered to have a range of learning disabilities—how to become competent, self-directed, successful learners. In response to the second question, most educators would probably agree that examining students' overall performance on objective measures would reveal who are the expert teachers. These two responses describe the teachers featured in this book.

In the third section of this book, I examine the qualities and capabilities of these expert literacy teachers. I have found concrete evidence that the characteristics and qualities of expert teacher reported in the literature (see Leinhart 1988; Schon 1990) are present in literacy teachers featured in this book. But I would go one step further than the researchers and say that the teachers in this book are more expert because they have successfully taught the lowest-achieving, most at-risk students how to read and write and enjoyed teaching them.

Chapter 8 focuses on the characteristics of expert literacy teachers' attitudes and assumptions about learning and teaching. Specific qualities are shared that contributed to their ability to help every low-achieving child they taught reach their full potential. In Chapter 9, expert teachers' knowledge base, rationale for actions, and understanding of when to act and when to observe are discussed. Chapter 10 pulls the chapters of this book together. It provides final perspectives on the brain, learning, and teaching and what this means for teaching low-achieving readers and writers. It is written with both parents and teachers in mind because parents are the child's first and most important teachers; their interactions with their children early on are fundamental to the child's potential academic, social, and emotional growth in the future.

I believe there are many uncharted areas of effectively teaching children to read and write that will be informed by new developments in brain research. These new findings will need to be incorporated into future educational and parenting practice. Today, educators are in a good position to begin this process. *Teaching Struggling Readers* is a plan of action for accomplishing this feat.

Chapter 8

Characteristics of Expert Teachers

Until recently research that examined expert teachers' practice focused on what they know, understand, and can do (Brophy and Good 1986; Dill 1990; Shulman 1987). Little attention was given to the social and emotional dimensions of learning, that is, to how expert teachers relate to children and promote their ability to understand, process, manage, and express themselves. Yet some researchers argue that we should want more from educational efforts than adequate academic achievement and contend that teachers will not achieve even meager success unless children believe that they are cared for and learn to care for others (Noddings 1995). Coles (1998) has found that social and emotional aspects of learning have a powerful effect on students' ability to learn how to read, especially those who are struggling.

Teachers' attention to the emotional side of learning facilitates emotional and intellectual growth. One teacher described this phenomenon in the following way. "Past experience teaching students who believed they could not learn to read and write taught me that how children feel about themselves and their teachers determines whether they will be successful or continue to fail to learn to read and write."

Authorities in the field of education agree with this teacher's position (Coles 1998; Gardner 1999). Cohen (2001) argues that students' "social emotional capacities powerfully affect, and even determine, their ability to listen and communicate; to concentrate, to recognize, understand, and solve problems, to cooperate, to modulate their emotional states, to become self-motivating and to resolve conflicts adaptively" (4).

Analyses of videotapes, on-site observations, and interviews with the teachers featured in this book reveal that they understand and value the social and emotional aspects of learning and they act upon this knowledge and belief. They know when to praise, encourage, demonstrate, challenge, and hold children accountable to enhance their self-understanding. In this chapter I (1) discuss the social and emotional dimensions of learning; (2) identify and discuss expert teachers' attitudes and beliefs about learning and teaching; (3) describe the characteristics of their teaching, specifically how expert teachers interact, support, and motivate students so that they become self-regulated, lifelong readers and writers; and (4) provide educational implications for parents and teachers.

The Importance of Social and Emotional Dimensions of Learning

The social and emotional dimensions of learning are at the heart of Vygotsky's theory of learning as exemplified in the zone of proximal development (see Chapter 3). He was particularly interested in how social interaction in small groups or dyads leads to higher mental functioning in the individual and how the external mediators and signs or tools (e.g., oral language, written text, books, materials) are used to assist the child in developing higher-order mental processes.

Vygotsky believed that higher mental function (e.g., monitoring behavior, choosing between alternatives, self-correction) must proceed through an external state of development because it is initially a social function. Thus, for Vygotsky, "external" means "social" (Wertsch 1985). Social interactions provide the platform for learning how to learn and for the development of self-reflection, responsibility, cooperation, and effective problem solving, and it is through social interactions that children develop and expand their capacity to learn.

It is important to realize that the very nature of social interaction involves emotional ties. We know that virtually all forms of learning take place within the context of a relationship with another and that learning won't happen unless the child feels safe—safe enough to listen and share herself

with the teacher. When teachers connect with and care about students, they are making a link that is determined by many factors: who the student is, who they are, and the nature of the context they are sharing with the student. The extent to which students feel connected to teachers and the extent to which they feel teachers are fair and care about them is significant to their progress.

I learned this lesson from Shirley Brice Heath, a well-respected anthropologist and linguist who studied the social, emotional, and learning contexts of three distinct groups of children, parents, and teachers in the South (Heath 1983). Shirley was invited to speak in an eminent scholar lecture series at Ohio State University. As I was driving with her from the airport to the hotel, she asked if it would be possible to observe a Reading Recovery lesson. The following morning we visited Sue, an RR teacher in the Columbus Public Schools. Sue provided a brief orientation to the thirty-minute lesson and then asked Shirley if she had any questions. Shirley had one question, "What do you know about this child?"

Sue commented that the little girl, Carrie, was shy and withdrawn. She had a difficult time speaking and explaining herself, but she had good ideas. Carrie had few literacy experiences prior to coming to school and was eager to learn. When the lesson was over, Shirley asked Sue questions about her interactions with the child at specific times throughout the lesson. For example, "Why did you tell the child something one minute and encourage her to try several ways to solve a problem the next minute? How did you decide when to tell, show, or wait for an answer? Why did you touch the child's arm when she appeared discouraged and other times asked her to persevere?" Sue's answers were thoughtful and introspective and revealed a clear rationale for doing what she did when she did it.

On our drive back to Ohio State, Shirley and I discussed the observation. She was impressed that Sue's first response about the child was related to Carrie as a person and not to literacy, although later on in the conversation Sue did talk about Carrie's knowledge of print. Shirley commented about nonverbal interactions and conversations between the teacher and child, specifically the tone and pitch of their voices, the hesitations, the eye contact, the overt moves—the subtle interactions I had overlooked.

What Shirley saw and heard in the RR lesson was not only what Sue said and did, but how she said and did it. By listening and watching Carrie closely, Sue was attempting to understand Carrie's perspective and how she changed to meet the demands of the task. Sue's moves were in response to the child's moves at the moment of action, just as two people move to the rhythm of the music when they dance. Shirley thought Sue had all the qualities and characteristics of an expert teacher. And what was more impressive is the fact that Sue was teaching a child who had a very low repertoire of early literacy skills.

I never forgot my experience observing an RR lesson with Shirley Brice Heath nor did I ever look at teacher and student interactions in the same way again. Shirley showed me the importance of the other side of teaching—the ways teachers develop collaborative social relationships with students that convey support and ownership in the learning process.

The ten teachers featured in this book not only have knowledge about how to teach reading and writing, they have a positive way of seeing, hearing, and conversing with students. And what they see, hear, and remember of the child's literacy development is what influences their interactions with the student. I believe that these ten teachers understood implicitly that the mind encompasses the very essence of humanity—intelligence, emotion, compassion, will, and creativity—and that they acted on these assumptions.

Expert Teachers' Assumptions About Learning and Teaching

Through years of effective teaching, these ten teachers have acquired three positive, self-fulfilling stances about learning and teaching, which are evident in their teacher-student interactions and conversations with children and colleagues. These expert teachers:

◆ expect the lowest-achieving children to learn how to read and write;
◆ know how to develop students' capacity to learn; and
◆ believe that they will teach them to read and write.

High Expectations

Why is it that some teachers do not believe a certain percentage of students in the regular classroom setting will learn to read? Allington and Walmsley (1995) suggest that teachers who believe that some children will never learn to read and write respond in ways that ensure the children's failure. One teacher commented,

> the reason some teachers have the attitude that certain children cannot learn to read or write is because they do not know how to teach them. They understand neither the reading and writing processes themselves nor what these processes look like as children become more proficient. Since they do not know how to teach children to attend to print, for example, they believe that the children cannot learn or that something is wrong with the child's brain. Their attitudes often change, however, once they are shown, through demonstration, ways to teach low-progress students.

This teacher's experience has shown that once unbelieving teachers successfully teach a struggling student to read, they will convince themselves that every child can learn if they have a teacher who knows what to do and doesn't quit trying.

Most of the teachers in Tommy's school did not think this "developmentally handicapped" child would ever learn to read and write. Karolyn, Tommy's RR teacher, wanted to change these negative perceptions and prove that he could learn. She forgot about the "developmentally handicapped" label that Tommy had for the last two years and treated him as she would any child she was going to teach.

> I kept reminding myself that it was possible for Tommy to reorganize his brain to read. I kept thinking that with my help and the right experiences he could replace and reorganize the inefficient brain structures with an assembly of neurons that would help him learn to read and write. That is exactly what happened. In less than five months, Tommy fit right in to the middle reading group in his first grade and he never

needed help in reading the rest of his elementary school years. I'll never doubt the plasticity of the brain and the fact that any child can learn how to read if the teacher knows what she is doing.

Kathy, a special education teacher, concurs with Karolyn. Kathy teaches physically handicapped children in the orthopedic unit in the morning and RR in the afternoon. She has taught children with multiple handicaps how to read and write. One child had spina bifida, and Michael, whom I will discuss throughout this chapter, had a large brain tumor removed when he was five years old. During the last seven years, Kathy and her colleagues have successfully taught every low-progress child in the orthopedic unit how to read and write. Kathy believes

> Any child can learn how to read and write when you supply what they have missing. For some children I might need to be a hand or arm, for another, such as Michael, I might need to be the child's memory for a while. Sometimes it does get discouraging when a child does not make the progress you think he should be making or you would like him to make. But you need to keep trying alternative ways to reach him and eventually it will happen. You will see the spark that shows a connection between what you said and what he did. And it takes time, so never give up.

Positive Mind-Set and Belief in Their Ability to Teach

These expert teachers shared Kathy's view that with time, patience, trying alternative ways to reach a child, and a belief that every child can be taught to read and write, all children can learn. They did not assume that something must be fixed before they could learn or that the children had a brain deficit or were missing something.

These feelings support the negative mind-set that is expressed by many low-

achieving students and are often revealed by the teacher in her interactions with the students. Instead, these teachers framed each child positively. Whether they were talking with the child or colleagues, there was no hint that the child was "diagnosed" learning disabled, unmotivated, hard to teach, developmentally handicapped, language delayed, having attention deficit disorder, or impaired in any way.

Kathy, Karolyn, and Maryann, another expert teacher, saw past the students' disabilities. They saw the child's potential and believed that the children could learn and that they could teach them. This positive mind-set and belief was contagious—the students' started to believe in themselves. Tommy said, "I knew I could learn to read because Mrs. King said I would learn. She believed in me so I believed in me."

Maryann remarked,

> I always ask myself who's standing behind me? If there is no one looking over my shoulder to take over where I left off, then it is up to me to keep teaching this child until she learns to read and write. If I do not teach this child, she might never get another chance.

These altruistic teachers shared a genuinely unselfish concern for the welfare of the children and put the children's welfare above their own. Their tenacity and willingness to go the extra mile helped them connect with students and find ways

Expert teachers believe every child can learn to read and write and enjoy teaching them.

to create learning opportunities that enhanced students' capacity to learn.

These teachers approached teaching with the attitude that they cannot control the circumstances that the child brings to the lesson, but they can control how they react and respond to those circumstances. Therefore, if the children were going to change their behavior, the teachers had to change their ways of interacting *first*. Teachers were as concerned with their students' self-confidence, self-efficacy, and self-esteem as they were with the children's reading and writing achievement. In the next section we take a closer look at what the expert teachers did to support and enhance students' social and emotional health and well-being.

The Social-Emotional Aspects of Teaching

How do expert teachers establish a collaborative partnership with the children, engage them in productive conversation, and motivate them to participate in literacy activities? These social-emotional interactions are essential for children to learn. Analysis of the videotapes and interview transcripts revealed six critical actions that each of the ten expert teachers took to support students' learning.

Establish Trusting Relationships

The expert teachers were able to develop a strong bond with the children. This bond helped students form a trusting partnership with their teacher. One of the first things they did was convey to the child that she was important. This message is frequently conveyed more by teachers' actions than by their words. One shy child made this point crystal clear.

Elizabeth entered first grade four weeks after school started. Records from her previous school indicated that Elizabeth was very low academically and that she was shy, withdrawn, and fearful. Her current classroom teacher said that when Elizabeth walked to the restroom or outside for recess, she "clung to the wall." Elizabeth only spoke to her classroom teacher and only when asked a direct question. She rarely spoke to her classmates or other adults, but when asked about Reading Recovery, she had the following to say:

"I like to come to the reading lesson because I know Mrs. Hundley really likes me and cares about me." When asked how she knew this, Elizabeth shared that her books, her magnet letters, her special pencil, and the writing book with her name on it were always on the table, ready for her. She also mentioned that the book she has to sit on to reach the table was placed on the chair and that Mrs. Hundley pinned her writing up on the wall. She commented that Mrs. Hundley always picked books especially for her, ones that they could talk about. Elizabeth believed that Sue Hundley was going to teach her to read and write because she was special and she knew she was special because "Mrs. Hundley told me so."

Elizabeth's discussion of the arrangements Sue made to get ready before she arrived showed that the child knew she was important and knew that the lesson was important as well. Elizabeth described not only how she viewed the teacher, but how the teacher viewed herself. Sue, the RR teacher, commented,

I was surprised to hear what Elizabeth said about our lesson. I knew she was new to the school and she started school late, which probably contributed to her uneasiness. She needed to feel more comfortable about leaving her room and going to another room for reading. I thought that if I had the room arranged with familiar materials, things that belonged to her, she would feel more secure. I was thinking that if I were in her shoes, seeing that the room was set up especially for me would make me feel like I belonged. I really didn't know if she noticed the room arrangement until I heard about what she said.

This teacher is able to take the perspective of the child. She thought about what it might be like to be enrolled in a new school, with new teachers and classmates. Children are more likely to thrive when they are in environments in which they feel they belong and when they believe that the teacher appreciates them. Sue was helping Elizabeth feel as though she belongs and is welcome, thereby alleviating her feelings of alienation. A teacher's small gestures—a smile, a touch on the shoulder, a friendly greeting—can have a major impact on helping students feel comfortable in a classroom. The expert teachers created trusting relationships by:

- showing compassion and empathy;
- demonstrating a strong sense of responsibility toward the students' achievement;
- not letting the children down;
- being reliable, organized, and predictable;
- addressing the students' emotional needs first;
- providing support and encouragement.

Show Genuine Interest in Children

In order to create and promote a responsible environment in which learning optimally takes place, children need to feel recognized, understood, cared for, and supported (Cohen 2001). The relationship between the teacher and students establishes the context for this to occur. Expert teachers create this context by showing genuine interest in what the child does, says, and thinks.

Michael had a brain tumor removed one year prior to his placement in Kathy's orthopedic classroom. Initially he would not communicate with Kathy or the other children in the room. He crawled around on the floor or sat in a corner sucking his thumb. Kathy was also his RR teacher, so they had many opportunities to work together throughout the day. Maryann, an RR teacher-leader, describes Kathy's way with children.

> Kathy knows how to invite a child to sit down and come with her to work. She finds some personal little thing about each child that makes her feel special. For example, Kathy knew that prior to his brain operation, Michael had traveled many places throughout the world with his parents. She used that information to engage him in conversation and to make very simple books for him to read. Michael had been to Paris, yet he was having this terrible time learning to read due to the brain injury. He was not interested in *I Can Read*, a simple text that describes a girl reading to her family members. Kathy had a way of relating things that she knew were important to Michael, such as his experiences traveling, and used them to write simple books. She explained to Michael why it was important to read

simple text about his travels. Once he had an explanation, Michael said, "OK, I will read easy books because they are about the trips I took with my family." Michael initially read personalized little books, which not only helped him learn how to read, but also enabled him to discuss and recall past experiences. The neurologist believed that it was the emotional connections revealed in conversations that triggered his recall.

Kathy commented that through their conversations about his family and their travels, Michael started to recall specific things he had done.

> I had to listen very carefully to his words and fill in the gaps. I could tell when he was drifting away and not attending. I would regain his attention and hold it by sticking to his interests, which wasn't hard to do because I knew them so well. I'll never forget the day he said, "I used to know how to play cards," and it was a certain kind of card game and he couldn't remember the name. He began to realize what he had forgotten, but as soon as he realized it, Michael began to turn to people for help and ask to have something shown to him again. For example, he might not be able to remember what word he wanted to use in his sentence but he would remember what letter it started with. I would give him several words until he remembered the one he wanted to say. The sentences we wrote every day were powerful ways to retrieve something he knew prior to his injury. We became very close. I took the time to listen and have a real conversation with him many times throughout the day. Children can sense that you truly care and they will start to trust you.

Before the Christmas break, Michael was released from RR reading as well as the average in the first-grade class. You never would have known he had a brain tumor. He became a very strategic reader and knew to ask for help when his memory lapsed. Because the tumor had been removed when he was only five, the neurologist believed that Michael would recover fully. Michael's family moved to another state, and it was not possible to follow up on his progress. Today he would be twelve years old.

Engage in Personalized Conversation and *Listen*

Language has its social basis in the form of conversations children have with teachers, and it is through these conversations that they become socialized into the school culture (Wertsch 1998). There are differences, however, in the nature, content, and substance of these classroom conversations. According to leading language researchers (Cazden 1988, 1999; Lindfors 1999) conversations that provide children with opportunities to contribute what they think, feel, and believe fuel both their curiosity about all aspects of the world they live in and their creativity in constructing and conveying their developing understanding of it.

But what do these conversations look like? Lindfors (1999) proposes that these conversations are acts of inquiry. She distinguishes between authentic and inauthentic teacher-student conversations, or acts of inquiry. Inauthentic conversations are designed by the teacher to seek or provide information and clear up confusion. The teacher views herself as the transmitter of a body of knowledge and set of skills deemed appropriate for that grade level. The teacher is the master of this body of knowledge that is transmitted to students. The teacher drives the agenda. In that role she gives students' information, questions, and elicits from students' answers to preconceived questions.

Authentic conversations, on the other hand, are not preconceived. The teacher is not solely a transmitter of knowledge or a questioner but a learning partner, a teacher-inquirer. The teacher-as-inquirer helps students develop conceptual knowledge and understandings by providing a living demonstration of inquiry acts, not preconceived formulated questions. The teacher and students reveal various perspectives and experiences, and explore and wonder about a range of possibilities. In this context, children construct their own understandings, bringing meaning to and making sense of their experiences (Lindfors 1999).

The following two book introductions distinguish authentic from inauthentic conversations. The teacher is introducing the book *Cookie's*

Week by Cindy Ward to a small group of low-achieving first graders.

TEACHER: Today we are going to read a story about a cat who gets into trouble every day of the week. What are the days of the week?
STUDENTS: [in unison] Monday, Tuesday, Wednesday, Thursday, Friday, Saturday, Sunday.
TEACHER: Let's look at the pictures and guess what is happening.
KAREN: Cookie is getting into trouble, I wonder why?
TEACHER: Let's find out. Look at the picture. What did Cookie do on Monday?
MIKE: Fall in the toilet.
TEACHER: What happened on page 3?
BILL: She knocked over a plant?
TEACHER: Where is the tricky word on that page?
KATE: There are two tricky words . . . *windowsill* and *knocked*.
TEACHER: I meant *knocked*. What is tricky about *knocked*?
MATT: Silent *k*.
TEACHER: Let's read the story and find out what happens on the other days of the week.

This teacher-student interaction has elements of an inauthentic conversation. One by one the children raised their hands and answered the teacher's directed questions. This was not a conversation but a series of questions that addressed the teacher's agenda. Karen had a genuine question but the teacher did not address it or perhaps she did not hear it. When Kate pointed out that there were two tricky words in the sentence, *Cookie knocked a plant off the windowsill*, the teacher disregarded her statement and told the children the tricky word that she had in mind.

Contrast this with the following book introduction, conducted with another small group of first-grade readers.

TEACHER: I couldn't wait for you to read this book, *Cookie's Week*. It is a story about a cat who gets into trouble. How many of you have a kitten or cat? [several hands fly up]
MICHAEL: My cat is Mitsy and she is always running after our dog. It is really funny!
KATHERINE: What's so funny?

MICHAEL: Cats are supposed to be afraid of dogs, but not Mitsy.

KEITH: My cat is afraid of dogs, she runs away from our neighbor's dog.

BETSY: I don't have a cat. My Mom says I'm allergic to them and besides they are sneaky.

KATHERINE: What do you mean sneaky? My cat isn't sneaky.

BETSY: Oh they sneak around the house and look at you from behind the couch and sometimes get into the garbage or knock stuff off the table when you aren't looking.

KEITH: I don't think that's being sneaky.

TEACHER: What would you call that, Keith?

KEITH: Just playful.

TEACHER: What do the rest of you think?

MICHAEL: Cats might be playful and sneaky.

KATHERINE: Michael's right, my cat is playful even when she's sneaky. We have lots of fun with her.

TEACHER: I bet you all have fun with your cats. Michael, you made an excellent point when you mentioned that cats might be sneaky and playful. Betsy, you mentioned something that happens in the story. I don't know if Cookie is both playful and sneaky in this story or not, I would like to know what you think.

KEITH: OK, let's read the story.

TEACHER: OK, lets read the story and think about what Cookie gets into and what is the consequence of each of her actions. Decide if Cookie is sneaky or playful and what made you think so. When you are done, we'll discuss why you thought Cookie was playful or sneaky or both playful and sneaky.

The preceding conversation has elements of an authentic act of inquiry. The children are talking to each other, not directing their comments to the teacher. The teacher has a tentative stance, which is a crucial part of the inquiry demonstration. She is wondering if Cookie was playful or sneaky and how the children would interpret Cookie's actions. She was probably not conscious of doing this, but as an active listener and inquirer, she followed the conversation led by the children.

The children understood that they would share their responses to the book they have read. They are reading to make a judgment about what is not there but implied. Inferring, or going beyond the literal meaning of the text, is one of the most difficult strategies for intermediate students to understand and grasp (Fountas and Pinnell 2001), yet this teacher was discussing inferencing with first-grade students.

This teacher is also gaining access to critical information about what the children know and think, which affected their motivation to read the story. This was evident in Keith's comment, "OK, let's read the story." The knowledge they shared came from the heart as well as from the head. The teacher's response demonstrates that feelings and factual knowledge are both important to comprehending. This conversation showed the children that their teacher was very interested in their thoughts and cared about what they had to say. If teachers want to form a collaborative partnership and know what is going on in students' minds, they have to create opportunities and conditions to share themselves and risk revealing themselves and their thinking (Johnston 1999; Lindfors 1999).

The expert teachers' book introductions were acts of inquiry. They invited children to speak and be heard, and they listened carefully to what they had to say. When asked how they engaged

Expert teachers know how to engage children in authentic conversation and how to listen.

and sustained children in conversation, the teachers had similar responses:

- personalize the conversation;
- talk about things the child is interested in that make the child happy;
- show your interest in the child as a person;
- ask for opinions;
- ask questions but don't ask twenty questions that require yes or no responses;
- assume an inquiry stance.

Most children are willing to share their ideas and experiences once they are provided the opportunity. Some children, however, are resistant and may be considered language delayed. The following example illustrates how to create opportunities for a "language delayed" child to converse.

Taylor Taylor rarely talked the entire time she was in kindergarten and was thus labeled language delayed. She lived with her grandmother and rarely spoke to anybody at home. Taylor's expressive language and concept knowledge was limited. She was very shy and withdrawn. The other teachers in the building decided that Carla was the only one who could reach Taylor because "she had a wonderful way of relating to children and bringing them out of their shell."

Carla took Taylor's hand as they walked to the RR lesson and after the lesson on the way back to the classroom. She would touch her arm, comment on how glad she was to see Taylor, and ask her what she had been doing. For the first couple of weeks Carla did all the talking.

Carla knew that Taylor would not respond or interact unless it was something that she knew. She tried to have her talk about herself, her likes, dislikes, and so on. Eventually Taylor began to tell her a few things about her life, and Carla would respond by sharing something personal about herself.

Carla was able to reach Taylor by arranging for her to be successful. She knew which thirteen letters Taylor knew, and so she arranged for her to contribute that knowledge whenever possible. She made many books that included Taylor as the main character. This made her feel important. If a task were too hard, Taylor would withdraw and quit immediately.

Carla prevented Taylor from struggling by joining her in problem-solving activities. "We can do this part together, Taylor," was frequently said, especially early on in lessons. Carla provided lots of specific praise when Taylor initiated any problem solving. She cared deeply about the future of this little girl, and she wanted Taylor to feel safe. Carla commented, "If children feel safe they will tell you about themselves, you just need to listen and respond to what they have to say, just like you do with any casual conversation."

Carla demonstrated a singularity of purpose: to help students feel successful. She acquired the reputation from colleagues throughout the state as the one teacher who could relate to any child, even those who were considered nontalkers. In order to accomplish this feat, Carla

- acts on the belief that children will make progress and converse with you only if and when they feel successful;
- allows children personal choice to talk about the books to make and sentences to compose and does not change their thoughts;
- encourages children to speak and listens to their responses;
- listens to be informed and transformed by what the children reveal;
- believes that she can reach the child through conversation.

Provide Feedback That Is Constructive, Targeted, and Positive

A critical underlying premise of Vygotsky's (1978) theory of learning and development is that children grow into the intellectual life around them. Children are always learning; in fact it is impossible to prevent them from learning. Teachers must learn how to construct the environment in which children will grow. They must learn how to create effective contexts and shape instruction to facilitate children's understanding of reading and writing processes through socially patterned interaction and feedback (Johnston 1998; Wertsch 1998).

From a Vygotskian perspective, language has its social basis not only in the conventions of its symbols (written and oral) but in the scaffolding (Bruner 1966) to children in the form of feedback. The child's individual mental functioning develops through experience with cultural tools (language, materials) in joint problem solving with more skilled partners working in the zone of proximal development (see Chapter 4). The following example illustrates this point.

MATTHEW: [reading] "and the lake got on" [immediately stops and looks closely at the text]

TEACHER: I am so glad you stopped, why did you stop?

MATTHEW: Because "and the lake got on the bike" doesn't sound right or make sense?

TEACHER: You are absolutely right, what would make sense?

MATTHEW: "And the woman," no that is wrong.

TEACHER: Keep thinking, you have the right idea, that [pointing to the picture in the text] looks like a woman. What else could you call a woman but begins with an *l*?

MATTHEW: *Girl*, no that word does not begin with a *g*, I can't get it.

TEACHER: I bet you can, you have the right idea. Can you think of another word for *girl* or *woman* that begins with an *l*? Look closely at the first two letters of that word to give you a start.

MATTHEW: La . . . la . . . Lady. That's it! And the lady got on the bike.

TEACHER: You were really thinking hard, are you right?

MATTHEW: Yeah, it all fits, and the lady got on and that is what happened in the story. I just never saw the word *lady* before. Now I know what the word *lady* looks like.

TEACHER: You sure do. I bet you are proud of yourself.

MATTHEW: Yeah, I am!

TEACHER: I'm proud of you too. You are a good problem solver.

In the preceding conversation, the teacher's feedback enabled the child to think differently and act. She did not tell the child the word *lady* but revealed how to think about alternative ways to solve the problem.

Cazden (1999) and Clay (1998) discuss different ways teachers can use feedback to scaffold students' processing while problem solving.

◆ They can "tell" the child the word or how to solve the problem and specifically talk her through the process. For example, the teacher might say, "What letter would you expect to see at the beginning of *woman*? Does that word look like *woman*?" If Matthew does not respond, the teacher might say, "Could that word be *lady*?"

◆ The teacher might "reveal" what needs to be done by the child to solve the problem, which

is what the teacher in the preceding example did. With the specific feedback, Matthew came to understand how to proceed as he tried *woman*, *girl*, and then, finally, completed a visual analysis of the unknown word and read *lady*. This action sequence was completed under scaffolded support. Clay (1998) argues that the active support demonstrated by the teacher in the preceding example should be done in the early formative stages of perceptual processing so that children make successful responses and learn how to choose between alternatives. Through these actions, Matthew will come to know how to complete the process without external support.

◆ The child could try to discover the solution to the problem alone. However, it is likely after receiving the scaffold feedback, Matthew will be able to complete a similar process unassisted.

The feedback Matthew received during the problem-solving attempts was also encouraging. It buttressed and strengthened the child's resolve and motivated him to keep trying. For example,

◆ "I am so glad you stopped."
◆ "You are absolutely right."
◆ "Keep thinking, you have the right idea . . ."
◆ "I bet you can [get it], you have the right idea,"
◆ "You were really thinking hard . . ."
◆ "I bet you are proud of yourself."
◆ "I'm proud of you too."
◆ "You are a very good problem solver."

If feedback reinforces progress, learning gains are forward thrusting. When gains are made by systematic reinforcement, teachers can observe the processes of movement through the zone of proximal development (Rogoff 1990; Tharp and Gallimore 1988).

Maintain Consistent Support, Expectations, and Limits

Children who struggle to learn how to read and write early on are generally deprived of self-esteem that accrues from successful learning and relationships. They become embroiled in negative spirals of failure, deepening emotional challenges, and continued failure that often results in behavior problems. Research studies have shown that in some cases, the real source of the problem is a child's difficulty learning to read and write (Coles 1998; Mate 1999).

Children's behavior, both positive and negative, is a form of communication that always has motivations and reasons (Deci, Koestner, and Ryan 2001). Some adults believe that children intentionally try to annoy the teacher. Leading child psychologists and physicians (Mate 1999; Greenspan 1997) argue that it is a mistake to think that anyone knows the intentions behind the actions of children; in fact, it gets in the way of seeing the child for who she really is. Moreover, the judgments that teachers deliver become the self-judgments children will carry into adult life.

To alter school failure, the teacher must provide and maintain consistent expectations, support, and encouragement. Psychologists generally agree that providing students with a framework within which to work and setting firm but reasonable rules and expectations for mature behavior is necessary to improve children's social emotional and cognitive growth and development.

The RR lesson establishes a structure within which to support and improve the students' behavior. Some children, however, continue to resist the teacher's attempts to organize, shape, and monitor their behavior. Katherine is one of these children.

Katherine Katherine had more than her share of negative experiences in her first few years in school. She experienced severe behavior problems in kindergarten and was suspended in first grade. One teacher described Katherine as the child from *The Exorcist*.

Katherine's RR teacher, Mary, suspected that her emotional outbursts were calculated to avoid reading and writing. During guided reading, for example, Katherine did little oral reading because when called upon she misbehaved. She tried similar tactics during RR lessons. After Mary confirmed that she was a good reader and that she would sound even better if she read *Mrs. Wishy-Washy* more smoothly and fluently, Katherine rebuffed her advice. "No [referring to fluent reading] I want to say it slow. You can't make me read that way. You can't tell me what to do. No, no I will not read. No way, no way. I'm going to get out of here!" Katherine was most uncooperative and refused to read *Mrs. Wishy-Washy*. She made no comment as Mary quickly read the rest of book fluently with expression.

Katherine's behavior changed dramatically during the writing portion of the lesson (Figure 8–1). Incredibly, four minutes after the exasperating time they shared during reading, Katherine became a different child. Mary set clear limits and direction to establish Katherine's job in the writing task even when Katherine continued to try to renegotiate. Mary was persistent and consistent in her responses to Katherine's attempts to control the situation. She had to use an extensive amount of positive reinforcement to keep Katherine on task and working with her. An examination of the practice page and the page where she wrote the sentence revealed a collaborative partnership between Katherine and Mary (Figures 8–2, 8–3).

Children attribute meaning to the experiences they have with teachers and, just like adults, have their own personal "take" on any particular experience (Mate 1999). Even though she balked during the familiar reading of the lesson, Katherine became more actively involved and successful during the writing portion of the lesson. I believe several teacher actions contributed to Katherine's shift in attitude and behavior during the lesson. The teacher

◆ knew what Katherine was capable of contributing and held her accountable for that contribution;
◆ frequently praised the child's contributions to the writing;
◆ provided specific praise tied to a student behavior;
◆ helped to regulate Katherine's mood by joining in to complete the hard part of the task so that the child could continue to think constructively;
◆ held the child responsible for her learning and behavior;
◆ persisted optimistically in frustrating circumstances and kept calm, tempered, and predictable;
◆ set limits and high expectations;
◆ cared about this child and the child knew it.

It is clear that the development of responsibility for learning is a primary task of students. However, some children must be shown how to assume this responsibility and be held accountable for their decisions and actions. This feat can only be accomplished through persuasion, not coercion. Recent research (Deci, Koestner, and

> TEACHER: Can you please tell me the sentence you want to write today.
>
> KATHERINE: "The frog jumped over the oranges then jumped under the oranges."
>
> TEACHER: You can write *the*, why don't you do that.
>
> KATHERINE: OK. [writes *the*]
>
> TEACHER: Let's write the word *frog* on the practice page. [makes four boxes; see Figure 8–2] Can you think about the sounds that you hear in *frog*?
>
> KATHERINE: It only has four parts.
>
> TEACHER: Yes, it only has four parts. See how clever you are? You are very good at hearing sounds in words. You can do this easily! You can hear the sounds in *frog* really well can't you?
>
> KATHERINE: Yeah [says *frog* slowly]
>
> TEACHER: What do you hear?
>
> KATHERINE: G.
>
> TEACHER: Good, where do you hear the *g*?
>
> KATHERINE: [points to the fourth box]
>
> TEACHER: Good. Put it in.
>
> KATHERINE: [writes the *g*]
>
> TEACHER: Try to say *frog* again and see if you can hear anything else.
>
> KATHERINE: [says *frog* slowly] I hear the *f*.
>
> TEACHER: Good, put the *f* in the box. I will finish it for you. [puts in *r* and *o*]. There it is—that word is *frog*. Put *frog* in your story.
>
> KATHERINE: [writes *frog*].
>
> TEACHER: Good job. Frog was in the story we read, wasn't he?
>
> KATHERINE: Yeah and you know the funny part was the frog jumped over the oranges.
>
> TEACHER: Yes, that was funny. Let's read your sentence so far. What word are we doing next?
>
> KATHERINE: [reads "the frog jumped"] We are doing *jump* next.

Figure 8–1. *The Impact of Specific Praise During the Writing Portion of the Lesson (Student Writing and Writing on Practice Page Is Illustrated in Figures 8–2 and 8–3.)*

Ryan 2001) found that perceived caring from teachers and parents is predictive of positive motivational outcomes for students that result in emotional, social, and cognitive growth.

When working with difficult-to-teach students, it is important to discuss effective techniques for managing behavior with parents, support staff, and classroom teachers. Consistency in teaching and managing student behaviors is required for positive outcomes to occur and be sustained. Katherine's story had a happy ending.

After Katherine started to make progress in reading and writing, her behavior in the classroom continued to improve. The recommendation for her to be placed at a special school for severe behavioral handicapped (SBH) children was withdrawn. Her first-grade teacher said to Mary, "I

wonder how many children we have labeled SBH whose biggest problem was that they didn't know how to read and write?" When Mary checked with Katherine's third-grade teacher on Katherine's progress in reading, her teacher said, "Her reading was great and her behavior was tolerable." Katherine remained at the school through third grade and then her family moved to another state.

Continue to Take Responsibility for Their Learning

Taking responsibility for one's own development and learning is essential to becoming a more proficient and expert teacher. It is through ongoing analyses, reflection, and conversation with others about their practice that teachers continue to

TEACHER: Good. What do you do? [makes boxes on the practice page for *jump*] What sound do you hear?

KATHERINE: [says *jumped* slowly] I hear a *p*.

TEACHER: Good, where do you hear it?

KATHERINE [points to the box and puts the *p* in]

TEACHER: Say it one more time and think what you hear.

KATHERINE: I hear a *j*.

TEACHER: Where do you hear it?

KATHERINE: [pointing to the first box] Here.

TEACHER: Good, put the *j* in the box. Say the word slowly again. What do you hear?

KATHERINE: [says *jump*] I can't get it. You say it.

TEACHER: I will say it with you. [they say *jumped* slowly together]

KATHERINE: I hear a *u*.

TEACHER: Oh yes, where do you hear a *u*? It is right here isn't it? [puts the *u* in the second box]

KATHERINE: Yes.

TEACHER: Let's say it again and see if you can hear this letter. [says *jumped* slowly, enunciating the *m*]

KATHERINE: I can't get it.

TEACHER: [writes the *m* in the third box] Do you know it now?

KATHERINE: Yeah it's an *m*.

TEACHER: That's right, just like the first sound in the word *me*. Write *jump* in your story. [says *jumped* and adds the -*ed*] It needs this on the end.

KATHERINE: [writes *jump* in the story. Teacher checks to make sure there is an -*ed* on the end.]

TEACHER: Lets do one more, let's try *over*. [makes three boxes on the practice page]

KATHERINE: I don't want to do it.

TEACHER: It only has three sounds, you can always do three!

KATHERINE: [says *over* slowly]

TEACHER: Good, you did it. That's an easy one for you, isn't it?

Figure 8–1 continued. *Part Two of the Writing Portion of the Lesson*

grow, develop, and expand their expertise (Lyons and Pinnell 2001). These ideas are not new. In 1916, John Dewey wrote:

> An ounce of experience is better than a ton of theory simply because it is only in the experience that any theory is vital and verifiable significance. An experience, a very humble experience, is capable of generating and carrying any amount of theory (or intellectual content), but a theory apart from an experience cannot be definitely grasped even as a theory. (169)

Expert teachers support and adhere to this idea of Dewey's. They continue to analyze, critique, and reflect on their teaching and invite other teachers to be partners in the evaluation of their teaching. They assume responsibility for their own development and learning and seek ways to continue to grow and better understand the complexities of learning and teaching processes.

Expert teachers become a community of learners, combining inside knowledge and outside knowledge (Lieberman and Miller 1999). Outside knowledge comes from reading current and seminal research on specific topics and forming study groups to discuss and critique this information. For example, a study group has met for the last three years to read and discuss current research in neuroscience focusing on brain growth and

KATHERINE: Yeah! [says *over* again]

TEACHER: What did you hear?

KATHERINE: [puts in the *o* and the *v*]

TEACHER: Very good and there's one part that you can't hear. [puts in the *-er*] Very good, Katherine, write that in your story. You heard all the sounds in *over* didn't you?

KATHERINE: Yeah but I made a little mistake. [referring to the formation of *v*]

TEACHER: That's OK, it looks good. You did a very good job on that. Read your story from the beginning.

KATHERINE: "The frog jumped over the oranges."

TEACHER: You can write the next word can't you?

KATHERINE: [writes *the* and starts to write the *o* for *oranges*]

TEACHER: That's right, *oranges* starts with an *o*. Very good. [writes the rest of the word *orange*] What is at the end of *oranges*?

KATHERINE: S [writes the *s* at the end of the word]

TEACHER: What comes next in your story?

KATHERINE: *Then.*

TEACHER: I will write *then*. What comes next?

KATHERINE: *Under.*

TEACHER: I'll write *under* for you. You can write the next word.

KATHERINE: Yeah I can! [writes *the*]

TEACHER: And what is your last word?

KATHERINE: *Oranges.* I can write the *o*.

TEACHER: I will finish the rest of the word. Very good writing today, Katherine. Read your whole sentence.

KATHERINE: [reads with assurance] "The frog jumped over the oranges and under the oranges."

Figure 8–1 continued. *Part Three of the Writing Portion of the Lesson*

development in the early years, emerging language and literacy development, teacher development, and Clay's recent books on literacy learning and changes over time.

But they also learn from inside knowledge by focusing on a particular area of study, for example, learning disabled or very difficult-to-teach students. After selecting the target population of students to study and investigate over a course of the year, the teachers meet periodically to analyze and discuss their lesson records and teacher-student interactions captured on videotapes and audiotapes. They assess how students' social, emotional, and cognitive needs are addressed and share alternative ways to support students' needs.

They do not give up on the children or themselves. Their spirit and desire to find out how to reach the children emotionally and teach them

how to become self-regulated readers and writers is ongoing and time-consuming, but they never quit. Every child became a reader and writer. The expert teachers also share a tremendous commitment to the children they taught. Maryann McBride captured the essence of this commitment.

Children take a big risk when coming to Reading Recovery. Teachers should do everything they can to make them feel that they care. Teachers must approach the child with respect and make it clear that you can help them learn to read and write. It is fun to think how wonderful these children are. You've taught a child that has made a difference in two lives—the child's life and your

Figure 8–2. *The Practice Page in Katherine's Writing Book (Note: Underlined Letters Written by Katherine; Numbers Indicate Order Used to Write Each Letter)*

Figure 8–3. *Katherine's Sentence (Note: Underlined Letters Written by Katherine)*

own. Teaching is an emotional commitment and an emotional task because you face lots of problems. Just think you have one time in this low-achieving child's life, that you can make them feel that they are the stars, the most important people on the face of the earth. Children do not often get that. Children know when you are invested in them.

Implications for Teachers and Parents

This chapter addresses dynamics of effective practice with a focus on characteristics of expert teachers' understandings about the emotional, social, and cognitive dimensions of learning. As a parent and teacher, I find having an awareness of and sensitivity to the juxtaposition of these aspects of teaching and their impact on learning most helpful. With respect to social and emotional learning, the expert teachers provided excellent examples to guide our thinking and to expand our understandings and appreciation of these essential dimensions of learning so that we are better prepared to teach every child to read and write. There are four critical lessons about social and emotional learning that parents and teachers can learn from these remarkable teachers.

1. *Build a supportive relationship with each child.* When you first meet children, get to know them and continue to personalize your interactions with them. Invite children to share something about their lives in school and at home. What do they like to do? What kind of books do they like to read or have their parents read to them? What have they written? What kind of music do they listen to? What are their favorite television programs or movies? How many people are in their family and what are their names? Do they have any pets? Find ways to communicate with children and draw upon their language and experience to facilitate the process. Persist in developing this relationship even under difficult circumstances. Developing a positive relationship builds trust and shows that you are genuinely interested in each child's future. Your efforts will speak volumes and be well worth your time and energy.

2. *Demonstrate your interest in children and your belief that children will succeed.* Convey that you truly care and that each child is important and worthy of your time and effort. Personalize the room and display students' work. Provide an uncluttered space for children to work in. Prepare well for each lesson. Children's time is as important as your time. Praise little successes, when warranted, and remind children often what they did right (even if it is minor). Many low-progress students lack self-esteem. Their self-perceptions are strengthened in environments where priority is placed on personalized experiences, respect, and involvement. They will become more secure, take risks, and attempt to resolve problems they encounter while reading and writing and feel free from fear and guilt if they experience difficulty. Expert teachers believe they can influence students' learning. Their actions and feelings build children's confidence and lead to more positive self-perceptions.

3. *Convey to children ownership in the learning process.* Many low-achieving students do not become active participants in the learning environment and when they become involved some are disruptive and try to undermine the teachers and other students' attempts to learn. Sometimes they refuse to participate in an activity. Do not let them withdraw. You owe it to children to include them in activities.

   Rather than retreat, punish, or give up on the student, establish roles and responsibilities for the student that are reasonable and attainable. Set limits and hold students accountable for their learning. As one child put it, "Mrs. K. told me her job and my job and we remind each other who is suppose to be doing what." When decision-making power and control rests only with parents or the teacher, children may develop feelings of personal incompetence and inadequacy. As a result they may eventually come to depend entirely on others for direction and develop "learned helplessness." Conversely, when individuals participate in making decisions, they are helped to feel that they can function independently and responsibly. This will enhance their self-perceptions. The vignettes and conversations reported in this chapter reveal how expert teachers work hard to help students participate and take responsibility for their own learning. They also persist in helping children achieve and expend additional effort when necessary to help them succeed.

4. *Value the students' diversity.* No two children are alike, nor do they learn the same way. Decide how approachable a student is and do not impose your feelings. Many children will sit close to the teacher and their arm or leg might be touching the teacher's. Others need space. The teachers in this book enjoyed working with students' ethnic, cultural, language, physical, and intellectual differences, and used those differences for their own growth. Teaching children from diverse populations affects the teachers' motivation and tenacity as well as the students.

In our society today, social and emotional learning is generally not valued and oftentimes not mentioned in educational communities, yet it is fundamental to all learning in the home and school. The clearer we are about how to create environments to develop social and emotional learning, the more able parents and teachers will be to further this development and facilitate the learning of all children, especially those who are struggling to learn.

Chapter 9

Knowledge, Thinking, Reasoning, and Practice of Expert Teachers

Explicit goals and standards about what students are expected to know and be able to do as a result of their education have been set for every student in every classroom (Ohanian 2000). As the demands on students become more rigorous, so too have the demands that classrooms be staffed with teachers capable of *teaching* students to achieve these standards. After two years of intense study of schools and schooling in the United States, the National Commission on Teaching and America's Future concluded that what matters most in educating students to meet the demands of the workforce in the twenty-first century is a competent teacher for every child (Darling-Hammond 1996).

What makes a teacher competent enough to be considered expert? What do expert teachers know and do that result in student learning? Research using classroom observations and laboratory settings has been conducted to answer these important questions. Most research focuses on what expert teachers know and can do. For example, Brophy and Good (1986) and Leinhart (1988) report that expert teachers have more content and skill knowledge than less expert teachers. This knowledge base and skill enables them to select and explain concepts and procedures that facilitate learning and engage students until they are able to learn specific content and develop specific skills.

Other researchers (Schon 1990; Shulman 1987) have found that expert teachers have not only accumulated extensive knowledge about their content area but they have acquired a comprehensive grasp of how students learn that enables them to create experiences that facilitate learning. The research cited provides a valuable contribution to helping us better understand what makes some individuals expert at teaching most students, but it does not address how they effectively teach those who are *failing* to learn. In today's changing world, teachers are expected to help every student, including those struggling to learn, to master more challenging material.

It is difficult to find any activity that does not require some, and often considerable, reading. Therefore, in order to accomplish this goal, every child must be taught how to read and write. If teachers are to create experiences that enable every student in the classroom to become successful readers and writers, they must know how to teach students who are having learning difficulties. All students depend on the teacher's skill and expertise to a certain extent. Students struggling to learn, however, are more vulnerable to instruction because they have not developed a strategic processing system that enables them to learn from the act of reading and writing itself (Clay 1991, 2001).

In my view, what is needed is a clearer picture of what expert teachers know, understand, and do to help the lowest-achieving students become proficient readers and writers. In Chapter 8, I discuss characteristics of expert teachers' personalities such as their will, tenacity, and ability to persevere until they reach and teach students who have repeatedly experienced failure learning to read and write. Chapter 9 provides an in-depth look at how expert teachers effectively and efficiently use their knowledge, judgment, and skills to facilitate the lowest-achieving students' capacity (will and skill) to become literate in a relatively short amount of time. In this chapter I (1) examine the knowledge base and skill of expert literacy teachers; (2) discuss how expert teachers use their knowledge, judgment, and skill to meet the individual learning needs of struggling learners; (3) describe how expert classroom teachers create a supportive learning environment for all children; (4) discuss experiences that facilitate the development of expert teachers' knowledge, skill, and judgment; and (5) describe, in conclusion, what teachers do and how they teach to demonstrate their expertise. The chapter shares expert teachers' personal reflections about their experiences working with difficult-to-teach students.

Expert Literacy Teachers' Knowledge Base and Skill

Research on effective teaching of RR students (Lyons 1991, 1999; Lyons, Pinnell, and DeFord 1993) and analyses of teacher-student interactions and interviews included in this book reveal that expert teachers' repertoire of knowledge is a tool whose meaning evolves through its use. The ten expert teachers in this book have drawn on their experiences teaching hundreds of hard-to-teach RR students on a daily basis, as well as teaching children in special education and primary classrooms for many years. They have acquired the ability to build new knowledge on what they already know. This process is active and ongoing; they accumulate knowledge case by case, every time they work with another student.

Because expert teachers are able to integrate new knowledge into existing knowledge to make sound judgments about what is relevant, they are more likely to meet the needs of a struggling student. Making connections between new and existing knowledge enables teachers to apply that knowledge in various ways to extrapolate and generalize information.

As revealed in the lesson transcripts presented in this book, teachers who become expert are able to make sound judgments about how to use their repertoire of knowledge. They can analyze where a student's processing is breaking down and determine what he needs to learn *next* that will be generative and suited for a particular purpose. They develop skills to prioritize and organize their knowledge and decide when, where, and how to use this knowledge to better understand and scaffold students' processing. The behaviors and reflections of the expert teachers also reveal that they share two fundamental assumptions about how children learn and how to teach them to read and write.

How Children Learn

Close examination of the interactions discussed in preceding chapters reveals expert teachers' belief that all children can and will learn and that it is the teachers' responsibility to find the best way to teach them. They recognize and seize powerful "teachable" moments to help students develop an effective processing system or network of effective problem-solving strategies.

Expert teachers do not focus on how teachers teach (e.g., questioning strategies, cooperative learning) but on how students learn as the basis for teaching. Students' behaviors while engaged in authentic reading and writing tasks inform how the teacher acts. As a result, the teacher finds and seizes the "teachable moment" within the context of what the student is doing at a particular moment in time. What makes teachers more expert is their ability to create and act during those teachable moments.

Expert teachers learn how to create teachable moments by connecting the curriculum (books and materials) to the personal learning needs of individual children through conversation. To begin the process, they find out what the children know and can do through informal assessments (Clay 1993a). They routinely analyze reading and writing samples of student work and conduct ongoing observations as children are engaged in various reading and writing tasks. This information is used daily to plan for instruction. Expert teachers ask themselves questions that focus on student learning. For example, they might ask:

◆ What is the child's understanding of this reading or writing task?
◆ How is the child attempting to solve the problem?
◆ What is the child finding difficult? Why?
◆ How many and what kind of attempts does the child use to resolve conflict?
◆ Is this task too difficult or easy for the child? Why?

After posing these questions, they observe carefully to seek answers, always keeping in mind that children's behavior changes while reading and writing different texts. The better they make these connections between what the child can do easily, the materials they select, and the language they use to engage the child in problem-solving activities, the more likely the student will learn.

In this inquiry process grounded in student behaviors, expert teachers are creating knowledge by observing student behaviors and then using it to inform their teaching. Observation, meaning making, studying, analyzing, and hypothesizing how the child will respond when presented with more challenging material are at the core of the expert teachers' work. One teacher described her process this way.

I knew that Marsha could match what she said to what she saw (one-to-one matching) when she read one line of text if the text had a predictable pattern, there were no more than three words of print per line, and the print layout was on the bottom of the page. I wanted to see if she could complete a return sweep and move her eyes to the second line of print. So I selected a book with one word on the second line that would complete the sentence so that it sounded right. If Marsha immediately reads the second line of print without hesitation, then she has pretty good control of left-to-right directional scanning. I need to introduce a book with a different print layout or more than three words on one line of print and one word on the second line. If she hesitates and moves to the left side of the page to begin to read the second line, left-to-right directional scanning on more than one line of print is beginning to be formed, but she needs more practice so I would continue to reinforce her processing on similar texts for awhile. If Marsha does not successfully complete a return sweep when she reaches the end of the first line of print, I need to do more explicit teaching, such as putting a green mark at the beginning of the second line of print so that her eyes would immediately go to the green mark and she will know where to begin reading. This technique will help to control her behavior until she completes the return sweep to the beginning of the second line of print without assistance. I will watch her eyes closely and as soon as I see that she is looking at the beginning of the second line, I will remove the green mark.

This teacher created an opportunity to observe the child's behavior when given a specific set of circumstances. She then discussed three probable scenarios with potentially different outcomes to assess Marsha's understanding of left-to-right directional scanning. The teacher has created an environment in which she can reflect and learn from the child. In this process of watchful waiting, she has devised three kinds of tentative ways to respond to the child's behaviors.

This teacher is an astute observer of children's reading and writing behaviors, which informs how and when she will respond. She understands the complexity of the learning and teaching process and how best to facilitate the child's active construction of these processes. She has developed the knowledge, judgment, and skill to create many zones of proximal development (Vygotsky 1978) to assess Marsha's processing and prompt her to act in such a way as to gain additional insights before she is able to appreciate the significance of her knowledge and skill on her own.

When teachers focus on learning, they develop a model of learning that views children not as the receivers of a body of information, but as meaning makers actively engaged in constructing their own understandings (Clay 1991, 2001; Resnick 1989). Advances in understanding the physiology of the brain and the relationship between emotional and cognitive development informs everything these teachers say and do. They use this broader knowledge base, skill, and judgment to design experiences that help all children, especially those who are having difficulty, become proficient readers and writers.

The Role of Experience in Teaching Children to Read and Write

The second assumption that underpins expert teachers' actions is related to creating a context for learning. As discussed in the first four chapters of this book, parents and teachers cannot prevent children from learning and they have tremendous impact on what children learn and how they learn it.

Dewey (1938) argues that it is not enough to insist upon the necessity of experience to learn, nor even of activity in experience. Everything depends on the quality of the context and experience that the teacher or parent arranges. According to Dewey (1938), high-quality experiences have two aspects. First, there is an immediate aspect of agreeableness, that is, the child enjoys the experience and it is well within his reach and ability to be successful with teacher or parent support. Second, the experience is problem centered and engages the student in an enjoyable way to solve the problem. When these two conditions are met,

experiences are educative, that is, they will influence subsequent experiences and promote future desirable experiences.

Wood, Bruner, and Ross (1976) added a third component necessary to educative experiences. They argue that an adult must engage in dialogue with the child in such a way as to provide the child with prompts that guide him from one step to the next. Bruner (1986) describes this experience as a "loan of consciousness" that gets the child through the zone of proximal development. Moreover, the language between teacher and child is a negotiation within a social setting and a feature of the lesson routine and procedure.

In addition to the preceding characteristics, expert literacy teachers revealed a fourth component of an educative experience: sound judgment and the skill to promote, support, and integrate social, emotional, and conceptual learning. Their language, juxtaposed with specific actions within a specific time frame, creates a culture of learning and provides opportunities for the child to develop conceptual knowledge and skill. Both teacher and child can then use these for further reflection and learning. The conversation between expert teacher Cheri and Megan exemplifies these four components of an educative experience.

Megan The three-minute conversation that is illustrated in Figure 9–1 took place immediately following Megan's independent reading of *Cookie's Week*, a level 10 text, which is equivalent to a first-grade primer. The plot of this story was discussed by a group of first-grade children in Chapter 8.

Megan initiated the conversation by discussing what she thought might happen on Sunday when Cookie was supposed to rest. This action shows her involvement and interest, her comprehension of the story, and her willingness to participate. Cheri showed genuine interest too, and continued to delve into Megan's thinking. The teacher's words validated and justified Megan's predictions about what Cookie would do on Sunday. Megan's choice to participate and the teacher's flexibility to allow for the child's choice is empowering and automatically makes the child an active participant, which is an essential condition for an educative experience. Early on in the lessons, Megan was reluctant to work with the teacher and found many different ways to avoid participating.

Text: *Cookie's Week* by Cindy Ward

MEGAN: [immediately after finishing the last two pages of the story] Tomorrow is Sunday . . . Maybe Cookie will rest! [picture shows the cat with one eye closed and the other eye open looking at a bee flying around] I don't think so!

TEACHER: Why don't you think so?

MEGAN: Because he's going to get into trouble in more places?

TEACHER: Do you see anything in the picture that makes you think that?

MEGAN: Yes, the eyes.

TEACHER: You're right, one eye's closed like he's asleep and the other eye is open. Does that give you a clue as to what is going to happen tomorrow?

MEGAN: Yes, he's going to get into trouble.

TEACHER: You understand the story well, Megan. You also did some really nice work as you read this story. I especially liked what I saw on page 17. You were checking not only to make sure the word made sense but looked right. You said, "Cookie went" and then you took a really good look. I even saw you take the word apart. What did you see in that word that you know?

MEGAN: *An* and *ran*.

TEACHER: You saw the *an* in *ran*, didn't you? I saw you get in there with your finger. The sentence is "ran into the closet." And you did the same thing here trying to figure out this word, didn't you?

MEGAN: Yes, *be . . . fore*. I saw the *be* and the *for* and it said *before*.

TEACHER: You are right. Good for you. Did it help to take the word apart like that? [Megan nods yes] I thought so. I especially liked what you did here because you stopped and noticed something. Sometimes you read so fast you don't check with your eyes, do you? You did a good job with that today, Megan. Where was the word that you left out here?

MEGAN: [points to *kitchen*]

TEACHER: You left that word out didn't you? Do you want to go back and try again?

MEGAN: OK.

✔	✔	✔	✔	✔		cupboard
"Cookie	got	stuck	in	a	kitchen	drawer."

TEACHER: Are you right?

MEGAN: Almost . . . *kit* . . . [takes word apart with her finger and pronounces *kit*]

TEACHER: [noticing that Megan is continuing to struggle] Oh, I liked the way you're doing that. You saw this part didn't you? [masking *kit*] What does that say? [Takes word apart with her finger, exposing *kit* and then covering *kit* and exposing *chen*. Waits.]

MEGAN: *Kit . . . kit . . . kitchen* . . . "kitchen drawer." [exclaims joyfully]

TEACHER: Are you right?

MEGAN: [nods with big smile on her face]

TEACHER: You figured it out, didn't you? Cupboard made sense but if you take a good look . . . could that word be *cupboard*?

MEGAN: Hmm, no because that word [referring to *drawer*] has a *d* . . . *cupboard* doesn't have a *d*.

TEACHER: That's right. There was another place that gave you some trouble. Do you see where it is? [turns to page 9]

MEGAN: [points to the word *upset*]

TEACHER: Do you remember what you said when you got to that part?

MEGAN: I said *up*.

Figure 9–1. *Transcript of Conversation Between Teacher and Student Immediately Following a Running Record*

TEACHER: Yes, you said *up* and then you stopped and said, "I wonder if it's a silent *e*. I wonder if it says this . . ." You were talking out loud, weren't you? You know what? Do you remember what we talked about if you stop too long and talk about the word, what happens?

MEGAN: I won't figure it out.

TEACHER: No, we probably won't figure it out because you've forgotten what the story's about. It gets us off to the wrong start, doesn't it? What would be a better thing to do rather than talking about it?

MEGAN: I could say that it says its own name . . .

TEACHER: [realizing that Megan is getting more confused, intervenes, writing *got, get* on the white board, pointing to *got*] Do you know this word?

MEGAN: *Got.*

TEACHER: Good, that word is *got*. What is this word? [points to *get* on the white board]

MEGAN: *Get.*

TEACHER: So this word [writing *set*] must be . . .

MEGAN: *Set.*

TEACHER: [adding *up* before *set*] And this word must be . . .

MEGAN: *Upset!*

TEACHER: That is what you should do, Sweetie, when you come to a word you are not sure of. What really is important is to start over and reread and then when you come to the problem word, think about what makes sense while you take the word apart. That will help you think about what will make sense and look right.

MEGAN: OK, I can do that.

TEACHER: You did a very good job problem solving today, Megan.

MEGAN: Thanks.

Note: [✔] means accurate reading. Substitutions are written over the word in the text.

Figure 9–1 *continued.*

After their conversation about the ending of the story, Cheri complimented Megan on using excellent problem-solving strategies while reading independently. Megan needed this reassurance. For the first six weeks they worked together, she was reluctant to initiate any move in either reading or writing for fear of making a mistake. Cheri did not perpetuate the problem by failing to validate Megan's emotional response. Instead, she developed a connection with her by accepting her inner fears and reassuring her that she would learn to read and write and that it was the teacher's responsibility to help her succeed. The social setting was pleasurable and mutually satisfying to both teacher and child.

The teacher's reassuring comments and specific references to Megan's problem-solving actions throughout their conversation bolstered her confidence, kept her attentive, and prevented her from quitting. This was apparent in Megan's body language. She sat up straight, pushed the sleeves on her sweater up so that they did not get in her way, held the book up, initiated independent processing by finding places in the text where she experienced difficulty, and smiled often, especially when she struggled and then self-corrected. These behaviors are in direct contrast to previous behaviors that suggested withdrawal and inattentiveness. For example, to avoid attending in earlier lessons, Megan would play with the teacher's necklace, cover her hands with her sleeves so that she couldn't point to the words, sit on her hands, yawn loudly, scratch her nose and arms, make faces, and play with the book and materials.

Cheri continually reminded Megan of the positive problem-solving activities she had already done. She was not giving blanket statements of praise such as "good job" or "good girl," which have little connection to Megan's real problem-solving competencies, attributes, or affects. Instead, the teacher conveyed the message that success is contingent upon a certain adherence to problem-solving abilities and she held Megan accountable for completing these activities. She also created opportunities for Megan to be successful.

The teacher restated Megan's successful attempts to take words apart while reading. For example, she complimented Megan for finding *an* in the word *ran*, as well as *be* in the word *before*. She then reminded Megan that she could use the same strategy to figure out *kitchen* and helped her to use this strategy, which Megan was able to do. The smile and pride on Megan's face after the teacher asked her, "Are you right?" was heartwarming. Sitting up in her chair and with a big grin on her face, Megan nodded yes.

The teacher had created an opportunity for Megan to have a successful experience in the context of both interpersonal interactions and interactions with materials. As a result, Megan's self-confidence and self-concept were bolstered. The last two minutes of their conversation revealed the impact of this positive experience. Megan volunteered more information than requested. She explained how her substitution of *cupboard* for *drawer* was incorrect because cupboard did not have a *d*.

The teacher, realizing Megan's rising confidence, was ready to present a learning challenge. She asked her to locate the place on page 9 where she had difficulty. Megan pointed out the word *upset*. This is the place where she hesitated and asked herself if the *e* in upset was silent. The teacher knew Megan was accustomed to using this inefficient processing behavior and that she had used it many times early on in lessons. When she stopped reading and focused closely on the word and talked to herself, Megan forgot the meaning of the story.

The teacher reminded Megan of her past experiences in forgetting the story and asked her what would be a better option than talking to herself and looking only at the word. The teacher, realizing that Megan's response, "I could say that it says its own name," was not productive and may be confusing her, intervened immediately by taking out the white board and clearly demonstrating a more efficient way to figure the word out, which Megan could easily do. This clear demonstration added to rather than took away from Megan's prior successful experiences. Cheri restated the value of taking words apart to analyze an unknown word and at the same time reassured Megan that she is competent and able to

solve the problem without teacher assistance. Megan learned how to approach new challenges confidently and at the same time draw upon the teacher for help and support when needed. Teachers must establish this important balance by providing children with many appropriate challenges and opportunities for success.

As indicated in the lesson transcript, Cheri was very specific and selective in prompting to Megan's error, that is, to the *next* move Megan needed to make to solve the problem. Megan could not retain many words, expressed by the teacher in the form of prompts, in short-term memory. The teacher did not "beat around the bush" or ask her a series of questions about what she had already done well.

Cheri initiated instructional moves that are automatic, fluid, and flexible. The instructional moves enabled her to perform teaching tasks without burdening her working memory. She has a repertoire of prompts in mind that are connected to the problem in context and that, when used, prompt Megan to think and act in a particular manner to facilitate productive processing.

Cheri's teaching illustrates the extent to which the process of exchange and negotiation, this cultural context that is being created on the spot, is a feature of the lesson routines and procedures. It is not simply Megan working in isolation through the lesson; the lesson itself is an exercise in collectivity, one that depends on Cheri's ability to be aligned with and responsive to Megan's mental state from moment to moment. This sharing of emotional space is called *attunement* and is necessary for the normal development of brain pathways involved in attention and emotional self-regulation (Mate 1999). The teacher is teaching Megan how to control her behavior, attend to and select information as needed, and disregard nonessential information. These actions will help Megan become self-regulated and independent.

The conversation between Megan and her teacher and their patterns of interaction include the following four main components of an educative experience. First, the experience was well within Megan's capabilities and control. Second, the experience was problem centered and engaged Megan in an enjoyable way to independently solve problems. Third, the experience involved a dialogue between the teacher and student that included prompts tied to action to flexibly guide the child's and teacher's thinking and next moves. Finally, the teacher used sound judgment and skill to promote, support, and integrate social, emotional, and conceptual learning upon which both teacher and child reflected and learned together.

When teachers and students are involved in educative literacy experiences, learning is accelerated and children develop processing strategies that are generative. The teacher integrates the cognitive, emotional, and social components of learning throughout the learning process. Providing intervention by focusing solely on the cognitive dimensions of the interaction without regard for unresolved emotional issues (the affective side of learning) greatly reduces the struggling student's chance for success.

Dewey (1938) addressed this idea by making a distinction between educative and noneducative experiences. He suggested that noneducative experiences often focused on the cognitive dimensions of learning, resulting in

◆ an increase in teachers' automatic skill in a particular direction that leads into a fixed routine and rut;
◆ the formation of a slack and careless attitude that modifies the quality of subsequent experiences, preventing children from revealing what they know;
◆ experiences that are disconnected from one another and are not linked cumulatively, which may artificially generate disintegrated habits.

Dewey's descriptions of a noneducative environment are in sharp contrast to the educative experience that Megan and Cheri shared.

Meeting the Individual Learning Needs of Struggling Readers and Writers

Expert teachers tailor their knowledge and develop the skills required to address individual learning needs. Each student constructs distinct pathways in his brain to develop a working system of neurons to read and write. At the same time, each student possesses a different level of skill with which to begin the process. These variations in performance are a function of the student's emotional state and how much support the

student receives from the teacher. The teacher must help the student construct a neural network that is in itself unique to the individual and thus requires a dynamic approach to teaching, one that constantly changes to meet the increasingly more complex challenges the student faces as he constructs meaning.

Three studies of the teacher-student interactions in RR lessons revealed that patterns of interactions and scaffolding shifted and changed over time as children demonstrated greater control of their learning through self-initiated actions. Hobsbaum, Peters, and Sylva (1996) identified three phases of teacher-student interactions as children became more competent during the writing portion of the RR lesson. In the first phase, the teachers closely monitored and structured the learning in the task and intervened often to scaffold the child's learning. In phase two, the children independently identified their needs and the teacher prompted the child to retrieve and make connections and helped them to remember what to write or how to act. During phase three, children exercised increasing control over their processing through the use of self-regulatory language and the teacher reacted or responded to the children's behaviors

In another study of teacher and student conversation during scaffold instruction in the writing portion of the RR lesson, Anderson (1997) found that children's ability to self-initiate control of the writing process was a function of the change in teachers' talk and ability to transition from more to less assistance. Moreover, the scaffold instruction within RR lessons facilitated children's writing progress in classroom journal writing.

In a study of scaffold instruction during the familiar reading and the new book reading portions of the RR lesson, Wong, Groth, and O'Flahavan (1994) found that teachers' "scaffolding" comments change as a function of the teachers' familiarity with the text. These three studies provide strong evidence that because children learn to read and write many different ways, instruction must be individualized to meet these differences. The message to teachers should be equally clear. No two children should be taught the same things, in the same sequence, in the same way, or using the same books and materials. Moreover, students' success is dependent on teachers' expertise to effectively analyze and assess children's behaviors and scaffold their learning.

The expert teachers featured in this book view learning to read and write as a dynamic process, that is, they moved beyond the static, one-dimensional, step-by-step approach to beginning reading instruction. As Clay (1998) points out, children take different paths to common outcomes and expert teachers operate from that theory. They understand, acknowledge, and recognize individual differences in students' learning patterns as they shift over time and use them constructively to scaffold their learning, which is evident in the following example.

David David knew where to begin to write a sentence in the writing book and how to write from the left to the right across a page, but did not control directional movement when reading a book. He needed to learn how to control directional movement—left to right, top to bottom, and return sweep to read the second line of print. David also needed to learn how to control one-to-one matching, that is, how to relate the visual information (what he sees) to auditory information (what he says) while reading. In order to accomplish this complex skill, David needed to learn how to segment his speech and coordinate his timing to link pointing (with his finger), looking (with his eye), and speaking (with his ear). Only when he is able to integrate these three sets of behaviors will David be able to control the directional movement required to make accelerated reading progress.

In the example illustrated in Figure 9–2, the teacher began teaching David how to control directional movement and one-to-one correspondence. She showed him his writing book and asked him where he begins to write a sentence. After David pointed out the top left-hand side of the page, his teacher explained that he should do the same thing when he reads a page in the book. Going from the familiar to the unfamiliar is an excellent way to make it easier for the child to learn. She also put a green dot on the left-hand side of the page to indicate where he should look to begin to read. Eventually David will learn to focus on a left page automatically, without thinking about where to look.

After placing a green dot to indicate where to start, David was asked to point out where he should begin reading. Once he correctly identified the place to begin, the teacher took David's finger to demonstrate early strategies of direc-

tionality and one-to-one matching of words read aloud to the words in print. She demonstrated left-to-right directional movement, matching his finger to the words on the page while saying each word and asking him to check the picture to see if what he read made sense. This routine was repeated on two pages.

The teacher wanted to determine if David could engage in the routine without help, so on the third page she asked him where to start and which way to go. He quickly pointed out where to start reading and which why to go so she asked him to read the page. David successfully completed the task. The teacher reinforced David's excellent processing, describing exactly what he had done successfully.

David's reading behavior on this particular day suggested that he had learned how to control his attention in the left-to-right serial order requirements of print. He demonstrated the integration and coordination of three sets of behaviors: visual attention to print—what he sees (occipital lobes); matching what he sees to what he says (temporal lobes); and left-to-right directional rules of position and movement—what his finger points to (parietal lobes). David was able to go through the routine established on the first two pages without the teacher's prompts. The teacher was flexible enough with her language and actions to withdraw support after David demonstrated he had some control over the action sequence. However, if he had faltered, the teacher would have intervened to help him to complete the process.

After reading the first two pages, the teacher was confident that David had established a coordinated stability and control over the left-to-right directional pattern. Now she is ready to select books that vary in print formats to assess his ability to use directional skills. David must encounter texts that vary in placement of the print on a page in order to gain flexibility in applying the directional principle when reading more than one line of text. The teacher's seemingly fluid and flexible prompting disguises the lengthy preparation and planning that she engaged in prior to teaching this lesson. She had to ask herself several questions. For example,

◆ What does David know about location of words on a page?
◆ Is there evidence that David has some control of directional movement (with regard to

Text: *The Birthday Cake* by Joy Cowley

TEACHER: [opening the writing book] David, when you wrote your sentence, "David likes to play football after school," where did you start to write the first word of the sentence?

DAVID: [pointing to the top left-hand side of the page in his writing book] Here.

TEACHER: That's right. When you read stories, you start to read in the same place. I am going to put a green dot to remind you where to start reading this book. The title of the book is *The Birthday Cake*. David, point to first word of the story and show me where you should start reading.

DAVID: [pointing to the left-hand side of the page] Here.

TEACHER: Good, that is right. What is that word, David?

DAVID: *A*.

TEACHER: [taking David's index finger] I will read the words and we will point to each word while I read. "A red cake." Read it with me while we point.

DAVID: [pointing with the teacher while the teacher reads] A red cake.

TEACHER: Good. Is that what you see in the picture? Are the lady and man putting a red cake on the table?

DAVID: Yes, here is the red cake. [pointing to the cake in the picture]

TEACHER: When we read the words on this page did the words you read match what you pointed to and what you said?

DAVID: I think so.

TEACHER: Yes they did. That was excellent reading work, David. Let's look at page 3. Where should we start now?

DAVID: I don't know.

TEACHER: Where did I put the green dot on the first page we read together?

DAVID: [pointing to the left side of the page] Here.

TEACHER: And which way did you move your pointer finger to read the words?

DAVID: This way. [moves his finger from left to right]

TEACHER: That's right. We have to do the same thing on this page. Which way do we have to go?

DAVID: [pointing left to right] This way.

TEACHER: That's right. What do we need to do to get ready to read this page? Put your pointer finger under the first word you will read.

DAVID: [points to the word *A*]

TEACHER: Good that is where you start. Look at the picture. What color do you think the next cake is going to be?

DAVID: Yellow.

TEACHER: Let's point and read the words together to see if you are right.

TEACHER/DAVID: [pointing to each word while reading the text] "A yellow cake."

TEACHER: Were you right? Did the man and lady put a yellow cake on top of the red cake?

DAVID: Yes.

TEACHER: And did the words we read match what we pointed to and said?

DAVID: Yes.

TEACHER: Let's turn the page and show me where you need to start reading.

DAVID: [pointing to the word *A*] Here.

TEACHER: That's right. Look at the picture and tell me what color of cake you think is going to be added next.

Figure 9–2. *Teaching for Strategies to Facilitate Left-to-Right Directional Movement*

DAVID: A blue one.

TEACHER: Where do you start reading? Which way do we go when we read?

DAVID: [pointing to the left side of the page and moving left to right]

TEACHER: That's right, you always begin reading at the left side of the page. Can you point to the words while you read them without my help?

DAVID: [pointing to each word while reading the text in a left-to-right sequence] "A blue cake."

TEACHER: That is very good, David. You pointed to every word going in the right way. When you read *A* you were pointing to the word *A*. When you read *blue*, you were pointing to the word *blue*. When you read the *cake*, you were pointing to the word *cake*. And you did that without my help. Very well done!

Figure 9–2 *continued.*

left to right, top to bottom, return sweep) when he reads or writes?

◆ What kind of book (characteristics of the text) will make it easy to teach David to locate the top-left starting point to begin reading?

◆ What specific language and actions will guide and control David's directional movement and help him to establish one-to-one correspondence?

◆ What external mediator (e.g., green dot) will facilitate David's ability to know where to begin reading?

◆ What evidence will I look for to determine if David controls directional movement and one-to-one correspondence?

◆ How will I alter my language and choice of book to withdraw support as David develops competence in controlling directional movement and one-to-one correspondence?

◆ What specific support can I use to help David reestablish the routine if he has a momentary skip or falters?

Expert teachers' knowledge is dynamic in that what they perceive and do at any moment in the lesson is rooted in what they assess while ob-

serving the child today and recalling past experiences teaching the child. For example, this teacher believed that after two pages of demonstration, David might be able to control directional processing without her assistance. The teacher believed this to be the case because David had no difficulty with left-to-right directional schema and return sweep when writing a sentence. Therefore, she did not wait until they read the entire book to find out if he was able to proceed without her help. The teacher also withdrew her support as soon as

Expert teachers closely observe and analyze children's processing while they read and write stories.

she observed that David was able to control left-to-right movement and return to the left side of the page to read the second line of print. He was beginning to develop the same consistency in his reading behavior that he had developed writing sentences.

The instructional moves of both David's and Megan's teachers may look routine and scripted as they demonstrate thinking, engage the students in deliberate practice, calibrate task difficulty, teach strategies directly, and withdraw support when the students' behavior suggests it is warranted. But these are the behaviors of vigilant expert teachers in action. They are building case knowledge about how to teach a specific process to a specific child for a specific reason.

They are experts at negotiating and mediating learning through conversation tied to specific action. Only when teachers are part of the action do mediational means come into being and play their role (Wertsch 1991). The language and other sign systems—for example, books and materials (dots)—have no power in themselves. It is only when they are tied to actions with others that opportunities for learning arise. Action and mediation determine meaning; they do not exist independently (Wertsch 1991).

Most of the examples in this book illustrate sociocultural settings, social languages, and mediated action involving one expert teacher or parent working with one low-achieving child. The following section discusses how expert classroom teachers can create a learning environment to support groups of struggling readers learn how to learn.

Creating a Supportive Learning Environment

Findings from fifteen years of longitudinal research examining how children become literate reveal that the single most important factor contributing to young children's success or failure in learning how to read and write is the teacher and the opportunities he provides for children to negotiate meaning through conversation (Wells 1986). Additionally, in order for the collaborative talk to have an empowering effect it must be based on the assumption that the learner has ownership of the task. Expert classroom teachers strive to ensure that children own the task by in-

corporating personal life experiences into the conversation. Introducing a book to group of children is an ideal place to initiate the process.

The book introduction can help students think about and anticipate what could happen in the story, ask themselves questions, make predictions of the outcome, and confirm or disprove their predictions. Yet some teachers are not aware of the power of the book introduction to help children construct meaning while in the act of reading. This became clear to me after I watched two teachers introduce the book *Peter's Move* to a small group of first-grade children.

On the cover of the book Peter is sitting on top of a box labeled "Peter's books." There is a suitcase, several boxes labeled "Peter's toys," and four stuffed animals with sad expressions on their faces. The first page of the book shows Peter's mother talking to her son, who has an apprehensive look on his face. The third page shows Peter sitting on his bed, feet firmly planted on the floor with the same sad expression on his face. The stuffed animals also look sad. Throughout the next several pages different family members (who are smiling throughout the story) are pictured packing up Peter's room. Peter is not helping. He is sitting on the bed. His face and the faces of his stuffed animals remain sad.

Several pages later, the moving van is parked in the front of the house. The movers are loading boxes into the moving van. The next page shows Peter standing in the middle of an empty room clutching his favorite stuffed animal, an alligator. Peter and the alligator retain their apprehensive, sad faces.

The next page shows the moving truck pulling up to the new house. Family members are in Peter's room unpacking his boxes. This time Peter is helping to unpack and putting things away. The next page shows Peter and his stuffed animals with smiles on their faces playing with his train. On the last page of the story, Peter is smiling again, this time reading a story to his stuffed animals, who are also smiling.

In the excerpt in Figure 9–3 one first-grade teacher is introducing *Peter's Move* to a small group of children in the middle (average) guided reading group. This book introduction was a picture walk that left few opportunities for the children to use their oral language and prior knowledge. The children were not allowed to anticipate what might happen next by predicting

TEACHER: This is a story about a child moving. Let's see what he packed to move to his new house. [asks each of the six children in the group to describe what Peter was packing up in each picture]

STUDENTS: Books, toys, stuffed animals.

TEACHER: Yes, that's right and Peter had to pack all his toys and things. What letter would you expect to see at the beginning of *packed?*

MARTHA: A *p.*

TEACHER: That's right, Martha, can you find the word *pack* on page 10?

MARTHA: Yes, here it is. [accurately finds *pack*]

TEACHER: Everybody find *pack* on page 10. Now find the word *unpack* somewhere at the end of the story.

KARL: It is on page 14.

TEACHER: That's right, Karl, Everyone find *unpack* on page 14. Read the story and find out what happened to Peter when he moved.

Figure 9-3. *First-Grade Teacher Introducing* Peter's Move *to Six Children in the Middle Reading Group*

and confirming their predictions in the text, or searching for additional information if there was a mismatch. They struggled during the first reading of the new book, relying for the most part on visual information. For example, Karl said, "Peter's room was *up*" instead of *empty.* Crystal read "two men *made* all the boxes" instead of "two men *moved* all the boxes."

Without knowing the gist of the story, the children did not learn how to anticipate what might happen, hypothesize what the words might be, and check their prediction with the words in the text. They were not able to use feed-forward mechanisms such as anticipation or prediction to keep their processing system efficient, even though they appeared to have developed an efficient system of strategies when they read some books. The children did not seem to understand the story, otherwise they would have monitored and corrected their behavior.

As shown in Figure 9–4, the book introduction of *Peter's Move* to another average group of first-grade students is quite different. The students' reading was fluent and there were several self-corrections. Every substitution was meaningful; for example, one student said *grandma* for *grammy.* Another read "He liked it *here*" instead of *there.* After the children had read the story, the teacher asked them what happened at the end of the story.

TEACHER: Did Peter change his mind about moving?

PATTY: Once he got to his new house he was really happy and so were his stuffed animals. He even helped his family unpack.

JASON: YES, he changed his mind, he likes his new house. I liked my house too after I made friends.

PATTY: So did I. It's fun to move.

The differences between these two book introductions are evident in the type of errors the children made while reading the story. Despite the fact that both groups of children were reading within the average range in their respective classroom, only those who experienced the second book introduction made meaningful substitutions. I believe several things may have contributed to these differences.

♦ Before mentioning the story, the expert teacher engaged the children by asking them to reflect and discuss their feelings about moving to another neighborhood. She also sustained the conversation by inviting children to respond to one another. This action suggested that she enjoyed the conversation and valued their input.

♦ The teacher continued to encourage the children to express their feelings and thoughts about moving. They responded to one an-

TEACHER: Patty, have you ever moved from one house to another house?

PATTY: Yeah, we moved from Leon Street to Wayne Street.

TEACHER: Do you remember how old you were when you moved?

PATTY: I think I was five.

TEACHER: Has anyone else moved to another street like Patty did?

JASON: No, but we moved to another state.

TEACHER: How did you feel about moving to another state, Jason?

JASON: Terrible. I hated leaving my school and my friends.

TEACHER: How did you feel leaving your old house, Patty?

PATTY: The same as Jason, I didn't want to go. I liked playing with the kids on my street.

TEACHER: Your new book is about a boy who moved, just like Patty and Jason did. The title of the book is *Peter's Move*. Let's look at the cover of this book. How do you think Peter feels about his move?

BETH: He doesn't want to go.

TEACHER: Why do you think that, Beth?

BETH: You can tell by the look on his face.

TEACHER: What do you think he wants to do?

MIKE: Stay in his old house.

TEACHER: Is that what you would want to do, Mike?

MIKE: Yes.

TEACHER: What two letters would you expect to see at the beginning of the word *stay*?

STUDENTS: St.

MIKE: [reads without prompt] "He wanted to stay in his old home." I was right!

TEACHER: Look through the next few pages.

STUDENTS: [look through the book without help]

TEACHER: What do you think is happening?

PATTY: Everyone helps him pack.

TEACHER: Do you think he has changed his mind about not wanting to move?

RODNEY: No, because he's not helping to pack and he looks sad.

TEACHER: Do you think he will change his mind and begin to feel better?

BRAD: I don't know, I was wondering why he looks better at the end of the story.

TEACHER: So was I. Why don't you read the story and find out.

Figure 9–4. *First-Grade Expert Teacher Introducing* Peter's Move *to Six Children in the Middle Reading Group*

other's ideas by raising questions or connecting their ideas to issues brought up during the discussion and justifying their responses.

◆ The teacher made sure that the children understood the plot and sequence of the story up to the climax. She provided an overview of the story structure and a familiar framework for the children so that they could anticipate and predict what may occur.

◆ This teacher was a good listener and an active participant. Her behavior suggested that she could learn from the students. Teachers who have this stance listen carefully to students' conversations and do not assume that they have all the answers.

◆ The teacher carefully selected one word, *stay*, for the children to locate after she asked Mike, "What do you think Peter wants to do?" The teacher used his response to have him locate the word *stay*. The word selected was critical to the main idea of the story and ensured that the children had the language required to get the meaning.

◆ The teacher did not come with a preplanned book introduction, although it was clear that she knew the story well. Her introduction did not interfere with the learner's thinking. She observed and listened to what the children were saying and together they had a genuine conversation. She was dealing with real-world situations and the answers came from the children themselves.

◆ There was a complex interplay among students and collective storytelling in their ongoing conversation that suggested trust and confidence in one another. This interplay promoted the development of various participants as well as the whole group. They were excited and eager to find out if their predictions about how the story ends were correct.

This expert teacher had provided a feed-forward system for the children to anticipate and predict the meaning of the story, which in this case was Peter's sadness, uncertainty, and anxiety about moving to another home. She also engaged the children by drawing on Jason and Patty's past experiences and how they felt about moving. These children identified with the main character in the story. They easily read the story, focusing on

meaning. They expected reading to make sense, which was obvious when Patty monitored her behavior and self-corrected without stopping the flow of the story.

The book introduction serves as the child's feed-forward system. This is Bruner's theory of serial order (which Clay has applied to describe how children learn to read). The child must have an understanding of the main idea of the story in order to connect with the author's message and gain meaning. And as I have discussed throughout this book, when children make emotional connections to the story they are reading and/or writing, they are more likely to comprehend, make inferences, and remember what they read.

Facilitating Expert Teachers' Knowledge, Skill, and Judgment

Several years ago, I was in a large hall listening to a lecture by an internationally known scholar and professor of psychology who has received numerous awards for his contributions to the understanding of the human mind. After the talk, a man stood and asked the professor, "What should I read to understand better how children learn to read?" He replied, "Teach a struggling child to read and then you will know what to read." The man replied, "I don't have time to teach young children." The professor commented, "Then you will not likely understand the complexity of the reading process." The man sat down.

I believe what the professor was trying to communicate is that adults cannot learn how young children develop an efficient processing system to read and write by reading articles and books about becoming literate. The best way to understand the complex learning processes involved in literacy acquisition is from firsthand experience observing changes in low-progress students' behaviors as *you* teach

Effective teaches provide interesting book introductions that make challenging texts accessible to children.

them to construct a complex network of strategies to reading increasing more complex texts. One teacher expressed her journey through this process in the following way:

> I taught first grade for eight years and was a reading specialist for about six years before I enrolled in the RR professional development courses. I had a master's degree in education and a reading specialist certification. But I never understood what it meant to teach young children how to read and write until I taught four of the lowest children in the first grade every day. By the time that year was over I had taught nine children how to read. The other half of the day I was a first-grade classroom teacher. I looked at my first-grade children differently. Some of those first graders were struggling and I would not have identified the problem prior to RR professional development. Mitchell, for example, found it difficult to analyze the sequence of sounds in words while reading. I was able to straighten him out quickly. He would have eventually figured it out on his own, but how much time would he have wasted? Today after fifteen years working with low-achieving students, I learn something new every day. Every time I teach a child struggling to learn, I am forced to look differently at another aspect of the of the reading and writing process and as a result I gain more insights into the complexity of literacy learning.

This teacher learned how to effectively teach low-achieving students to read and write in a year-long series of graduate-level RR courses (Pinnell, Fried, and Estice 1990). The two-semester courses focus on recent theories and research about learning, language development, emergent literacy, phonemic awareness, spelling, comprehension, and reading and writing difficulties. Simultaneously, the teacher works individually with four low-achieving students in a school setting. Similar to the way physicians and surgeons are prepared to work with patients, RR teachers learn how to use their course knowledge to respond to situations while observing and discussing teacher and student interactions from behind a one-way viewing glass. These live demonstration lessons involving a teacher teaching a low-progress student are critical to developing teachers' conceptual and practical knowledge about literacy learning and effective teaching practices.

The demonstration lessons provide the framework within which new knowledge can be associated with prior knowledge in two fundamental ways. First, the RR teachers develop understandings about the reading and writing process by direct observation and analysis of learning-in-progress. They learn how to observe, analyze, and discuss a student's behavior and use that discussion to infer the student's "in the head" processing. The teachers' perceptions and inferences about a student's processing oftentimes arise from different and/or multiple perspectives because they are consciously relating student behaviors from the demonstration lessons to their daily teaching of four RR students. Thus, teachers' discussions about what the observed child controls and needs to learn how to control *next* is grounded in their work with students.

Second, while observing and discussing teacher-student interactions from behind the one-way glass, teachers are encouraged to approximate and generate hypotheses about what the student controls and provide alternative explanations for the student's behavior, with supporting evidence. As they respond to colleagues' inferences about how the teacher is creating opportunities for the student to develop a self-extending system of reading and writing behaviors, teachers begin to collectively construct chains of reasoning to help themselves and each other better understand how beginning readers learn how to learn (Lyons 1994b).

Creating opportunities for teachers to develop chains of reasoning to theoretically explain and infer a student's processing is a gradual and complex process. A teacher-leader[1] is facilitating the conversation among colleagues. The teacher-leader begins to weave together, expand, clarify, and restate fellow teachers' comments so that they move from describing a student's behavior; to inferring the underlying perceptual and cognitive processing of the student signaled by the particular behavior; to thinking theoretically about the student's processing; and finally, to identifying the most powerful teaching procedures for enabling the student to use what he knows to gain new understandings.

Initially the teacher-leader structures the teachers' learning by linking streams of thought. However as the year progresses, teachers learn how to structure their own learning. By collectively constructing chains of reasoning while observing, analyzing, and discussing student-teacher interactions in progress from behind the one-way viewing glass, teachers refine what they already know into a more coherent theory of learning and teaching upon which to act (Lyons 1993, 1994b). They are actively involved in a social construction of knowledge.

After the initial year of training is complete, RR teachers engage in ongoing professional development that focuses on recent research in language, learning, and literacy. Meanwhile, they continue to refine their knowledge and hone their skills by observing and analyzing teacher and student interactions from behind a one-way viewing glass.

Conclusion

Analyses of the teacher-student interactions of the ten expert teachers revealed that they have a complex body of knowledge that enables them to make sound judgments about learning and develop efficient and effective skills to teach the lowest-achieving children to read and write. After observing many lessons, analyzing over sixty videotapes, and interviewing these expert teachers, I found six major points of convergence about how they think, reason, and act.

First, they have a thorough understanding of reading and writing at the acquisition stage and know how these processes change over time as children become more proficient. These understandings permeate the expert teachers' talk, thinking, decision-making, and practice. In addition to this knowledge, the expert teachers know how to facilitate and promote children's learning by adjusting their assistance to meet children's changing level of performance, always keeping in mind the children's emotional needs and their zones of proximal development.

Second, the expert teachers assess children's progress and identify roadblocks to learning. They recognize when children's processing is efficient and when it is not, and create opportunities geared to the limited repertoire of knowledge children bring to the literacy task. Moreover, the expert teachers understand the nature of the problem-solving tasks and determine how children are attempting to solve the reading or writing problem, which helps to pinpoint what the children need to learn *next*.

Third, the expert teachers know how to provide a dynamic, flexible scaffold that assists children in mastering new competencies and when it is too difficult for a child, they adjust the task so the demands at a specific moment are appropriately challenging. Every day they systematically observe and evaluate what children can do independently and use this information to inform their teaching the following day.

Fourth, expert teachers are reflective before, during, and after the lesson. They discuss, analyze, and evaluate the effect of their teaching on children's progress. They make good teaching decisions to assist children "on the run" while teaching and change their plans and actions "on the run" as children's behavior dictates. Expert teachers are able to determine, from a myriad of instructional approaches, the one or two procedures that are most likely to help children to develop a strategy for independent problem solving and recognize when children have acquired a generative processing system.

A fifth characteristic that these expert teachers share is that they never stop working to make the children's experiences positive and rewarding. They understand that in order to learn, children must be attentive, active, and successful. To accomplish this goal, they make a point of knowing the children well, engaging them in meaningful conversations about their interests, attending to their emotional responses and feelings, and following their behavior closely to make sure that they are successful as soon as they begin to work with them.

Finally, these expert teachers have an intangible quality. They convey through their actions and words that these very low-achieving children can and will learn and that they will find a way to teach them. They often commented that they had to reanalyze what they were doing because it was not working and try something else. They were tenacious and committed to finding a way to teach the children to read and write, and they enjoyed the challenge of problem solving. They also comforted the children and reassured them that they were making progress every day.

According to Darling-Hammond (1996) what matters most in student learning is a competent teacher, an individual who has developed the capacity to help the majority of students reach levels of competence and skills that were once thought to be within the reach of only a few. I firmly believe that these expert teachers fit that description and much more. They taught students who were thought to be incapable of learning how to read and write as well as the average children in the classroom.

Providing a list of performance characteristics for other teachers to model and emulate will not ensure students' success. What will ensure success is helping teachers

◆ develop the understanding and ability to focus on the learner, not the method or materials;

◆ collaborate with colleagues to create environments that support optimal learning of every student;

◆ realize that each student has a different way of learning; and

◆ understand that there is no one right way to teach every student how to read and write.

Expert teachers' focus is not on identifying one right method or set of materials that work for all children; that would be a waste of money, time, and effort. Rather, the focus is on acquiring the knowledge and skills to make sound judgments and create environments that scaffold student learning and maximize children's opportunities to learn. Teacher expertise develops case by case through experience. Optimal learning contexts must evolve; they are not mandated.

Endnote

[1] Teacher-leaders (TL) teach the yearlong RR teacher classes. Their training includes RR teacher and TL advanced course work. They continue to work with the lowest-achieving students as long as they are teacher-leaders.

Chapter 10

Putting It All Together: Perspectives on the Brain, Learning, and Teaching

For the last ten years scientific research on the organization, operation, and functions of the brain has accelerated. Advances in technology have enabled neuroscientists to observe and analyze the activity of the conscious brain.

Instead of speculating and making educated guesses about how an individual learns or remembers, neuroscientists can now examine specific changes in the neurons of brains while individuals learn new tasks and recall previously learned information (Ratey 2001). Some neurologists (Damasio 1994, 2000) conclude that we are beginning to unravel the mystery long associated with the concept of mind. Defined in the third edition of Webster's New World Dictionary (Neufeldt 1988) as the "thinking and perceiving part of consciousness," the mind is unique to every individual and encompasses how one thinks, feels, wills, and acts.

In the past, educators have elevated the cognitive aspect of the mind above the emotional aspect, and this has had a profound influence on schooling. Today, research in neuroscience proves that children's home and school experiences produce actual changes in brain function and anatomy (Mate 1999). This suggests that parents and teachers are having an impact on how children's minds grow and are formed every time they interact with them. What parents and teachers do and say can either support or hinder the development of children's malleable minds.

Building anything, including a mind, requires an understanding of how it works. Pediatricians, psychiatrists, and neurologists who routinely work with children experiencing learning difficulties observe the daily emotional and physical stress their young patients experience (Greenspan 1997; Levine 2002; Mate 1999). They are pleading that recent discoveries about the developing mind and workings of the brain become available to those who have the most impact on children's learning—educators and parents (Mate 1999). Medical technology is changing the way we look at the brain. It should be positively transforming our understanding of teaching and learning as well, especially when teaching students struggling to learn.

Teaching children to read and write is critical to the future success and prosperity of people from every cultural community in the world. Educators must not only learn what to teach and how to teach it, they must also know *why* they are doing it. This final chapter discusses five major principles about teaching and learning derived from recent research in neuroscience (Figure 10–1). I believe if parents and teachers incorporate these principles into their daily interactions with children, they will create opportunities for all children to grow, learn, and thrive emotionally, cognitively, and socially.

These five principles are an outgrowth, integration, and expansion of ideas presented in preceding chapters. This chapter (1) describes each principle; (2) discusses why it is important to understand and use each principle to guide parents' and teachers' work with children considered difficult to teach; and (3) draws educational implications and applications for each principle so that parents and teachers can create environments that maximize children's learning potential.

The Brain Is Complex

The first principle derived from recent discoveries in neuroscience is that the brain is a very complex, adaptive, working assembly of neurons that interact to form thoughts and actions. Moreover, this complex working system has the capacity to function on many different levels and in many different ways simultaneously. Because the brain is a parallel processor, different regions and components of the brain are interacting at the same time on the same sensory input from the environment. Thus, learning engages the entire physiology of the brain at once. The first four chapters of this book describe, through example, how various regions of the brain interact simultaneously to produce thoughts, emotions, memories, and imagination as the entire assembly of neurons interacts with and exchanges sensory information with its environment.

Why Is It Important to Understand the Complexity of the Brain?

It is important to know about the brain's complexity because understanding this phenomenon can improve educational practice, especially for children who are struggling to learn. In many classrooms, children who do not learn required material in a specified amount of time are considered to have a deficit; that is, something is wrong with their brains. Teachers and parents begin to look for reasons for children's learning problems. Some believe that heredity plays a role in their inability to learn, and therefore do not expect much from the child's educational experiences. Recent discoveries about how the brain is organized and functions have debunked three previously held beliefs and challenged scientists' thinking about learning and the mind-brain-body connections during the learning process. Once revealed and understood, they should change how parents and teachers work with children struggling to learn.

1. The Brain Is Wired for Life. The long-held belief that the brain is hardwired at birth and remains that way until old age is inaccurate. Recent

1. The Brain Is Complex.
2. The Brain Is Social and Emotional.
3. Emotions and Thoughts Interact, Shape Each Other, and *Cannot* Be Separated.
4. Learning Is an Individual Constructive Process.
5. Children's Self-Concept Determines Their Motivation to Learn.

Figure 10–1. *Five Principles of Learning Derived from Recent Mind/Brain Research*

research has shown that the brain is remarkably plastic. For example, it has been found after studying hundreds of stroke patients that the brain can often compensate for damage to speech and motor centers by rerouting nerve signals through new pathways. This finding is consistent with my mother's full recovery from her first stroke (see Chapter 1). If the brains of individuals who have been traumatized by a stroke can be rerouted to form new pathways to learn, the intact brains of students certainly can reorganize to learn something new in the same way. Every child has the potential to learn how to read and write.

2. Individuals Are Born with a Set Number of Neurons, Which Die as One Ages.

The idea that neurons cannot regenerate is also inaccurate. Researchers investigating the thinking and memory systems of aging adults (McKhann and Albert 2002) proved that the adult brain contains cells capable of dividing and becoming healthy new neurons. This discovery was even more dramatic because these viable new cells were found in the hippocampus, a brain region crucial to memory and learning in individuals over seventy years old.

If neural cells in the hippocampus region of the brain can divide and reproduce anew in men and women who have reached their senior years, how is it possible that some children "lack brain power" and therefore cannot learn as well as others? How many parents and teachers have given up on children because they thought they couldn't learn? Examples from expert teachers described in Chapters 4, 5, 6, 7, 8, and 9 prove otherwise.

3. Studying Individual Parts of the Brain Explains the Whole.

Until recently, regions of the brain were studied in isolation in order to explain cognitive functions or operations such as learning and memory. New discoveries in neuroscience reveal that earlier studies were based on faulty assumptions about how individuals learn. With the assistance of technology, scientists today are convinced that emergent properties of the brain as a whole working system cannot be recognized or understood when only parts of the brain are examined (Ratey 2001). Until educators come to terms with the multifaceted nature of the brain's functions and with the fact that learning involves the integration of the whole brain, including its emotional and cognitive dimensions, students who are having difficulty learning will continue to fail.

Implications from Recent Brain Research for Working with Children Struggling to Learn

These three myths about learning and the brain have influenced educational practice for years. Educators generally painted a dismal picture of teaching the lowest-achieving students. The longer students failed to learn to read and write, they said, the harder it will be to teach them. Moreover, it will be virtually impossible for them to catch up and read and write as well as their peers.

Fortunately, this bleak view is misguided. Recent research has shown that the brain is highly plastic and capable of reorganizing and rebuilding itself. Furthermore, the evidence strongly suggests that the earlier children are provided help, the quicker they will catch up to their peers and learn from regular classroom instruction (Clay 1991, 2002). But this can only occur when children are working in nonthreatening, emotionally supportive environments with teachers who have high expectations that the children will learn and that they can teach them (Levine 2002).

The Brain Is Social and Emotional

The second critical new insight from brain research is that social relationships and interactions with others profoundly influence learning. For the first two years of life, infants' brains are in the most flexible, pliable, impressionable, and accepting state that they will ever be. The social learning that takes place in infancy through the mutual expression of affect between parent and child impacts the child's future learning potential (Gopnik, Meltzoff, and Kuhl 1999). Furthermore, attunement affects the development of affective communication and is partially dependent upon social opportunities and emotional connectedness with others.

Why Is It Important to Understand the Social-Emotional Brain?

Neurologists (Damasio 1994, 2000) have found that the implicit emotional memories processed by the amygdala system of the brain connect to the hippocampal system, producing a memory of the experience. If the social interactions involved during the experience are traumatic, the implicit emotional memory-processing system operating through the amygdala system and the explicit memory about the emotional interaction function in parallel, resulting in diminished learning (LeDoux 1996). The example of my futile attempts to learn trigonometry discussed in Chapter 4 makes this point. Conversely, when interactions between parent and children or teachers and students are positive, emotional connectiveness occurs and learning is enhanced. The following example demonstrates how positive affective interactions can actually result in an increase in the development of brain tissue.

Gail and Her Son—A Parent's Story During the summer of 1997, I developed and taught a graduate-level course at the University of Maine. Gail enrolled in a one-week summer institute connected with the course that met from 8:30 A.M. until 4:30 P.M. every day. The course was designed to help teachers and parents learn how to create contexts for effective literacy learning and teaching. It was an introductory course to the developing brain with emphasis on the relationships between the emotional, social, and cognition dimensions of learning. Students read research and current theories related to the neuropsychology of learning, social/emotional learning, and effective teaching. The students submitted a final paper that synthesized the research that was presented and discussed in class and drew personal or professional applications for their work with children and adults. Gail's paper was one of the most memorable ones I received. The following excerpt is printed with her permission.

Making an Emotional Connection. Will They Learn Better?

I believe that recent developments in brain research has brought teaching to the brink of a transformation, letting teachers move beyond the tradition and folk-wisdom to a blending of science and art. What does this mean to me? There are many developments in brain research, but the most poignant for me are those concerning the emotional component of learning potential. I had never planned for or thought about the emotional piece of learning before. I have always been aware of the need for my second-grade classroom to be a safe place, where students could be comfortable, able to take some risks, but all in a tightly controlled setting. The differ-

ence in my classroom this year (after taking the summer course) has been a major effort on my part to create an atmosphere of trust, happiness, joyful activities, meaningful tasks, and to provide lots of opportunities for success. I now believe that new learning needs to be celebrated—attaching a joyful connection to new knowledge, both my students' and mine. This emotional piece will help them learn better and me learn how to teach better.

Why do I believe this way? A better question might be, how could I believe otherwise? My current philosophy and practice have evolved as a result of the course work I had this summer and personal experiences I have had during the three months following the course. The personal experience involved a day-long series of tests on my eight-year-old son by a pediatric neurologist.

My son has been diagnosed with many development problems. At age three, the work began when we realized he couldn't hear. One doctor led to another as we tried to get his hearing fixed. We were referred to speech and language therapists, occupational therapists, special education teachers, and finally psychiatrists. Mark's hearing difficulties were coupled with delays in language acquisition, fine and gross motor delays, and problems with math, writing, and social interactions at school.

During the course, I experienced an emotional response to what we were learning about at-risk students, the problems with medicating children, and the proliferation of AD(H)D diagnosis for boys from single-parent households. One day after class I told you briefly of my son. At the time, I was struggling with a new psychiatrist wanting to medicate Mark with Ritalin and antidepressants. You asked if Mark had been evaluated by a pediatric neurologist and he had not. I made the appointment that day.

The newfound understandings I received during your summer course on how the brain works made my discussions with the pediatric neurologist incredibly meaningful and gave me the background to ask some questions that helped clarify my understanding of my son. After the entire test, the neurologist informed me that Mark tested consistently two years behind his peers in everything except reading. In reading he tested slightly above grade level. The tests included language development, math, reading, writing, social, fine motor, and gross motor skills. We were baffled by his reading ability and talked about the possible explanations for some time.

My initial questions revolved around discovering any interventions or therapies that could bring some of his weak spots closer to age appropriate levels. Dr. Rioux gently explained that with all the interventions Mark had received (speech and language therapy, occupational therapy, and special education support), he had probably made all the gains he could. He suggested that those school based interventions would have shown better results if there was any hope of them working. Dr. Rioux held a similar belief as you do, that is, the way "in" to children with major learning problems (for him, boys with developmental delays) was through some kind of emotional connection. Based on our conversation, he felt that Mark was not happy in school. Mark held very negative feelings about school and his role there. Dr. Rioux believed that Mark would always be a couple of years behind.

I asked Dr. Rioux how he could explain Mark's development in reading, and there came the magic word. He hypothesized that for Mark, there was a strong emotional attachment to reading. He explained that our reading time together (every day at bedtime) was probably the "ultimate intervention" because of the emotional connection we shared. He went on to talk about the implications for Mark's development through puberty and beyond.

Dr. Rioux suggested that the most powerful new learning for Mark would come through something he loved. During the whole discussion, I had mental pictures of Luria's map of the functional organization of the brain and the discussion we had about how positive emotions helped to myelinate the pathways in the brain. Being a skeptic at heart, I decided to dig a little further and see what I could find out about the connection between emotions and cognitive development, which I was now beginning to believe.

The more I thought about what Dr. Rioux called "the ultimate intervention," the more I wondered how it worked and why. If I could think in terms of making that kind of connection with my own children and my students, perhaps I could make it easier for them to learn. I decided to reread the readings from the summer course. Everywhere I looked I found evidence of the power of emotion on cognitive processes. Not every author called this connection the same thing, but different voices all led to the same conclusion.

Meadows (1993) says that the social aspect of teaching and learning cannot be ignored. These social occasions help students to make the emotional connections required to learn. Rogoff (1990) believes that along with this social relationship comes great responsibility for decisions that include the tacit structuring of everything teachers say and do and the arrangements of the activities. If teachers believe that activities must be meaningful to warrant attention and lead to satisfaction, then a more thoughtful approach to each activity given to students is required (Rogoff 1990). Marie Clay wrote that before decisions about instruction can be made, it is a teacher's responsibility to give considerable thought to the environment she creates for each student. Ensuring that each task makes sense and offers the student an opportunity to make meaning will make that task worthy of the students' attention (Clay 1991). Durden and Mackay (1995) contended that it is the teacher's responsibility to make the optimal match between students' needs (both emotional and academic) and the appropriate challenge for them.

[Gail goes on to write about the changes she has made to the culture and environment in her second-grade classroom as a result of the new insights she has gained about the importance of attending to the emotional and social dimensions of learning. Her paper concludes with the following paragraph.]

As I bring my discussion of this very personal journey to a close, I would like to say that the summer institute course literally changed my life in many ways. It came at a time when I was exploring my understanding of my own son and these insights lit a rocket underneath me. I have received an incredible amount of feedback from colleagues and parents at their delight in the individual attitudes my students are showing about school and the personality my classroom has developed. I work hard each day to see each student as an individual, and to do everything I can to meet their individual needs. At present, I have never felt so fulfilled from what I do each day. I have the confidence that lets me go to sleep every night knowing my judgments are enlightened ones.

Mark's and Gail's Lives Five Years Later Mark is thirteen years old and will begin eighth grade in the fall of 2002. He is well traveled and well read. Mark still experiences some learning difficulties; however, standardized tests scores show that he is reading and comprehending as well as students in college. Although he continues to struggle with peer relationships, Mark has developed a secure friendship with one boy. They share a love of history and current events, and while some students are playing four square at recess, it is not unusual for the two of them to be having a discussion about politics. Mark enjoys spending time with adults, and outside school, he is poised and self-confident.

In the summer of 1999, Gail was transferred from teaching first and second grade to fifth grade. I asked her about the transition from teaching primary to intermediate age students. She wrote the following response:

It was a scary time for me. So much of my life had been spent learning about how young children learn—I wasn't sure I would find the same kind of success with beginning middle school students. At our particular school, fifth grade was a time of transition for our students. Grades 1–4 are all multi-aged. Grade 5 is the first time the students have an opportunity to form an identity as a group. It is the first year they receive grades and can participate in our school's music and sports programs.

In fifth grade most students are beginning puberty. It is the beginning of a whole new phase of their emotional lives. I discovered with great relief that students in fifth grade need to have an emotional connection to their learning, just as they did in first and second grade. Fifth graders are beginning to learn about themselves as people, forming ideas about likes and dislikes. It became clear in that first year that fifth graders were ready, willing and able to pursue independent studies.

It was the beginning of a whole new phase of my own professional development as well. Giving students the opportunity to pursue their own interests through inquiry-based classrooms was proof enough for me that when students study what they have questions about, the learning that results is genuine and lasting. For me it's further proof that when there is a positive emotional involvement attached to any learning opportunity, student achievement goes through the roof.

Parents talk about how happy they are with their children's performance—watching them rise to challenges over and over again. The students leaving fifth grade attended science and math camps in the summer (by choice). They demonstrated that they were developing a love of learning.

As Gail's personal story conveys, the experiences she and Mark shared while reading and responding to books throughout his early childhood and elementary school years paid huge dividends in his academic, social, and emotional development. Gail's understanding of the emotional side of learning early on in his life enabled her to respond empathetically to his pressing needs both cognitively and emotionally. He was able to approach new challenges confidently and at the same time draw upon her for support and help when needed.

Gail's experiences with Mark had an impact on her teaching first-, second-, and fifth-grade students. Just as she did with her son, Mark, Gail is helping these students develop an inner sense of who they are, what they feel, and what is important in their lives. This can only be done in an environment in which the emotional and cognitive dimensions of learning are embedded in classroom activities. In this rich context, students are able to become actively involved in the process of learning. They will gain pleasure and satisfaction from academic content and, out of that stimulation, acquire intrinsic motivation to continue learning.

The Social and Emotional Brain: Implications

In the last two years, studies using sophisticated brain scans have revealed that good instruction can actually result in positive changes in brain structure and increase neural development (Ratey 2001). It is also possible to see increases in brain tissue when parts of the brain get properly stimulated after having been neglected. This is incredible information and positive news for the thousands of parents and teachers working with children struggling to learn. I would hasten to add, however, for instruction to be good, teachers and parents must attend to the affective as well as the cognitive dimensions of learning. Gail's story and the expert teachers' description of teaching discussed in each chapter in this book provide some guidance on how to accomplish this feat.

Emotions and Thoughts Interact, Shape Each Other, and <u>Cannot</u> Be Separated

The third principle emerging from new technological advances in mind/brain processing is that emotions and thoughts are processed simultaneously, from birth throughout life. Until recently, the majority of books that focus on cognitive development did not mention the interplay of emotion and cognition. This glaring omission reflects an almost complete failure to recognize any affective streak in cognitive development (Meadows 1993). Research in neuroscience (Damasio 2000) has proven that cognition (reasoning) cannot be separated from emotion and that they are totally dependent on each other for learning.

Why Is It Important to Understand How Emotions and Thoughts Commingle?

Recent findings in neurological research (Damasio 2000; Levine 2002; Ratey 2001) provide hard evidence that what children learn is heavily influenced and organized by emotions and that emotions color how the information is received, assembled, interpreted, understood, and used. Furthermore, these positive or negative emotional reactions to events are observable in infancy. Infants react emotionally to notable changes in their environment: if their goals are blocked, they react negatively; if their goals are reached and confirmed, they respond positively.

In the first chapter in this book, I discuss my son Kenny's cognitive and emotional development as he learned to identify and categorize buttons found in my grandmother's button jar. Observing his behavior once again, we can speculate on how his emotions and thoughts were interconnected and could not be separated.

The Button Jar Experience Revisited The moment he saw the buttons scatter on the floor, Kenny showed great joy and excitement as he translated the sensory input from his eyes and ears into thoughts. His facial expressions, screams of delight, rhythmic voice, dancing eyes, and uncontrolled movement of his entire body as he watched the buttons scatter on the floor were emotional responses to what he saw and heard.

Kenny immediately took the initiative to crawl after each button. He raced successfully to a button, but had difficulty coordinating his fingers to pick it up. Kenny's frustration showed in the frown on his face and the anger in his voice as he babbled at the buttons and me. Gradually he became more skilled at picking up the buttons and returning them to the jar. His facial expressions and the animation in his voice as he babbled nonstop were emotional reactions to feeling successful. As the tasks became more complex (e.g., finding the one button that did not belong in a specific pile), he was working toward a different goal. With each new challenge and successful completion of a task, Kenny became more animated and excited about the accomplishments, suggesting that his thoughts and emotions were working in concert. He was also functioning to maintain and respond to my emotional responses, which were evident in my facial expressions, tone of voice, and body movements.

Together we were also developing an attachment or bonding with each other. Kenny was developing an internalized working model of how to relate to me, and I was attempting to try and figure out how to relate to him. As we both came to know each other, we were better able to understand each other's expectations and limits. This was apparent when we had our first major confrontation.

Even though he could not yet talk, Kenny could make himself understood. He communicated joy and happiness when we were both picking up the buttons and putting them into the jar. He interpreted my response to his actions by smiling and laughing as we put each button away. His emotional response to our interactions changed, however, when I had to put the button jar away because he was continuing to put buttons in his mouth. He was mad at me and at the same time probably sad about relinquishing a positive relationship and interactions we shared. Kenny showed helplessness, frustration, and anger by throwing a tantrum when he could not get his way.

Once he realized that I could not be convinced to continue playing the game, the tantrum stopped and he started to cry. This response made me feel terrible; however, I knew not to give in or "crying to get my own way" behavior would continue every time he wanted something. I did, however, reassure him in a positive, calm way, that we would continue to play with the buttons once he stopped putting them in his mouth. I also reminded him that we stopped playing because I was afraid he could choke on the button and get hurt. I believe he understood what was required of him to continue to play with the buttons because his expression changed and the crying stopped.

Kenny's thoughts and interpretations of my thoughts were governed by and expressed through emotion. Early childhood research reveals that infants are extremely aware of and sensitive to nonverbal expressions of emotion because that is the only way they have to understand their environment and individual's responses and reactions to situations that take place in this context (Greenspan 1997). Kenny was beginning to develop the ability to use emotional signals appropriately. He was also learning how to attend particularly closely to emotion-arousing situations and my response to his behavior while engaging is various activities with the buttons.

The emotional confrontation Kenny and I experienced while playing the button jar game continued to reverberate long after the event. He learned that there was a reason why the button jar had to be put away for awhile and that crying would not help to change my mind. I learned that if I gave him a reason for a decision he was more likely to respond in a positive manner and that it was important to his social and emotional development to hold him accountable for his behavior. I believe the emotional climate that was set that day paid dividends throughout the years.

Implications

Researchers believe that thinking and reasoning evolve to a highly complex level because individuals have to live in social groups and what they learn depends upon their ability to observe, interpret, and use emotional signals appropriately (Damasio 2000; Meadows 1993). Two critical findings about teaching and learning derive from the research showing that emotion and thought cannot be separated and that learning depends on an individual's ability to interpret and respond to emotional signals. First, what children learn depends on how parents and teachers communicate verbally and nonverbally. Second, learning is profoundly influenced by the nature of the social relationships children have with parents, caregivers, and teachers.

Children Observe and Interpret Nonverbal Signals The idea that it is impossible to separate thoughts from emotions has been repeatedly proven in studies of the brain (see discussion in Chapters 1 and 4). Research in neuroscience also reveals that the brain processes both information that is conscious and within the immediate focus of attention, and information that emerges in the larger peripheral areas of the sensory cortex where teaching and conversation occur (Ratey 2001). It is the unspoken words and actions, moreover, that determine how children interpret parents' and teachers' feelings about what they are saying and doing. For example, a large sigh and frown from a parent who is repeatedly asked by her young child to read a book signals to the child that reading a story is a chore, a job to be done. According to Mate (1999), children who struggle to learn tend to be most sensitive and react more strongly to parents' and teachers' nonverbal cues.

Adults reveal their inner attitudes, beliefs, and prejudices every time they interact with children, and most children read the subtext. These social exchanges and interactions have a powerful impact on students' ability to attend, sustain attention, and learn, which in turn has an impact on their motivation to learn, what they learn, and how much they learn. Due to a myriad of reasons, parents and teachers may not be able to change their feelings, but they should pay attention to the emotional subtext of their lessons and interactions with children.

Small verbal and nonverbal exchanges between parent and child or teacher and student have an emotional subtext. For example, if a three-year-old becomes frustrated while putting a puzzle together and asks her busy father for help, she could receive two different responses that have two different subtexts. Her father might stop what he is doing and approach his child immediately and with excitement in his voice ask, "How can I help you?" The subtext of this response is that the child is more important than the work father is doing, he understands his child's frustration and wants to alleviate it quickly, he is delighted to be asked for help, and he will be here to help whenever the child becomes frustrated again.

Another reply may convey a different message to the child. The father looks at his frustrated child and says in a loud angry voice, "Don't bother me now, can't you see that I am busy? I have many more important things to do than help you with a puzzle. Figure it out for yourself." The subtext of this response is that the father's job is more important than helping the child put the puzzle together, and he is not available for help. When the child finds difficulty, it is up to her to figure out a solution. Children who routinely receive the second response begin to believe this to be typical behavior from adults, and it may mold their emotional expectations about relationships for many years or until another adult or peer changes their expectation (Goleman 1995). If the father is not able to stop what he is doing when the child asks for help, a better response would be, "Please wait a few minutes until I am done working on the lawnmower and I will be happy to help you."

Social Relationships Profoundly Influence Learning The connectedness of the cognitive and emotional areas of the brain (see Chapter 4; Damasio 1994, 2000) implies that there is an intimate and immediate interplay between emotion and cognition in both the short-term and long-term interactions that take place in early childhood. As O'Leary (1997) documents in her descriptions of teaching five low-achieving children how to read and write, some children struggling to learn are raised in loving families, but have had few opportunities to interact with print prior to entering first grade. Other children are raised in highly literate families with high expectations and many literate opportunities in preschool, but are still the lowest-achieving children in first grade.

Teachers must be able to meet the individual learning needs of all low-achieving children, no matter what their cultural background or literacy history. They must understand that children learn to read and write in many different ways and assemble different working neural systems as they become literate (Clay 1998, 2001). In order for children to be successful, teachers must provide social and emotional support while creating different learning environments to address children's idiosyncratic needs.

Due to the complexity of reading and writing processes, children must acquire the ability to select from a repertoire of strategies ones that are appropriate for a certain set of circumstances. A more expert person must carefully scaffold children whose repertoire of strategies is very limited

Expert teachers provide emotional support to children.

construct representations of their experience through language, symbols, music, art, and so on. From a constructivist perspective, learning is a self-regulatory, self-organizing, and internal restructuring process through which individuals negotiate meaning by representing their ideas and experiences with symbols that are specific to their culture and environment (Wertsch 1991).

Studies of how the brain organizes and processes information reveal the constructive nature of complex processes involved in learning to read. Anderson (1992) found that myelination of neurons in the visual cortex and the development of the frontal lobes in the cerebral cortex enable individuals to form mental images of abstract symbols, such as letters and words, and from these to construct knowledge and understandings. Individuals can then act on these mental images and reflect on how they acted upon them, and through this process acquire new or transformed knowledge and understandings.

Children must not, however, learn solely how to attend to and process the information contained in the print (letters, spaces, words) on the page. They must also comprehend the meaning in those abstracted print symbols used to form words on the pages of a text, which is an individual constructive process in itself. The text is the preliminary blueprint on which the construction of meaning is initiated, but the information inside the text, that is, the print symbols, the linguistic structures, and so forth, must be combined with information in the mind of the reader, which is outside of the text. The information in the mind of the individual reader is derived from the reader's prior knowledge and experiences. It is in the individual's constructive processes of combining information *in* the text with information *outside* of the text—in the reader's mind—that a complete and adequate representation of the author's meaning is formed (Spiro et al. 1995).

The notion that reading is an individual constructive process is also reflected in Clay's (1991)

or inflexible until they are able to support their own processing when the expert other is no longer available. In the interview in Figure 10–2, one expert teacher, Mary, discusses how she established a positive interactive context to scaffold a difficult-to-teach student by demonstrating the task and making it easy and manageable. Mary created opportunities for Collin to be successful the first time they worked together. She set clear expectations, made tasks simpler when necessary to prevent frustration, and held him accountable for his behavior. This kind of context facilitates learning because positive affective social interactions are initiated early in lessons.

Learning Is an Individual Constructive Process

The fourth principle supported by neuroscience is the notion that learning is a constructive individual process. Constructivism is a theory about knowledge and learning that is based on the later work of Piaget (1977) and Vygotsky (1978) as well as the thinking of those who have studied the role of representation in learning (Bruner 1973, 1986; Gardner 1985; Goodman 1984). Human beings

CAROL: Mary, of the hundreds of videotapes of hard-to-teach children I analyzed, Collin was by far the most difficult. What made him so tough to teach?

MARY: He had great difficulty writing and could not write his name legibly. He had difficulty holding a pencil and moving it to write. But that wasn't his biggest problem. The biggest problem was his behavior.

CAROL: Did you notice a difference in his behavior once he was able to control the movement of the pencil to write his name?

MARY: Yes, once he was able to control his pencil he did start working harder. He noticed that he was able to do something that was really hard for him to do. In Roaming Around the Known, he could not form any letters. I had to put a sticker of an animal on a piece of paper and then say, "I'm going to make tall grass for the lion to sit on." I would make straight lines that started at the top and came down. Then he would make the straight lines but I had to remind him to always start at the top of the paper and come straight down. Then I would say, " Oh, I am going to draw some rocks." I would draw circles on the paper and then he would do it. That's how I got him engaged and able to control some movements in making letter like forms. I would say "Oh, let's put some berries on the grass" so he could make a dot. He was not writing any letters, except C in his name and that became the key letter to build on for him. When he was writing with me he would work, but in the classroom he did very little. He would draw and scribble some letters. I thought the biggest stumbling block to his learning would be motor development, but once I started with the letter formation he started to make progress and he saw it himself. I showed him how to use a piece of tag board for a spacer. I never handed him the spacer but just set it on the table for him to use. One day he noticed that he had written three words and he did not use the spacer. He said "I didn't even use that spacer." I said, "Well that must mean you don't need it anymore, you're spacing with your eyes."

CAROL: You made the task easy for him from the first day he put a mark on the paper by demonstrating how to make the grass from the top down. That was a manageable and successful task on which to build. Those little successes add up and probably motivated him to continue. The movement pattern helped him know where to attend and what to attend to as he made those basic marks needed to form letters.

MARY: Yes, and his behavior was better when he was writing also. But behavior was still the biggest problem. Getting him to problem-solve. As soon as he had a problem he got frustrated. He would beg me sometimes. He would say, "Tell me what this says, and I will read it to you." But I knew that he had this wonderful memory so if I did that he could remember what I said and he would never learn how to read. He could remember the story and get it almost right when he read the next day, but he wasn't learning how to read. I had to get him out of language pattern books because he would pick up the pattern right away. He would read it but not look at the words.

CAROL: How was his directional behavior in reading? Could he control left-to-right directional movement by pointing to each word?

MARY: He had difficulty with one-to-one matching and pointing to the words. He could not point with his index finger because his fingers were short and his hands were so chubby. When he pointed to the words he covered them up and then could not see them. So I asked him to point with his little finger and that helped him. After awhile, I asked him to read with his eyes but he resisted. So I made a deal with him to use his eyes on one book only, to which he said OK.

CAROL: You made the task more manageable and he successfully read one book with his eyes.

MARY: Yes, and then one day he read two books and then three books without pointing. I don't think he realized it. For every shift he made, I said we would start with just one thing that was a bit hard for him.

CAROL: You held him accountable for a more advanced task and set him up for a little success.

MARY: Yes, in a smaller task. I knew that he would eventually use his eyes alone to read all his books.

Figure 10–2. *Teaching Collin—When Behavior Is the Major Problem*

CAROL: Collin's writing has improved so much that you would never have know that he had a difficult time forming letters. (See Figure 7–6.) Yet it was through writing that he learned to read.

MARY: Yes, and writing is where he was successful first.

CAROL: Why was writing so beneficial to his ability to read?

MARY: I think because it was easier to see progress. When he was finished writing a sentence, he had a product, he could see something that he accomplished. Collin had very good ideas and language skills and I supported him a lot. He wanted to use longer, harder words and I just wrote them in so that his wonderful stories would not be simplified. He could always read the sentence because it was his language. But he did not show his classroom teacher what he could do. (See Figure 7–5.) When I found out what he was doing in the classroom, the teacher and I talked and we made sure he put effort into his classroom writing as well.

CAROL: He could see his improvement over time. You didn't try to simplify the sentence, which showed you valued his ideas. He also had you, a captive audience, to read the sentence. He knew somebody was going to read the sentence, which probably built his self-esteem. You gave him a purpose for writing. In the classroom his journal was not read by anyone so he might not have been motivated to show what he could do. But some teachers resist asking struggling students to write a story. Why?

MARY: I don't know but I think some educators are missing the boat. Writing keeps kids interested and holds their interest because it is their story. The sentence holds the meaning and structure and frees their attention to deal with the print and it is the print that is difficult for them. After Collin learned to hear and record sounds in words it was much easier for him to read.

CAROL: Throughout my analysis of the videotapes and during the interviews with expert teachers, I found some traits you shared. First, you all had high expectations for children and your ability to teach them to read and write. Second, you all showed great determination in finding out how you can reach and teach the children. Third, you set expectations for them. What expectations did you set for Collin?

MARY: One expectation I had was that he did not have tantrums in school anymore. He was in first grade and he was done with that. Now it was time to learn to write and read. And he agreed.

CAROL: Did you set expectations for Collin in reading and writing?

MARY: Yes, but I always had to give him a reason for what I was asking him to do.

CAROL: Maybe resistant children like Collin need to know why you are asking them to do something. Saying, "Do this because I said so," or "Because I am your teacher" isn't going to work.

MARY: Right. You do it because you will learn how to figure out a word. And once kids see that you were right and that they were learning how to figure out a word, then they would abide by what you were prompting them to do.

CAROL: You also helped the children reflect on their processing. Not all the time, just when you thought that the child might not know what he did that was right.

MARY: Yes, you need to clarify the children's learning. Collin had a consistent habit of looking at me as soon as he had difficulty during reading. The consistent appealing for help took his eyes off the text and interrupted any chance for successful problem solving. We made an agreement that during his first reading of his new story for the day, I would sit directly behind him instead of beside him. This would help him remember not to look at me but would also assure him that I was watching carefully. I would give him brief praise when he took problem-solving action on his own or I would suggest to him a possible action to take to solve an unfamiliar word. At the end of the first reading of the story, we would have a chat about what he did well on his own and what he learned how to do that might help another time. So far, Collin is the only child I have taught that I had to move my seat to help them break the habit of looking at me for help and instead learn to do independent problem solving.

Figure 10–2 *continued.*

CAROL: You give children an awareness of what they have done. We all do things without thinking about it. And then someone makes a positive comment about your work and you think, I never thought about that before.

MARY: Yes, that happened to me. A colleague was watching me teach an RR child who was a second-language learner and said that I did a nice job of restating the sentence in a clear phrase so that the child could think of the next part to write. I never thought about what I was doing, but he noticed and commented how much it helped the child. Now I am very aware of that behavior and encourage other teachers to not ask the child what is the next word, but restate a phrase of the sentence and that next word will just come out of their mouth.

Figure 10–2 *continued.*

definition of reading: "Within the directional constraints of the printer's code, language and visual perception responses are purposefully directed by the reader in some integrated way to the problem of extracting meaning from cues in a text, in sequence, so that the reader brings a maximum of understanding to the author's message" (6). From this perspective, learning is a constructive process of meaning making that is unique to the individual.

Why Is It Important to Understand the Constructive Nature of Learning?

I believe there are five critical reasons why understanding the constructive nature of learning is critical to parenting and teaching (Figure 10–3).

1. Children Construct Conceptual Knowledge

It is only within the constructive process that children develop conceptual knowledge. Parents and teachers cannot do it for them. When children learn a concept, they are able to self-organize and independently generalize the learned concept to another context, which is at the heart of learning to become independent and self-regulated.

For example, to read a simple book in English requires that the emergent reader learn several concepts about direction. The left page is read before the right page; start at the top of page and read to the bottom of page; read each line of print from left to right; when you get to the end of the first line of print return to the left of the next line and start reading again; always read from the left to the right across a word. Each concept is taught by guiding the movement of the child's hand while reading. Through repeated patterns of movement, the child will automatically learn directional behavior and in time her brain will form a memory trace of these sequence of movements.

Concepts about direction will be held in long-term memory to be recalled without conscious thought. The child's brain had to construct these movement patterns to develop the memory trace. Therefore the focus of instruction should be on concept development that is generative, rather than on discrete skills.

2. Children Construct Conceptual Knowledge by Engaging in Concrete, Contextually Meaningful, Problem-Solving Activities

Parents and teachers are in ideal positions to create environments where children can engage in problem-solving activities that enable them to construct possible responses, raise their own questions, construct their own concepts and strategies, and take ownership of their ideas. A critical factor in de-

◆ Children construct conceptual knowledge.
◆ Children construct conceptual knowledge by engaging in concrete, contextually meaningful, problem-solving activities.
◆ Children assimilate previously learned information to learn new concepts and information.
◆ To construct their own understandings, children must engage in a sustained focused conversation with a more capable other.
◆ Learning involves active children reorganizing their thinking and constructing knowledge.

Figure 10–3. *What Teachers and Parents Should Know About the Constructive Nature of Learning*

termining how successful children will become in acquiring conceptual knowledge is the competence of adults to scaffold their thinking. Parents and teachers who demonstrate the task and engage the child in active participation facilitate the constructive process (Clay and Cazden 1990; Rodgers 2000).

A mother who takes a toddler's finger and points to each word while reading, "Where is the puppy going to look for his food?" helps the child develop directionality, a concept critical to reading. When she asks, "Where do you think the puppy is going to look for the food?" the child will learn how to think about and answer the problem. The child learns that her opinions are accepted and valued and that reading involves predicting what might happen in the story.

3. Children Assimilate Previously Learned Information to Learn New Concepts and Information

Once parents and teachers understand the nature of the constructive process, they will realize that learning new information must occur within the context of what an individual already knows and be assimilated into previously learned information so that it can be used in a different situation. The mother's question to her toddler is providing an opportunity for the child to use prior experiences she has had feeding her puppy to predict where the dog dish might be found. The mother has seized an opportunity to teach the child concepts critical to becoming literate, that is, how to use prior knowledge to anticipate, predict, and infer what might happen in a story.

If learning involves *self*-organization and internal *self*-structuring of an assembly of neurons in the brain, some might ask, What do social interaction and language mean to learning? The simple answer is: everything—if the conversation engages the learners in problem-solving experiences such as this mother has done and the scaffold helps children develop more complex reasoning and become independent. In an award-winning research study, Rodgers (2002) found that the type and quality of the teacher talk within scaffolded instruction determined if the lowest-achieving RR students became successful independent readers. This finding supports an earlier experimental study designed to examine the effectiveness of one-to-one instruction in RR as compared to three other instructional models for early intervention (Pinnell et al. 1994).

4. To Construct Their Own Understandings, Children Must Engage in a Sustained Focused Conversation with a More Capable Other

The mutual compatibility of individuals' language and use of words would not be possible without social interaction. The process that leads to such capability is not one of telling, but a process that gradually evolves until it achieves a relative fit and understanding between individuals. It is critical that parents and teachers learn how to negotiate with children so that they can facilitate this process.

For example, Kenny's definition of *crowd*, which he acquired after we observed a crowd at the parade, was idiosyncratic and not appropriately used the following morning when he tried to describe a man's face (see Chapter 3 for a discussion of this example). Through our conversation about the word and its appropriate use, however, Kenny began to systematize and generalize this new knowledge and understand when to use the word and in what context. Through repeated use and reassurance that others could understand what he meant when he used the word *crowd*, Kenny learned how to use the word in context. I doubt that these understandings would have come about, especially at this time in his young life, without our conversations.

5. Learning Involves Active Children Reorganizing Their Thinking and Constructing Knowledge

When teachers and parents understand that learning is a constructive process, not a maturation process, they modify their attitudes about teaching (von Glasersfeld 1995, 1996). They begin to realize that children may perceive their environment in ways that are very different from that intended by the teacher or parent. For example, one teacher described an incident when she asked the child to show her the first part of the word and he showed her the first letter of the word. When she said, "No that isn't the first part of the word, that is the first letter of the word," the child replied angrily, "Well, how many letters are in the first part . . . two, three, four?" After the student's question, the teacher realized that she had assumed that he knew what she meant when she said, "Show me the first part of the word." That child's question forced the teacher to rethink the language she used and the tasks she asked students to do. The teacher also realized the importance of showing or demonstrating a concept before expecting the child to respond successfully.

Applying Constructivism to Education

Learning is not the *result* of development; it *is* development (Vygotsky 1978). To learn, children construct their own meaning by inventing and self-organizing. To understand development from a sociocultural perspective, teachers and parents must examine how children's participation in an activity changes over time (Clay 2001; Rogoff 1990). Moreover, they must provide opportunities for students to shift their understandings by engaging them in conversations and scaffolding their actions to help them identify their own problems, seek and ask their own questions, generate their own hypotheses in response to their questions or problems, test their hypotheses and accept or reject the results, and provide alternative solutions to the problem and/or questions.

There are some general ideas that are applicable to teaching all children, especially those who are struggling to learn how to construct their own understandings. I emphasize struggling students because oftentimes the least able children receive a set of instructional techniques or programs delivered in a prescribed way by teachers who follow a script. The five suggestions in Figure 10–4, adapted from Fosnot (1996), are offered to those who want to work with children in a more constructive way.

Make Many Attempts to Understand Children's Understandings In order to be most effective, teachers and parents should try to understand children's conceptual world and knowledge *before* they begin to teach or work with

them. They should also have an idea of the behaviors that would suggest children have acquired conceptual understandings and watch for these changes to occur during social interactions with them. Moreover, when teachers or parents are able to take children's perspectives and understand the reasons for their thinking, they are more likely to facilitate changes in children's ways of thinking and help them learn. For example, I had to try to understand what Kenny meant when used the word *crowd* to describe a man's face. Facilitating change will happen only if parents and teachers have some ideas about the domains of experience and concepts a child has already acquired and uses.

Reject the Notion That Children can Incorporate Exact Copies of Adults' Understandings for Their Own Use Parents and teachers who operate from a constructive perspective understand that meanings are constructed through social interaction and conversation while actively engaged in specific tasks. Their actions counter the widespread myth that conceptual knowledge can be directly transferred from teacher to students in the same prescribed sequence and structure for every student in any context.

Choose the Language You Use to Scaffold Children's Learning Carefully Language is a tool that enables teachers and parents to orient children's construction of concepts by providing multiple opportunities for them to construct new and more complex understandings through joint problem-solving activities. Their words are chosen carefully and are designed to elicit a response that will allow children to construct new and more complex understandings by building on existing knowledge. Examples of teacher-student conversations (see Figure 9–2) demonstrate how the specificity of the language not only follows, but is tied to the student's actions and influences and accelerates their thinking and behavior.

Create Challenging Learning Environments Challenging experiences stimulate thought, provide opportunities for children to generate and explore possibilities, and promote inquiry. When students are challenged they are also more likely to make errors. Mistakes or errors are to be valued and perceived as opportunities to stretch children's thinking, not something to be avoided. It is through partially correct responses that teach-

---

> ◆ Make many attempts to understand children's understandings.
> ◆ Reject the notion that children can incorporate exact copies of adults' understandings for their own use.
> ◆ Carefully choose the language you use to scaffold children's learning.
> ◆ Create challenging learning environments.
> ◆ Provide opportunities for reflection.

Figure 10–4. *Teaching Children in a Constructive Way*

ers know what children can do independently. Using what is partially known enables teachers to demonstrate how to help children successfully resolve conflicts and complete their processing.

Provide Opportunities for Reflection The brain looks for patterns within which to organize and retrieve information. Through reflection and thinking about possible applications of their learning, children learn how to generalize information and apply their conceptual knowledge in another domain or to a different set of circumstances. For example, in Chapter 9, Figure 9–1, Cheri was trying to help Megan learn how to analyze an unknown word *upset* by thinking about a word she knew that was almost like part of the unknown word. Cheri wrote two of Megan's known words on the white board . . . *got* and *get*. After Megan read the words, Cheri guided her in a reflective process whereby Megan was able to understand if she changed the *g* in *get* to an *s*, the word would be *set*. And if she added *up* to the beginning of *set*, she would know that the unknown word is *upset*. This reflective process taught Megan a strategy for problem-solving unknown words that she could then generalize and use in similar circumstances at another time.

their competencies and achievements. They have self-confidence and self-respect. Children with low-self esteem do not think very highly of themselves and exhibit the opposite kind of behaviors.

Studies of infants reveal that the quality and characteristics of children's early experiences with their caregivers shape their emerging self-concept in fundamental ways (Lewis and Brooks-Gunn 1979). Children who experience responsive, caring relationships develop a positive self-image and self-esteem that will influence and impact their later social interactions and relationships.

Children who have histories of sensitive care and have securely attached to their caregivers see themselves as worthy. They consistently behave in a confident, independent manner, suggesting that they have good self-images. They also have realistic appraisals of their current knowledge and skills and when faced with difficulty they are motivated to try harder to surmount challenges (Berk 2001). They tend to be more positive and confident in their interactions with others, show empathy, and are more motivated to engage in conversations and interactions with others, which are essential for learning (Levine 2002).

Children's Self-Concept Determines Their Motivation to Learn

The final principle derived from research in neuroscience that should inform the teaching and learning process is related to the development of children's self-concept. According to Webster's New World Dictionary (Neufeldt 1988), self-concept is an individual's image of self. Some researchers have defined self-concept as an individual's awareness and evaluation of herself (Lewis and Brooks-Gunn 1979). Closely tied to self-concept is self-esteem. Self-esteem has to do with children's evaluations or judgment of their own worth as well as the affective reactions and feelings associated with those judgments (Berk 2001). While many factors affect self-esteem, early relationships and reflective feedback from significant others are fundamental influences on self-esteem and impact children's self-concept. Children with high self-esteem are satisfied with

Independent Mikey would rather read than drink his bottle before bed.

Attachment studies reveal that children with histories of insensitive care see themselves as unworthy (Mate 1999). They tend to avoid interactions with others, lack empathy, and are less confident and resourceful. These children generally exhibit behavior that suggests they have low self-worth and poor self-images. Children with low self-esteem do not think very highly of themselves. They expect rejection and tend to elicit rejection from others. These children are passive and less likely to engage in conversation with adults or peers and may be hostile, defiant, and aggressive (Berk 2001).

Why Is It Important to Understand How Self-Concept Impacts Motivation?

My purpose in discussing how early experiences with caregivers impact young children's self-concept and self-esteem is *not* to imply that children with poor self-images or low self-esteem are more difficult to teach or cannot learn, but quite the opposite. While they may be more challenging, children with low self-esteem are in such need of reassurance that little successes they experience while interacting with a warm teacher or parent will permeate their thinking and motivate them to continue to work with the adults. Moreover, the sooner they experience positive reinforcement for their efforts, the more likely their attitudes and beliefs about their self-worth will escalate. One of the expert teachers commented, "He was so unsure of himself during the first few weeks of lessons that he would always check my face to see if his self-corrections were right. As soon as I reassured him that he was correct, he sat up taller, spoke louder, and seemed to gain a surge of energy. The look of determination on his face was inspiring."

The second reason for discussing this research is that teachers and parents need to understand why some children may be having difficulty learning and what they can do to turn the situation around. Research in neuroscience (Chapters 1 and 2) confirm that experience shapes and organizes the brain. Due to the brain's great plasticity, positive experiences will reroute and reorganize its structure. The emotional feeling of success during positive interactions with parents and teachers stimulates growth of nerve cells in the brain and releases neurotransmitters that directly impact learning: endorphins, dopamine, and seratonin, each of which promote the development of new connections in the prefrontal cortex (Mate 1999). These reward chemicals are released when children experience joy after they have successfully learned something that initially they found difficult. These kinds of experiences will greatly improve children's self-esteem and self-concept. The more often children feel successful and competent, the more motivated they are to continue working with adults to continue and sustain the feeling. The expert teachers have demonstrated clearly how to effectively work with hard-to-teach children, most of whom had behaviors suggesting that they had low self-esteem.

Implications for Motivating Children with Low Self-Esteem and Poor Self-Concepts

The likelihood that children struggling to learn to read and write have low self-esteem and poor self-concepts is generally high because they have probably experienced failure many times. When teachers and parents create environments that incorporate the following three suggestions, they will motivate children to persevere until they are successful and in the process greatly improve their self-esteem and self-concepts.

Provide a Safe Learning Environment All learning takes place within the context of a relationship with another. Unless children and adults feel safe enough in this environment, they will not learn. What does it mean to feel safe? After observing lessons, watching videotapes of the expert teachers many times, and interviewing them about their practice, I believe the following descriptors are indicators of a safe environment. A safe environment is a place where:

◆ you aren't afraid to share your ideas or concerns;
◆ someone listens to you and talks directly to you . . . not at you;
◆ you can ask a question and no one says or shows nonverbally that it isn't important;
◆ people smile often, laugh out loud, and show they enjoy your company;
◆ people show that they like you and say you have good ideas;
◆ you aren't afraid to show that you do not know something;
◆ you have time to think;
◆ you aren't picked on, embarrassed, humiliated, or bullied;

- you aren't afraid to show what you know or don't know;
- you feel secure and wanted;
- people show that they respect for you and others in the class;
- everybody gets along with each other most of the time;
- you feel like you belong;
- people take care of each other.

A safe environment has a profound effect on how students feel about themselves and the learning process. When children (and adults) feel good about themselves, they are motivated to learn and continue to be motivated throughout the learning process.

Set Reasonable Expectations for Mature Behavior and Academic Skills

In a safe environment, children's self-esteem will flourish if teachers and parents set reasonable expectations for learning and behavior and hold them accountable. One teacher commented after the child fell off his chair "accidentally" for the third time that day, "Michael, you have been in first grade for three days and first graders do not fall off their chairs." To which the child replied, "I can behave like a first grader from this day forth!" The teacher replied, "I knew you would be a responsible first grader, I could tell the first day we met." This teacher let Michael (and other children in the classroom) know in a firm and appropriate way her expectations for classroom behavior.

The teacher must also establish reasonable expectations for children's learning goals. In order to set these expectations, teachers must know what the children know and can do as well as what they will need to learn *next* to advance their thinking and skills. There should be enough challenge and the teacher should also be reasonably certain that the child can attain the goals with minimal teacher support. Using something the child knows is the best way to assure that this will happen. The conversation between Cheri and Megan (see Figure 9–1) illustrates how this is done. Cheri used two known words to teach Megan how she could use words that she knew to figure our unknown words.

The teachers' expectations for Michael and Megan were reasonable and well within their ability to achieve. The teachers' conversations let the children know that they believed they could succeed, which motivated the children to strive

for the attainable goals and in the process their self-esteem increased. Their self-esteem was earned through commitment, responsibility, and mastery of meaningful skills (Damon 1995).

Praise Children's *Real* Achievements

Too often well-intentioned parents and teachers praise children for minor things or for things that are not real achievements. It does not take children long to know that no matter what they do they will hear "Excellent." When such a phrase is used often, it means nothing. False compliments can actually undermine or call into question children's self-worth.

One child told her mother angrily, "Getting ten wrong on that paper is not excellent, you always say that and it isn't excellent." This mother accepted everything the child did as wonderful. In this case, the child reprimanded her mother for the behavior. Some children, however, have a distorted view of their capabilities because the teacher or parent has provided so much praise so often that the children have an inflated sense of self-esteem, which has been shown to be linked to adjustment problems (Berk 2001).

Parents and teachers who overpraise or give unearned praise are oftentimes hindering rather than helping children's motivation and self-esteem. Praise that is earned and specific, on the other hand, motivates students and bolsters self-esteem and self-concept. When a child has successfully self-corrected while reading, the teacher's comment, "I am so pleased that you looked carefully at that word, thought about whether that word looked right and made sense, and then fixed it!" is specific and earned. Examples of earned, specific praise are included in the transcripts of lessons in this book.

One of the most destructive things parents and teacher can do is react impatiently or harshly when children make mistakes. Comments such as "You're just lazy," "Can't you do anything right?" undermine positive teacher-student and parent-child relationships and destroy self-esteem and motivation.

One of the most positive things parents and teachers can do is to encourage in very specific ways children who are struggling and trying hard to succeed. Positive reinforcement boosts morale and motivates children to continue to try. And when they have completed and accomplished a hard-earned task, parents, teachers, and children greatly appreciate congratulations for a job well done.

It is critical that teachers and parents learn how to support children's fragile self-concepts and increase their self-esteem. There is a strong link between children's self-esteem and accomplishments. Consequently, parents and teachers should try to build children's self-esteem with praise and reassuring comments when they are earned. Moreover, feedback from others continually influences the children's developing images of themselves.

Real self-esteem can grow only from the mastery of genuine challenges, which in turn will greatly improve self-concept (Greenspan 1997). If teachers and parents have responsive and positive interactions with children, the child's self-concept will follow a positive course; with criticism and ridicule, the opposite will occur. It is also important for parents and educators to realize that as children grow older, it becomes more and more difficult to change their self-concepts.

Conclusion

Brain-based research provides solid evidence that virtually every child is capable of learning how to read and write. Under the right circumstances, all but those who have severe neurological problems (no more than 1 to 2 percent of the population) can learn to read and write in the primary grades, which will serve as a basis for success in the later grades. The recognition of this fact is essential to the education of students who are considered at risk of school failure after three years of formal schooling. Allowing large numbers of children to leave the primary grades with minimal skills ensures them a life of school failure, as well as probable poverty and long-term dependence on society, the consequences of which are disastrous to the well-being of the nations of the world.

Throughout this book, I have cited concrete data from neuroscience that proves unquestionably that emotion cannot be removed or divorced from the learning process and that it is through social interactions with caring adults that children learn how to learn. I have also provided many examples of teaching sessions to prove that classroom and Reading Recovery teachers can and do successfully teach children from diverse socioeconomic, language, and cultural backgrounds to

read and write. Although some children featured in this book are from middle-class families, most were poor and minority children. Some children were handicapped; for others, English was not their first language.

Quantitative standardized test scores provide more evidence that the children the expert teachers taught—and many other low-achieving children, except for the very few with more severe neurological problems—can learn to read and write if their teachers have *high expectations; the necessary knowledge about the emotional, social, and cognitive dimensions of learning;* and *skills in teaching the reading and writing processes.* Yet despite the evidence from research in neuroscience, and the practical examples derived from expert teachers' practice, some educational systems are supporting a "one-size-fits-all" approach for teaching beginning reading and writing. The idea that there are individual differences in learning is not considered. Moreover, there is no mention of the social and emotional role of learning in beginning reading instruction. Children and teachers are expected to be robots with minds that are little more than receiving and delivery machines for information. Parents and teachers should question any program that promotes whole-class teaching of a prescribed, sequential curriculum of skills.

Children who struggle do not learn how to read and write from all teachers, especially those who have low expectations and believe that some children cannot learn because they do not have the brain power or come from mainstream cultures. Children learn best if they are fortunate enough to have teachers like those featured in this book, who have the following characteristics:

- ◆ They like children and have an investment in their future.
- ◆ They help children feel confident, safe, and secure.
- ◆ They believe in themselves and in their ability to teach.
- ◆ They do not give up and will not let children down.
- ◆ They enable children to construct their understandings and knowledge through social interactions while engaged in a joint problem-solving activity.
- ◆ They challenge, motivate, and always encourage children to try.

- They engage children in activities and point out what to attend to, in what way, when, and for how long.
- They point out what children already know and can do.
- They care about children's welfare and show it.
- They demonstrate high expectations in children's ability to learn.
- They demonstrate confidence in their own ability to teach all children to read and write.
- They provide learning opportunities and experiences that maximize students' learning potential.

Unfortunately, there are teachers who may have the skills, but lack high expectations that the children can learn. If the teacher does not expect children to learn, it is most likely that they will not. An intelligent person is not motivated to invest energy in a cause he or she believes is fruitless.

In my view, every educational system designed to serve the needs of the society and the children within that society must pay attention to research on how the mind works and the brain develops and functions. When this happens, society will be compelled to recognize the social, emotional, and cognitive dimensions of learning and address individual differences. Moreover, teachers will be encouraged to create bridges between the very different experiences of individual learners and use a variety of instructional approaches to build on their culture, knowledge, and interests. Teachers must understand how their students think and learn as well as what they know and can do independently. Unless this is done, many children will not be able to realize their full potential and learn to read and write.

I agree with Dr. Stanley Greenspan, who argues:

> Our schools' failure to educate masses of children fully capable of learning is not the result of overemphasis on unearned self-esteem or touchy feely frills, but from reliance on a model (of education) that ignores the nature of the learning process. (Greenspan 1997, 213)

Index of Illustrative Examples

References

Adams, M. J. 1990. *Beginning to Read: Thinking and Learning About Print*. Cambridge, MA: MIT Press.

Allington, R. L. 2001. *What Matters Most for Struggling Readers*. New York: Longman.

Allington, R. L., and S. R. Walmsley. 1995. *No Quick Fix: Rethinking Literacy Programs in America's Elementary Schools*. New York: Teachers College Press.

Anderson, N. 1997. Reconstructing Scaffolded Writing Instruction from Reading Recovery. Unpublished doctoral dissertation, Ohio State University, Columbus.

Anderson, O. R. 1992. "Some Interrelationships Between Constructive Models of Learning and Current Neurobiological Theory, with Implications for Science Education." *Journal of Research in Science Teaching* 29: 1037–58.

Askew, B. J., I. Fountas, C. A. Lyons, G. S. Pinnell, and M. Schmitt. 1998. *Reading Recovery Review: Understandings, Outcomes, and Implications*. Columbus, OH: Reading Recovery Council of North America.

Athey, I. 1985. "Reading Research in the Affective Domain." In *Theoretical Models and Processes of Reading*, edited by H. Singer and R. Ruddell, pp. 527–57. Newark, DE: International Reading Association.

Bandura, A. 1997. *Self-Efficacy: The Exercise of Control*. New York: W. H. Freeman.

Beane, J. A. 1990. *Affect in the Curriculum: Toward Democracy, Dignity, and Diversity*. New York: Teachers College Press.

Berk, L. E. 2001. *Awakening Children's Minds*. New York: Oxford University Press.

Brophy, J. E., and Good, T. L. 1986. "Teacher Behavior and Student Achievement." In *Handbook of Research on Teaching*, 3rd ed., edited by M. C. Wittrock, pp. 328–76. New York: Macmillan.

Bruner, J. S. 1966. *Toward a Theory of Instruction*. Cambridge, MA: Harvard University Press.

———. 1973. "Organization of Early Skilled Action." *Child Development* 44: 1–11.

———. 1983. *Child's Talk: Learning to Use Language*. New York: Norton.

———. 1986. *Actual Minds: Possible Worlds*. Cambridge, MA: Harvard University Press.

Bruning, R., G. Schraw, and R. Ronning. 1995. *Cognitive Psychology and Instruction*. Englewood Cliffs, NJ: Prentice Hall.

Cazden, C. B. 1988. *Classroom Discourse: The Language of Teaching and Learning*. Portsmouth, NH: Heinemann.

———. 1999. "Revealing and Telling: The Socialization of Attention in Learning to Read and Write." In *Stirring the Waters: The Influences of Marie Clay*, edited by G. Gaffney and B. Askew. Portsmouth, NH: Heinemann.

Clay, M. M. 1973. *Reading: The Patterning of Complex Behavior*. Auckland, New Zealand: Heinemann.

———. 1975. *What Did I Write*? Auckland, New Zealand: Heinemann.

———. 1979. *Reading the Patterning of Complex Behavior*. Auckland, New Zealand: Heinemann.

———. 1987. "Learning to Be Learning Disabled." *New Zealand Journal of Educational Studies* 22: 155–73.

———. 1991. *Becoming Literate: The Construction of Inner Control*. Portsmouth, NH: Heinemann.

———. 1993a. *An Observation Survey Of Early Literacy Achievement*. Portsmouth, NH: Heinemann.

———. 1993b. *Reading Recovery: A Guidebook for Teachers in Training*. Portsmouth, NH: Heinemann.

———. 1998. *By Different Paths to Common Outcomes*. York, ME: Stenhouse.

———. 2001. *Change over Time in Children's Literacy Development*. Portsmouth, NH: Heinemann.

Clay, M. M., and C. B. Cazden. 1990. "A Vygotskian Interpretation of Reading Recovery." In *Vygotsky and Education*, edited by L. Moll, pp. 206–22. New York: Cambridge University Press.

Cohen, J. 2001. *Caring Classrooms/Intelligent Schools: The Social Emotional Education of Young Children*. New York: Teachers College Press.

Coles, G. 1987. *The Learning Mystique: A Critical Look at Learning Disabilities*. New York: Fawcett Columbine.

———. 1998. *Reading Lessons: The Debate over Literacy*. New York: Hill & Wang.

Cowley, J. 1980. *Mrs. Wishy-Washy*. Auckland, New Zealand: Shortland Press.

———. 1986. *The Birthday Cake*. San Diego, CA: Wright Group.

Cunninghan, P. A., and R. A. Allington. 1994. *Classrooms That Work*. New York: Harper Collins.

Damasio, A. R. 1994. *Descartes' Error: Emotion, Reason, and the Human Brain*. New York: Avon Books.

———. 2000. *The Feeling of What Happens*. London: Vintage.

Damon, W. 1995. *Greater Expectations: Overcoming the Culture of Indulgence in America's Homes and Schools*. New York: Free Press.

Darling-Hammond, L. 1996. "What Matters Most: A Competent Teacher for Every Child." *Phi Delta Kappan* 78: 193–200.

Deci, E. L. 1980. *The Psychology of Self-Determination*. Lexington, MA: Heath.

———. 1995. *Why We Do What We Do: Understanding Self-Motivation*. New York: Penguin Books.

Deci, E. L., R. Koestner, and R. Ryan. 2001. "Extrinsic Rewards and Intrinsic Motivation in Education: Reconsidered Once Again." *Review of Educational Research* 71: 1–27.

Deci, E. L., and R. M. Ryan. 1985. *Intrinsic Motivation and Self-Determination in Human Behavior*. New York: Plenum Press.

DeFord, D. E., C. A. Lyons, and G. S. Pinnell. 1991. *Bridges to Literacy: Learning from Reading Recovery*. Portsmouth, NH: Heinemann.

Dewey, J. 1916. *Democracy and Education*. New York: Macmillan.

———. 1938. *Experience and Education*. New York: Collier Books.

Diaz, R. M., C. J. Neal, and M. Amaya-Williams. 1990. "The Social Origins of Self-Regulation." In *Vygotsky and Education*, edited by L. Moll. New York: Cambridge University Press.

Dill, D. D. 1990. *What Teachers Need to Know: The Knowledge, Skills, and Values Essential to Good Teaching*. San Francisco, CA: Jossey-Bass.

Durden, W., and L. Mackay. 1995. "Rediscovering Self-Reliance in Education: The Optimal Match." *Phi Delta Kappan* 77: 250–51.

Dweck, C. S. 1998. "The Development of Early Self-Conceptions: Their Relevance for Motivational Processes." In *Motivation and Self-Regulation Across the Life-Span*, edited by J. Heckhausen and C. S. Dweck, pp. 257–80. New York: Cambridge University Press.

Ellis, A. W. 1984. *Reading, Writing, and Dyslexia: A Cognitive Analysis*. London: Erlbaum.

Fosnot, C. T. 1996. *Constructivism: Theory, Perspectives, and Practice*. New York: Teachers College Press.

Fountas, I. C., and G. S. Pinnell. 1996. *Guided Reading: Good First Teaching for All Children*. Portsmouth, NH: Heinemann.

———. 2001. *Guiding Readers and Writers Grades 3–6: Teaching Comprehension, Genre, and Content Literacy*. Portsmouth, NH: Heinemann.

Freud, S. [1923] 1947. *The Ego and the Id*. London: Hogarth Press.

Fullerton, S. K. 2001. "Achieving Motivation: Guiding Edward's Journey to Literacy." *Literacy Teaching and Learning* 6: 43–71.

Gardner, H. 1985. *Frames of Mind: Theory of Multiple Intelligences*. New York: Basic Books.

———. 1999. *The Disciplined Mind: What All Students Should Understand*. New York: Basic Books.

Ginsburg, M. 1972. *The Chick and the Duckling*. New York: Aladdin.

Goldberg, H. K., G. B. Shiffman, and M. Bender. 1983. *Dyslexia: Interdisciplinary Approaches to Reading Disabilities*. New York: Grune & Stratton.

Goleman, D. 1995. *Emotional Intelligence: Why It Can Be More Than IQ*. New York: Bantam Books.

Goodman, N. 1984. *Of Mind and Other Matters*. Cambridge, MA: Harvard University Press.

Gopnik, A., A. N. Meltzoff, and P. K. Kuhl. 1999. *The Scientist in the Crib: Minds, Brains, and How Children Learn*. New York: Morrow.

Greenspan, S. I. 1997. *The Growth of the Mind and the Endangered Origins of Intelligence*. Reading, MA: Addison-Wesley.

Guthrie, J. T., and A. Wigfield, eds. 1997. *Reading Engagement: Motivating Readers Through Integrated Instruction*. Newark, DE: International Reading Association.

Halliday, M. A. K. 1975. *Learning How to Mean: Explorations in the Development of Language*. London: Edward Arnold Ltd.

Heath, S. B. 1983. *Ways with Words. Language, Life, and Work in Communities and Classrooms*. New York: Cambridge University Press.

Hobsbaum, A., S. Peters, and K. Sylva. 1996. "Scaffolding in Reading Recovery." *Oxford Review of Education* 22: 17–35.

James, A. 1995. *Peter's Move*. Lexington, MA: D. C. Heath.

Johnston, P. 1999. "Unpacking Literate Achievement." In *Stirring the Waters: The Influences of Marie Clay*, edited by G. Gaffney and B. Askew. Portsmouth, NH: Heinemann.

Johnston, P., and R. L. Allington. 1991. "Remediaton." In *Handbook of Reading Research*, Vol. 11, edited by P. D. Pearson, pp. 984–1012. New York: Longman.

Juel, C. 1988. "Learning to Read and Write: A Longitudinal Study with 54 Children from First Through Fourth Grades." *Journal of Educational Psychology* 80: 437–47.

Katz, L. 1977. *Talks with Teachers*. Washington, DC: NAEYC.

Katz, L., and J. N. M. Gottman. 1991. "Marital Discord and Child Outcomes: A Social Psychophysiological Approach." In *The Development of Emotion Regulation and Dysregulation*, edited by J. Garber and K. A. Didg, pp. 129–66. New York: Cambridge University Press.

Knapp, M. S., P. M. Shields, and B. J. Turnbull. 1997. *Academic Challenges for the Children of Poverty: Summary Report*. Washington, DC: Office of Policy and Planning, U.S. Department of Education.

Kuhl, P. K. 1998. "The Development of Speech and Language." In *Mechanistic Relationships Between Development and Learning*, edited by T. J. Carew, R. Menzel, and C. J. Shatz, 53–73. New York: Wiley.

Leaming, H. 1974. *Pat's New Puppy*. Glenview, IL: Scott Foresman.

Learning Disabilities—A Barrier to Literacy Instruction. 1995. Washington, DC: International Reading Association.

LeDoux, J. 1996. *The Emotional Brain: The Mysterious Underpinnings of Emotional Life*. New York: Touchstone.

Leinhart, G. 1988. "Situated Knowledge and Expertise in Teaching." In *Teacher's Professional Learning*, edited by J. Calderhead. London: Falmer Press.

Levine, M. 2002. *A Mind at a Time*. New York: Simon & Schuster.

Lewis, M., and J. Brooks-Gunn. 1979. *Social Cognition and the Acquisition of Self*. New York: Plenum Press.

Lieberman, A., and L. Miller. 1999. *Teachers Transforming Their Work and Their World*. New York: Teachers College Press.

Lindfors, J. W. 1999. *Children's Inquiry: Using Language to Make Sense of the World*. New York: Teachers College Press.

Luria, A. R. 1969. "Speech Development and the Formation of Mental Process." In *A Handbook of Contemporary Soviet Psychology*, edited by M. Cole and I. Maltzman. New York: Basic Books.

———. 1973. *The Working Brain: An Introduction to Neuropsychology*. New York: Basic Books.

———. 1976. *Cognitive Development: Its Cultural and Social Formations*. Cambridge, MA: Harvard University Press.

———. 1979. *The Making of Mind: A Personal Account of Soviet Psychology*, edited by M. Cole and S. Cole. Cambridge, MA: Harvard University Press.

———. 1980. *Higher Cortical Functions in Man*. New York: Consultants Bureau.

Lyons, C. A. 1991. "A Comparative Study of the Teaching Effectiveness of Teachers Participating in a Year-Long and Two-Week In-Service Program." In *Learner Factors/Teacher Factors: Issues in Literacy Research and Instruction*, edited by J. Zutell and S. McCormick, pp. 367–75. *Fortieth Yearbook of the National Reading Conference*. Chicago, IL: National Reading Conference.

———. 1993. "The Use of Questions in the Teaching of High Risk Beginning Readers: A Profile of a Developing Reading Recovery Teacher." *Reading and Writing Quarterly* 29: 1–42.

———. 1994a. "Reading Recovery and Learning Disability: Issues, Challenges and Implications." *Literacy Teaching and Learning: An International Journal of Literacy Learning* 1: 109–119.

———. 1994b. "Constructing Chains of Reasoning in Reading Recovery Demonstration Lessons." In *Multidimensional Aspects of Literacy Research, Theory and Practice,* edited by D. Leu and C. Kinzer, pp. 276–86. *Forty-Third Yearbook of the National Reading Conference*. Chicago, IL: National Reading Conference.

———. 1995. An Analysis of Literacy Behaviors of Reading Recovery Children Who Are Hard to Teach. Paper presented at the International Reading Association Annual Conference, San Antonio, Texas.

———. 1998. "Reading Recovery in the United States: More Than a Decade of Data." *Literacy, Teaching and Learning: An International Journal of Early Reading and Writing* 3: 77–92.

———. 1999. A Study of Expert Reading Recovery Teachers Attitudes, Understandings, and Practices. Paper presented at Victoria Early Literacy Seminar, Melbourne, Australia.

Lyons, C. A., and J. Beaver. 1995. "Reducing Retention and Learning Disability Placement Through Reading Recovery: An Educationally Sound, Cost-Effective Choice." In *No Quick Fix: Rethinking Literacy Programs in America's Elementary Schools*, edited by R. Allington and S. Walmsley, pp. 116–36. New York: Teachers College Press and International Reading Association.

Lyons, C. A., and G. S. Pinnell. 2001. *Systems for Change in Literacy Education: A Guide to Professional Development*. Portsmouth, NH: Heinemann.

Lyons, C. A., G. S. Pinnell, and D. DeFord. 1993. *Partners in Learning: Teachers and Students in Reading Recovery*. New York: Teachers College Press.

Malcomb, M. 1983. *I Can Read*. Wellington, New Zealand: Department of Education.

Maslow, A. H. 1954. *Motivation and Personality*. New York: Harper & Brothers.

Mate, G. 1999. *Scattered: How Attention Deficit Disorder Originates and What You Can Do About It*. New York: Penguin Putnam.

McKhann, G., and M. Albert. 2002. *Keep Your Brain Young*. New York: Wiley & Sons.

McQueen, P. J. 1975. Motor Responses Associated with Beginning Reading. Master of Arts thesis, University of Auckland Library, Auckland, New Zealand.

Meadows, S. 1993. *The Child as Thinker: The Development and Acquisition of Cognition in Childhood*. New York: Routledge.

Neufeldt, V. 1988. *Webster's New World Dictionary*. 3rd ed. New York: Simon & Schuster.

Nicholls, J. G. 1983. "Conceptions of Ability and Achievement Motivation: A Theory and Its Implications for Education." In *Learning and Motivation in the Classroom*, edited by S. G. Paris, G. M. Olson, and H. W. Stevenson, pp. 221–37. Hillsdale, NJ: Erlbaum.

Noddings, N. 1995. "Teaching Themes of Care." *Phi Delta Kappan* 76: 675–79.

Ohanian, S. 2000. "Goals 2000: What's in a Name?" *Phi Delta Kappan* 81: 344–55.

O'Leary, S. 1997. *Five Kids: Stories of Children Learning to Read*. Bothall, WA: The Wright Group/McGraw-Hill.

Paley, V. 1981. *Wally's Stories*. Cambridge, MA: Harvard University Press.

Parris, S. G., B. A. Wasik, and J. C. Turner, 1991. "The Development of Strategic Readers." In *Handbook of Reading Research* 11, edited by R. Barr, M. Kamil, P. Mosenthal, and P. D. Pearson, pp. 609–49. New York: Longman.

Paterson, K. 1977. *Bridge to Terabithia*. New York: Crowell.

Pert, C. B. 1997. *Molecules of Emotion: Why You Feel the Way You Feel*. New York: Scribner.

Peters, C. 1995a. *Willy the Helper*. Lexington, MA: Heath.

———. 1995b. *My School*. Lexington, MA: Heath.

Piaget, J. 1977. *Equilibration of Cognitive Structures*. New York: Viking.

Pinnell, G. S. 1997. "Reading Recovery: A Review of Research." In *Handbook of Research on Teaching Literacy Through the Communication of Visual Arts*, edited by J. Flood, S. Heath, and D. Lapp. New York: Macmillan Reference Series on Educational Research.

Pinnell, G. S., M. D. Fried, and R. M. Estice. 1990. "Reading Recovery: Learning How to Make a Difference." *The Reading Teacher* 43: 282–95.

Pinnell, G. S., C. A. Lyons, D. E. DeFord, A. Bryk, and M. Seltzer. 1994. "Comparing Instructional Models for the Literacy Education of High-Risk First Graders." *Reading Research Quarterly* 29: 9–39.

Ratey, J. J. 2001. *A User's Guide to the Brain*. New York: Pantheon Books.

Resnik, L. B. 1989. *Knowing, Learning, and Instruction: Essays in Honor of Robert Glasser*. Hillsdale, NJ: Lawrence Erlbaum.

Robinson, S. E. 1973. Predicting Early Reading Progress. Master of Arts thesis, University of Auckland Library, Auckland, New Zealand.

Rodgers, E. M. 2000. "Language Matters: When Is a Scaffold Really a Scaffold?" In *Forty-Ninth Yearbook of the National Reading Conference*, edited by T. Shanahan and F. V. Rodriquez-Brown, pp. 78–90. Chicago, IL: National Reading Conference.

Rogers, C. R. 1961. *On Becoming a Person*. New York: Houghton-Mifflin.

Rogoff, B. 1990. *Apprenticeship in Thinking: Cognitive Development in Social Context.* New York: Oxford University Press.

Ruddell, R. B., and N. J. Unrau. 1997. "The Role of Responsive Teaching in Focusing Reader Intention and Developing Reader Motivation." In *Reading Engagement: Motivating Readers Through Integrated Instruction,* edited by J. T. Gutherie and A. Wigfield, pp. 102–25. Newark, DE: International Reading Association.

Ruff, H. A., and K. R. Lawson. 1990. "Development of Sustained, Focused Attention in Young Children During Free Play." *Developmental Psychology* 61: 85–93.

Schon, D. A. 1990. *Educating the Reflective Practitioner: Toward a New Design for Teaching and Learning in the Professions.* San Francisco, CA: Jossey-Bass.

Shannon, T., and R. Barr. 1995. "A Synthesis of Research on Reading Recovery." *Reading Research Quarterly* 30: 958–96.

Shulman, L. S. 1987. "Knowledge and Teaching: Foundations of the New Reform." *Harvard Educational Review* 19: 4–14.

Skinner, B. F. 1968. *The Technology of Teaching.* New York: Appleton-Century-Crofts.

Slavin, R. E., and O. S. Fashola. 1998. *Show Me the Evidence! Proven and Promising Programs for America's Schools.* Thousand Oaks, CA: Corwin.

Smith, F. 1994. *Understanding Reading.* Hillsdale, NJ: Lawrence Erlbaum.

Snow, C. E., S. M. Burns, and P. Griffin. 1998. *Preventing Reading Difficulties in Young Children.* Washington, DC: National Academy Press.

Spear-Swerling, L., and R. J. Sternberg. 1996. *Off Track: When Poor Readers Become "Learning Disabled."* Boulder, CO: Westview Press.

Spiro, R. J., P. J. Feltovich, M. J. Jacobson, and R. L. Coulson. 1995. "Cognitive Flexibility, Constructivism, and Hypertext: Random Access Instruction for Advanced Knowledge Acquisition in Ill-Structured Domains." In *Constructivism in Education,* edited by L. P. Steffe and J. Gale. Hillsdale, NJ: Lawerence Earlbaum.

Teale, W. H., and E. Sulzby. 1986. *Emergent Literacy: Writing and Reading.* Norwood, NJ: Ablex.

Tharp, R. G., and R. Gallimore. 1988. *Rousing Minds to Life.* New York: Cambridge University Press.

Vellutino, F. R. 1979. *Dyslexia: Theory and Research.* Cambridge, MA: MIT Press.

von Glasersfeld, E. 1995. *Radical Constructivism: A Way of Knowing and Learning.* London: Falmer.

———. 1996. "Aspects of Constructivism." In *Constructivism: Theory, Perspectives, and Practice,* edited by C. T. Fosnot. New York: Teachers College Press.

Vygotsky, L. 1978. *Mind in Society: The Development of Higher Psychological Processes.* Edited and translated by M. Cole, V. John-Steiner, S. Scribner, and E. Souberman. Cambridge, MA: Harvard University Press.

Ward, C. 1988. *Cookie's Week.* New York: G. P. Putnam's Sons.

Wasik, B. A., and R. E. Slavin. 1993. "Preventing Early Reading Failure with One-to-One Tutoring: A Review of Five Programs." *Reading Research Quarterly* 28: 179–200.

Weaver, C. 1994. *Success at Last: Helping Students with AD(H)D Achieve Their Potential.* Portsmouth, NH: Heinemann.

Weiner, B. 1992. *Human Motivation: Metaphors, Theories and Research.* Newbury Park, CA: Sage.

Wells, G. 1986. *The Meaning Makers: Children Learning Language and Using Language to Learn.* Portsmouth, NH: Heinemann.

Wertsch, J. V. 1985. *Vygotsky and the Social Formation of Mind.* Cambridge, MA: Harvard University Press.

———. 1991. *Voices of the Mind.* Cambridge, MA: Harvard University Press.

———. 1998. *Mind as Action.* New York: Oxford University Press.

Wildsmith, B. 1991. *Cat on the Mat.* Amherst, NY: Creative Edge.

———. 1991b. *If I Were You.* Austin, TX: Steck-Vaughn.

Wong, S. D., L. A. Groth, and J. F. O'Flahavan. 1994. Characterizing Teacher-Student Interaction in Reading Recovery Lessons. National Reading Research Center Report No. 17. Athens, GA; College Park, MD: Universities of Georgia and Maryland.

Wood, D. 1998. *How Children Think and Learn.* Oxford: Blackwell.

Wood, D. J., J. S. Bruner, and G. Ross. 1976. "The Role of Tutoring in Problem Solving." *Journal of Child Psychology and Psychiatry* 17: 89–100.

Ysseldyke, J. E., and B. Algozzine. 1983. "LD or not LD: That's Not the Question!" *Journal of Learning Disabilities* 16: 29–31.

Index

capacity, in self-regulation, 71
caregivers, self-esteem of child and, 185–86
category systems, 16–17, 20, 45–46
Cat on the Mat (Wildsmith), 30
Cazden, C. B., 144
cerebellum, 28f, 35f, 62f, 64f
    motor orientation and, 27, 29
    movement and, 36, 40
cerebral cortex, 10f
    motor areas of, 35f
    outer layer, 9–10, 62f
cerebral dominance, 10–12
cerebral integration, 12–13
cerebral specialization
    language production and, 12
    learning and, 12–13
    memories and, 12
cerebrum, 9
challenge
    in learning environments, 184–85
    level of, 41
    motivation and, 83–84, 92
    self-esteem and, 188
characters (in stories), conversations about, 41
Chicago, University of, 45
cingulate gyrus, 32f
    executive organization and, 27, 32
    functions of, 32
    motivation and, 80
clapping, syllables, 103–4
Clay, Marie M., 2, 18, 21, 38, 39, 88, 91, 94–95, 96, 97, 102, 105, 115, 128, 144, 148, 160, 174, 179, 182
cognitive development. *See also* thinking
    defined, 96
    in developmentally handicapped children, 123–24
    dual coding with emotions, 61
    emotions and, 60–61, 174–76, 176–79
    experience and, 68
    functional organization of the brain and, 20
    neurology and, 61–63
    reading and, 96–97
    reasoning, 47–48
    in students with AD(H)D, 114–16, 118–19
    in students with learning disabilities, 128–30
    teacher-student interaction and, 75
    writing and, 114–16
cognitive theory of motivation, 78
collaborative writing, 86–87
communication. *See also* conversations
    with hard-to-teach students, 107
comprehension
    by learning disabled (LD) students, 126
    motivation and, 88–89
concept development, 45–46
conceptual knowledge
    assimilation of, 183
    construction of, 182
    problem-solving and, 182–83

confusion, perception adjustment and, 18
consistency
    in limits, 144–46
    for students with AD(H)D, 130
    for students with learning disabilities, 121–22, 123, 130
constructivism, 179–85
    applying to education, 184–85
    learning and, 182–84
    theory of, 179, 182
content knowledge, 152, 153
context, for learning, 155
conversations. *See also* social speech
    about story characters, 41
    authentic, 141–43
    communicating ideas through, 51
    expert teachers and, 155–59
    inauthentic, 141–42
    instructional effectiveness and, 183
    interest shown in, 140–41
    language development and, 46–48
    listening in, 141–43
    literacy success and, 163
    motivation and, 87–89
    personalized, 141–43
    recommendations for parents and teachers, 56
    scaffolding and, 183, 184
    socialization through, 141
    value of, 141, 183
Cookie's Week (Ward), 141–42, 155–57
corpus callosum, 9, 10f, 28f
Cowley, Joy, 101, 118, 161
cueing systems, 131
Cunningham, P. A., 2

Damasio, Antonio, 60
Darling-Hammond, L., 169
deaf children, gestures used by, 45
de-automatization of performance, 55–56
Deci, Edward, 78, 83
defensiveness, of hard-to-teach students, 104
dendrites
    aging and, 13
    defined, 14
    growth of, 14
    hemisphere use and, 12
    signal transmission and, 15f
details, left cerebral hemisphere and, 9
developmentally handicapped (DH) children, 110
Dewey, John, 147, 155, 159
diencephalon, 9
directional movement
    constructive nature of learning and, 182, 183
    expert teachers and, 160, 162–63
    learning about, 100–102
discipline, motivation and, 82
distractions, for students with learning disabilities, 130–31
diversity, in students, 151
dopamine, 186
    cingulate gyrus and, 32
    defined, 14

Down to Town (Cowley), 101
dual coding, of experience, 61, 65
Durden, W., 175
dyslexia, 110

early reading
    learning behaviors, 97
    progress predictors, 39
embarrassment, 66
emotional development
    characteristics of, 117
    in developmentally handicapped children, 123–24
    scaffolding and, 118–19
    in students with AD(H)D, 114–16, 118–19
    in students with learning disabilities, 128–30
    teacher-student interaction and, 75
    through writing, 114–16
emotional memory. *See also* memory
    characteristics of, 67–68
    right hemisphere and, 12
emotions. *See also* negative emotions
    amygdala and, 63–64
    attention and, 73
    cognitive development and, 174–76, 176–79
    defined, 59
    dual coding with cognitive development, 61
    endocrine system response to, 60
    expert teachers and, 135
    of hard-to-teach students, 101–2
    individual differences in, 58
    interpreting, 59–60
    learning and, 1–32, 58–61, 65–66, 72–73, 90–91, 95–96, 107, 136–37, 174–79
    limbic system and, 30
    memory and, 12, 65–68, 72–73
    motivation and, 80–81
    motor development and, 35
    neurological roots of, 61–63
    regulation of, 61
    social interaction and, 136–37
    thinking impaired by, 59–60
    zone of proximal development and, 91
endocrine system, 60
endorphins, 186
engagement, encouraging, 27
environment. *See also* responsive learning environments
    exploring, 41
    learning and, 151
    motivation and, 84–92, 92
    richness of, 18–19, 23, 41
    stimulation provided by, 16–17
    for students with AD(H)D, 112–14, 117
    for students with developmental handicaps, 120–23
episodic memory, 67
errors
    anticipating, 90–91
    book introductions and, 164
executive organization, 27, 32–33